UNDERSTANDING READING COMPREHENSION:

Cognition, Language, and the Structure of Prose

Edited by

James Flood, *San Diego State University*

For the IRA Cognitive Psychology and Reading Comprehension Committee

Published by the
INTERNATIONAL READING ASSOCIATION
800 Barksdale Road, Box 8139, Newark, Delaware 19714

116253

INTERNATIONAL READING ASSOCIATION

Copyright 1984 by the
International Reading Association, Inc.

Library of Congress Cataloging in Publication Data
Main entry under title:

Understanding reading comprehension.

Includes bibliographical references.
1. Reading comprehension. 2. Reading, Psychology of.
I. Flood, James. II. International Reading Association.
LB1050.45.U53   1984   428.4   83-10847
ISBN 0-87207-736-5

Contents

Foreword

> "Every man who knows how to read has it in his power to magnify himself, to multiple the ways in which he exists, to make his life full, significant and interesting." *Aldous Huxley*

Since it is the aim of all teachers to make the lives of their students "full, significant and interesting," the teaching of reading has been of prime concern to educators around the globe. And, the essence of reading is comprehension—ascertaining meaning. Certainly, in the past decade comprehension has been the most discussed and researched topic among professionals interested in the teaching of reading. Authorities from many different disciplines have contributed to the better understanding of the complex process that comprises reading comprehension.

In this volume, James Flood, aided by the IRA Cognitive Psychology and Reading Comprehension Committee, has compiled the writings of some of the most prominent scholars in the areas of cognition, language, and the structure of prose, with one section of the book devoted to each of these topics.

Thus, the first section of the book gives us insight into the comprehension process through the eyes of the cognitive psychologist. What exactly is happening in the minds of children as they read *The Wizard of Oz*? Although no one can provide a definitive answer to this question, the psychologists and researchers in the first section offer some interesting research-based hypotheses.

Overall language development and its relation to reading is the focus of the second section of this book and Paula Menyuk, Peter and Mary Salus, and Thomas Sticht provide interesting perspectives from a linguistic vantage point. Finally, in the last section of the book, researchers examine the effect that the actual text has on the comprehension of the reader.

Certainly, this book will be a necessary addition to the libraries of all educational researchers and practitioners interested in the field of reading. Reading this work should help all of us better understand the comprehension process and, through this better understanding, improve instruction for our children.

Readers of *Understanding Reading Comprehension* will want the companion volume entitled *Promoting Reading Comprehension*, which is also edited by James Flood and available from the International Reading Association. *Promoting Reading Comprehension* presents an historical accounting of instructional approaches to the teaching of comprehension as well as insights into effective approaches for the present and future.

Jack Cassidy, *President*
International Reading Association, 1982-1983

Acknowledgement

The editor would like to express appreciation to Jacqueline Collins for her thorough and diligent work in proofreading this manuscript.

IRA PUBLICATIONS COMMITTEE 1983-1984 Joan Nelson-Herber, State University of New York at Binghamton, *Chair* • Phylliss J. Adams, University of Denver • Janet R. Binkley, IRA • Faye R. Branca, IRA • Martha Collins Cheek, Louisiana State University • Susan Mandel Glazer, Rider College • Jerome C. Harste, Indiana University • Nelly M. Hecker, Furman University • Roselmina Indrisano, Boston University • Douglas Inkpen, G.B. Little Public School, Scarborough, Ontario • Lloyd W. Kline, IRA • Eleanor Ladd, University of South Carolina • James R. Layton, Southwest Missouri State University • Irving P. McPhail, Johns Hopkins University • Nancy Naumann, North Haven, Connecticut, Board of Education • Caroline Neal, West Virginia College of Graduate Studies • P. David Pearson, University of Illinois • María Elena Rodríguez, Asociación Internacional de Lectura, Buenos Aires • Betty D. Roe, Tennessee Technological University • S. Jay Samuels, University of Minnesota • Ralph C. Staiger, IRA • Sam Weintraub, State University of New York at Buffalo.

Introduction

The comprehension of written discourse requires readers to use their cognitive and linguistic abilities while processing text which has specific structural organizations. These three elements, the cognitive ability of the reader, the linguistic ability of the reader, and the structural organization of the text are the foci of this volume.

Although reading comprehension can be defined in many ways, it can be argued that competent, effective comprehension is both constructive and interactive.

Comprehension is a constructive process in the full sense of the term. A text can be thought of as a set of building blocks: letters, words, sentences, paragraphs, chapters. The writer arranges these elements into patterns designed to communicate a message. The reader gains an understanding by using the text as a model to guide construction of a parallel image in the mind. Good writers are not completely explicit; like skilled block-builders they bridge many spaces for both economy and aesthetics. Moreover, competent readers do not examine all of the individual blocks. Some blocks are recognized as configurations and handled as chunks; others are superfluous and can be ignored altogether.

Competent readers, in undertaking to comprehend a text, rely on blueprints based on knowledge acquired during school and home experiences. Skilled writers work from a similar set of blueprints. To the extent that both readers and writers work from the same plan, all is well. Readers can analyze the textual information in a planned way, guided throughout by a knowledge of the overall structure, and mindful of checkpoints along the way that help insure that they remain on the right path.

Comprehension is also interactive; it entails both the analysis of text structure and the examination of preexisting memory structure. The preceding emphasized the importance of planning in the analysis of text structures. Human memory is also a repository for substantive knowledge, some of which is experiential (in the sense of naturally occurring and not fully examined) and some of which is abstract (in the sense of academic, secondhand, and rational). Whatever the source of knowledge, it appears that most of what we remember is retained according to some organized schema, prototype, conceptual network, hierarchy, or matrix. (This generalization is less true for those fleeting experiences that permit recognition but not reproduction). A distinctive element in comprehension is the process by which readers map the segments of text onto preexisting substantive knowledge. It is possible to carry out the formal structural analysis of text, yet fail to relate the information to the structure of what is already known.

This volume contains articles written by educators, linguists, psychologists, and artificial intelligence experts on these issues within the field of comprehension research. The volume consists of three major parts: cognition, language, and the structure of prose.

Part One, "Focus: Cognition," contains papers that examine reading comprehension as a cognitive phenomenon. Rumelhart's paper discusses broad issues of reading comprehension within a cognitive psychological framework; it uses schema theory as a unifying explanatory force for understanding story processing. Baker and Brown's article on cognitive monitoring explains current metacognitive theory and reviews ways in which reading comprehension occurs. De Beaugrande's article raises new issues and doubts about the certainty of a "linear processing" explanation of the reading phenomenon. Spiro's article on consciousness in comprehending texts reminds readers of the necessity for integrating elements of conscious awareness into theories of reading comprehension. Dehn's article offers new insights into our understanding of reading comprehension by examining the ways in which computers have been used to interpret texts.

Part Two, "Focus: Language," contains three articles on the relationships between important aspects of language study and reading. In her paper on language development and reading, Menyuk reviews the literature on the relationships between oral language and reading; she concludes that the successful reader must bring selected categories of linguistic awareness to consciousness while processing the texts. Salus and Salus offer an explanation of lexical storage, organization and access and its relation to reading. Sticht's article examines simultaneous reading and listening tasks within the framework of a developmental model of reading. He concludes that competent reading and auding rates are the same because they use the same linguistic and conceptual bases.

Part Three, "Focus: The Structure of Prose," consists of four articles on the ways in which texts are organized, the relationship between structure and reading comprehension. Calfee and Curley present a taxonomy of prose structures from a psychological perspective; they focus on the factors within a text that facilitate or impede comprehension. Hasan argues that cohesion is the phenomenon on which the foundation of coherence rests within a text. She maintains that textual coherence is a function of the degree of interactive cohesive chains within a text. Kintsch and Miller's paper examines the question, "What makes a text readable?" from a cognitive perspective. Chall's article on readability discusses views in which discourse analysis may be integrated into formulae for measuring text difficulty.

The entire volume is intended to illuminate our current understanding of the ways in which the reader's cognition and language and the text's structure affect the processing of prose.

J.F.

PART ONE   Focus: Cognition

Rumelhart presents a detailed account of a schematic-theoretical model of reading. He cites several studies that have been conducted by himself and others at the Center for Human Information Processing in the processing of stories. His analogy of a reader being like a detective in search of a set of consistent clues to be reconstructed in a logical manner is particularly helpful in understanding some properties of the nature of understanding.

Understanding Understanding

David E. Rumelhart
University of California at San Diego

What is understanding? How do we make sense out of what we read or are told? I believe that over the past several years a substantial consensus has arisen in the field of cognitive science about the broad outlines of this process (Fillmore, 1975; Minsky, 1975; Rumelhart, 1977; Rumelhart & Ortony, 1977; Schank & Abelson, 1977). In this paper I wish to sketch the basic features of those outlines and to show how this sketch can be given some reality by a careful analysis of the interpretations people actually make of stories and story fragments.

Consider the following brief fragment of a story.

> Mary heard the ice cream truck coming down the street. She remembered her birthday money and rushed into the house.

Upon hearing just these few words most readers already have a rather complete interpretation of the events in the story. Presumably Mary is a little girl who wants to buy some ice cream from the ice cream vendor and runs into the house to get her money. Of course, it doesn't *say* this in the story, there are other possibilities. Mary could be afraid that the ice cream vendor might *steal* her birthday money. Still, most readers find the first interpretation most plausible and retain it unless later information contradicts it.

Consider, in contrast, the following story fragment.

> Mary heard the bus coming down the street. She remembered her birthday money and rushed into the house.

Upon hearing a fragment such as this, most people get a rather different notion of what the story might be about. The story fragment is less coherent. For most, Mary is older. Rather than the 4 to 8 year old of the previous paragraph, Mary is now at least a teenager and possibly even an adult. Moreover, the quantity of money is somewhat greater. Almost surely the money is not needed to buy passage on the bus itself—somehow bus fare is too mundane for birthday money.

Consider still another variation on this same story.

> Mary heard the ice cream truck coming down the street. She remembered her gun and rushed into the house.

Here we get a rather different interpretation again. Is Mary going to rob the ice cream vendor? Does she fear for her life? Note how the modification of a single word or phrase signals an entirely different interpretation. What sort of process could account for such radical differences? Surely, it cannot be a process which takes word meanings and parlays them into sentence meanings and then into text meanings.

The purpose of this paper is to explore the processes involved in these examples, to give a general account of these processes, and to describe some experiments I have been doing in an attempt to understand them more fully.

To begin, let me lay out a general theoretical account of the comprehension process as I understand it and then turn to some data which help explicate this process.

A Schema-Theoretic Model of Understanding

In my attempts to account for these phenomena I have found it useful to appeal to the notion of *schemata*. Before proceeding with a discussion of comprehension itself, it might be useful to explicate my notion of schemata.

A schema theory is basically a theory about knowledge—a theory about how knowledge is represented and about how that representation facilitates the use of the knowledge in particular ways. According to schema theories all knowledge is packaged into units. These units are the schemata. Embedded in these packets of knowledge, in addition to the knowledge itself, is information about how this knowledge is to be used.

A schema, then, is a data structure for representing the generic concepts stored in memory. There are schemata representing our knowledge about all concepts: underlying objects, situations, events, sequences of events, actions, and sequences of actions. As part of its specification, schema contains the network of interrelations believed to normally hold among the constituents of the concept of question. A schema theory embodies a *prototype* theory of meaning. That is, inasmuch as a schema underlying a concept stored in memory corresponds to the meaning of that concept, meanings are encoded in terms of the typical or normal situations or events which instantiate that concept.

. Perhaps the central function of schemata is in the construction of an interpretation of an event, object, or situation—in the process of comprehension. In all of this, it is useful to think of a schema as a kind of informal, private, unarticulated theory about the nature of the events, objects, or situations we face. The total set of schemata we have available for interpreting our world in a sense constitutes our private theory of the nature of reality. The total set of schemata instantiated at a particular moment in time constitutes our internal model of the situation we face at that moment in time or in the case of reading a text, a model of the situation depicted by the text.

Thus, just as the activity surrounding a theory is often focused on the evaluation of the theory and the comparison of the theory with observations we have made, so it is that the primary activity associated with a schema is the determination whether it gives an adequate account for some aspects of our current situation. Just as the determination that a particular theory accounts for some observed results involves the determination of the parameters of the theory, so the determination that a particular configuration of schemata accounts for the data presently available to our senses requires the determination of the values of the variables of the schemata. If a promising schema fails to account for some aspect of a situation, one has the options of accepting the schema as adequate in spite of its flawed account or of rejecting the schema as inadequate and looking for another possibility. Therefore, the fundamental processes of comprehension are taken to be analogous with hypothesis testing, evaluation of goodness of fit, and parameter estimation. Thus, a reader of a text is presumably constantly evaluating hypotheses about the most plausible interpretation of the text. Readers are said to have understood the text when they are able to find a configuration of hypotheses (schemata) which offer a coherent account for the various aspects of the text. To the degree that a particular reader fails to find such a configuration, the text will appear disjointed and incomprehensible.

Schemata are like theories in another important respect. Once they are moderately successful, theories become a source of predictions about unobserved events. Not all experiments are carried out. Not all possible observations are made. Instead, we use our theories to make inferences with some confidence about these unobserved events. So it is with schemata. We need not observe all aspects of a situation before we are willing to assume that some particular configuration of schemata offers a satisfactory account for that situation. Once we have accepted a configuration of schemata, the schemata themselves provide a richness which goes far beyond our observations. Upon deciding that we have seen an automobile, we assume that it has an engine, headlights, and all of the standard characteristics of an automobile. We do this without the slightest hesitation. We have complete confidence in our theory. This allows our interpretations to far outstrip our observations. In fact, once we have determined that a particular schema accounts for some event we may not be able to determine which aspects of our beliefs are based on direct information and which are merely consequences of our interpretation.

On Getting Some Evidence

I have been investigating story comprehension for several years and have developed a story grammar (Rumelhart, 1975) which has proven useful in the analysis of story comprehension and recall. More recently (Rumelhart, 1977), I have recast that original work in the general framework described and have developed a model capable of accounting for the kinds of summaries people give to very simple stories. Although this general approach to story understanding and story memory has proven popular, I have been dissatisfied with the work on two accounts:

1. Although much of the work (including my own) has focused on the process of story understanding, most of the experiments employed postcomprehension measures. Usually the measures have employed story recall and occasionally they have employed summarization. I have wished increasingly for truly "on-line" measures of comprehension.
2. The story grammar approach has tended to focus on abstract features of story comprehension. By its nature, the story schemata I (and most others) have studied offer a very general account of the structure readers see in stories. This generality is a plus in the sense that the schemata are very generally used, but they are a minus in the sense that they ignore the vast amount of other information which subjects can and do bring to bear in understanding stories.

In the series of studies described in this paper, I set out to study this process of hypothesis generation and evaluation during the process of comprehension. Perhaps the simplest way to determine what people are thinking while they are understanding is to ask them.

The basic experimental paradigm involved presenting subjects a series of stories a sentence at a time and, after each sentence, asking them WHO they thought the characters under discussion were, WHAT they felt was going on in the story, WHY the characters behaved as they did, WHEN they think the event described took place, and WHERE they think the story is set. A series of ten pairs of stories and/or story fragments were prepared. Most of the stories were based on initial segments of actual short stories written by well-known authors. The segments were edited slightly so that an alternate version of each story could be created through the modification of one or two words or phrases. The two story versions were designed, like the example story fragments at the beginning of this paper, so that the modification led to a rather different interpretation of the whole story. Each subject read one version of each one of the ten different stories. In order to assess the effects on comprehension of the line at a time interpretation procedure, some subjects were presented the stories two lines at a time, some were presented four lines at a time, and still others were presented the whole story at one time.

Two results emerged immediately from this procedure:

1. The process is very natural. Subjects report that it is very easy to describe the hypotheses that come to mind as they read. Unlike problem solving where the collecting of protocols seems to interfere with the process, our evidence indicates that, if anything, it actually improves comprehension.
2. Subjects show a remarkable degree of agreement. With just three or four subjects the broad outlines of the sorts of results generally obtained become clear.

Perhaps the best way to illustrate the procedure and the kinds of results obtained is by example. Read the following sentence which is the first line from one of my stories.

I was brought into a large white room and my eyes began to blink because the bright light hurt them.

Consider this sentence and what scene comes to mind. There was a good deal of agreement among my subjects. Almost without fail, people belived that this was either an INTERROGATION situation in which the protagonist is being held prisoner, or it is a HOSPITAL scene in which the protagonist is a patient. It is interesting that when asked (after they had finished the story) why they thought it was whatever they thought, almost all reported it was the *bright lights* or the *large white room* which had tipped them off. In point of fact, further experimentation seems to indicate that it was the *was brought* which was the key, putting the protagonist in a passive situation. The large white room and bright lights simply further specify the basically passive situation aroused by the particular construction.

The OIL CRISIS Story

As a second example, consider the following brief passage used in my experiment.

> Business had been slow since the oil crisis. Nobody seemed to want anything really elegant anymore. Suddenly the door opened and a well-dressed man entered the showroom floor. John put on his friendliest and most sincere expression and walked toward the man.

Although merely a fragment, my subjects generated a rather clear interpretation of this story. Apparently, John is a car salesperson fallen on hard times. He probably sells rather large, elegant cars. Suddenly a good prospect enters the showroom where John works. John wants to make a sale and to do that he must make a good impression on the man. Therefore he tries to appear friendly and sincere. He wants to talk to the man to deliver his sales pitch, so he makes his way over to the man. Presumably, had the story continued John would have made the sales pitch and, if all went well, sold the man a car.

How, according to the theory described, do people arrive at such an interpretation? Clearly, people do not arrive at it all at once. As the sentences are read, schemata are activated, evaluated, and refined or discarded. When people are asked to describe their various hypotheses as they read through the story, a remarkably consistent pattern of hypothesis generation and evaluation emerges. The first sentence is usually interpreted to mean that business is slow because of the oil crisis. Thus, people are led to see the story is about a suffering business which is somehow dependent on oil. Frequent hypotheses involve either the selling of cars or of gasoline. A few interpret the sentence as being about the economy in general. The second sentence, about people not wanting elegant things anymore, leads people with the gas station hypothesis into a quandary. Elegance just doesn't fit with gas stations. The gas station hypothesis is weakened, but not always rejected. On the other hand, people with hypotheses about the general economy or about cars have no trouble incorporating this sentence into their emerging interpretation. In the former case, they conclude it means that people don't buy luxury items and, in the latter, they assume it means that people don't buy large, elegant cars much anymore. The third sentence clinches the car interpretation for nearly all readers. They are already looking for a business interpretation—that probably means a SELLING interpretation—and when a *well-dressed man* enters the door he is immediately labeled as someone with MONEY—a prospective BUYER.

Rumelhart

The phrase *showroom floor* clearly invalidates the gas station interpretation and strongly implicates automobiles which are often sold from a showroom. Moreover, the occurrence of a specific event doesn't fit at all well with the view that the passage is a general discussion of the state of the economy. Finally, with the introduction of John, we have an ideal candidate for the SELLER. John's actions are clearly those stereotypic of a salesperson. John wants to make a sale and his "putting on" is clearly an attempt on his part to "make a good impression." His movement toward the man fits nicely into this interpretation. If he is a salesperson, he must make contact with the customer and deliver the stereotypic "pitch."

Qualitatively, this account fits well with the general theoretical approach I have been outlining. The process of comprehension is very much like the process of constructing a theory, testing it against the data currently available, and as more data becomes available, specifying the theory further—i.e., refining the default values (as perhaps was the case when those holding the "car hypothesis" from the beginning encountered the sentence about nobody wanting anything elegant anymore). If the account becomes sufficiently strained, it is given up and a new one constructed or, alternatively, if a new theory presents itself which obviously gives a more cogent account, the old one can be dropped and the new one accepted.

But where do these theories come from? These theories are, of course, schemata. Presumably, through experience we have built up a vast repertoire of such schemata. We have schemata for car salespersonnel, the kinds of motives they have, and the kinds of techniques they employ. We have schemata for the "oil crisis" and what kinds of effects it has on what kinds of businesses. We have schemata about business people, the kinds of motives they have, and the kinds of responses they make to these motives. The knowledge embedded in these schemata forms the framework for our theories. It is some configuration of these schemata which ultimately forms the basis for our understanding.

But how does a relevant schema suggest itself? Presumably, it is the bottom-up observation that a certain concept has been referenced that leads to the suggestion of the initial hypotheses. The notion that business was slow suggests a schema about business and the economy. Since the slowness was dated from the occurrence of the oil crisis, it is a natural inference that the oil crisis was the *cause* of the slowness. Thus, a BUSINESS schema is activated. The particular TYPE of business is presumably a variable which must be filled. The information about the oil crisis suggests that it may be an oil-related business. Thus, readers are led to restrict the TYPE variable of the BUSINESS schema to oil-related businesses.

At this point, after the bottom-up activation of the high level BUSINESS schema has occurred, this schema would generate a top-down activation of the various possible oil related businesses. Prime candidates for these are, of course, automobile related businesses. Of these, selling gasoline and automobiles are the most salient.

When the second sentence is encountered, an attempt is made to fit it into the schemata currently considered most promising. As discussed, this information could serve to further restrict the TYPE variable in the automobile BUSINESS schema, but doesn't fit well with the gasoline business schema.

The BUSINESS schema presumably has a reference to the BUY or SELL schema. Once activated, these schemata search for potential variable bindings. In the case of the automobile business, the MERCHANDISE variable is bound to be an automobile. The second sentence suggests an elegant automobile. When the third sentence is encountered, the reader has not yet found a candidate for BUYER or SELLER. The sentence about a well-dressed man immediately suggests a potential BUYER. The phrase "showroom floor" offers additional bottom-up support for the automobile hypothesis. In fact, it is a strong enough clue itself that it can suggest automobile sales to a reader who currently considers the alternative schema more likely. We thus have a BUYER and some MERCHANDISE. The well-dressed quality of the BUYER is consistent with our view that the MERCHANDISE is elegant and, therefore, expensive (being well-dressed suggests MONEY). We need only a SELLER—i.e., an automobile salesperson. Readers probably already bring a relatively complete characterization of the "default value" for a car salesperson. We need but little additional information to generate a rather detailed description of goals and motives.

It is, in general, a difficult matter to analyze freeform responses of the sort obtained in this experiment. I have, however, devised a data representation scheme which allows the tracking of a subject's hypotheses through a story. The basic idea is illustrated in Figure 1. At any point in time a subject's hypothesis state can be characterized as a region in a multidimensional hypothesis space in which one dimension is time (or place in the story) and the other dimensions represent the subject's momentary beliefs about WHO the characters are, WHAT is

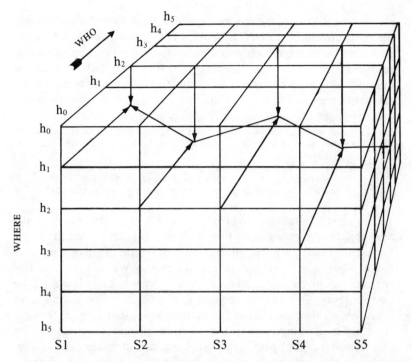

Figure 1. A representation of a subject's shifting hypotheses while reading a story. One dimension represents the sequence of sentences in the story. The other two dimensions represent a subject's hypotheses with respect to WHO the characters are and WHERE the action is taking place. The vector passing through the space represents a possible sequence of hypotheses.

going on in the story, and WHERE the story is set. Just two dimensions, WHERE and WHO, are illustrated in the figure. Each point in the space represents a possible hypothesis at some point in time. A particular subject's sequence of hypotheses can be represented as a path passing through the space. We can imagine that at particularly critical times during the reading of the story the path will turn sharply in several dimensions. At the start, we might imagine that different subjects would occupy a fairly wide region of the space. By the end, all of the paths for the different subjects should have converged on one or two points in the space. The dimensions, other than the dimension of time, are purely nominal and subjects often hold several hypotheses at once (i.e., they occupy not a point, but a region of the space). Nevertheless, this general representation proves useful in charting subjects' changing hypotheses.

I will illustrate the general form of analysis by looking at some of the results from the "Oil Crisis" story. In order to analyze the data, the responses for each question were categorized and for each subject it was recorded which of the responses was given. For example, there were five different categories of answers to WHERE the story took place. The five categories were:

1. *Indefinite*—when subjects said they had no clear idea.
2. *Gas station*—when subjects believed the action was occurring at a gas station.
3. *Showroom*—when subjects believed the action took place in an automobile showroom.
4. *Luxury store*—when subjects believed the action took place in a luxury store such as a jewelry store or a fancy furniture or clothing store.
5. *Nation*—when subjects believed the story was a general statement about the national economy.

Figure 2 illustrates the patterns of responses observed from the ten subjects who read this version of the story. Each line on the graph represents a pattern of responses. The number on the lines represents the number of subjects showing that pattern. We can see that five subjects had no clear idea where the events were taking place after the first sentence. One subject thought from the start that it was in an automobile showroom. After the first sentence, four subjects thought the story was taking place in a gas station. We can see that after the second sentence four people thought it was an automobile showroom,

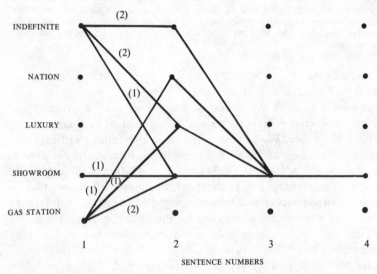

Figure 2. Set of paths through the hypothesis space for the question WHERE the "Oil Crisis" story was taking place.

three thought it was a luxury store, two were still indefinite, and one thought it was a general discussion of a national economy.

There is not space to illustrate the whole pattern of results for this story, so now I turn to discussion of a second story which shows a more dramatic pattern of results.

The DEAR LITTLE THING Story

Consider the following story used in my experiment.

1. Dear little thing.
2. It was nice to feel it again.
3. She had taken it out of its box that afternoon, given it a good brush, and rubbed life back into its dim little eyes.
4. Little rogue! Yes, she really felt that way about it.
5. She put it on.
6. Little rogue, biting its tail just by her left ear.
7. When she breathed, something gentle seemed to move on her bosom.
8. The day was cool and she was glad she had decided on her little fur.

The results for this story are particularly interesting. As people read the story they form clear impressions of certain aspects of the story, but none of them consider the possibility that the story might be about a fur until the fifth line of the story, and for some, this is not clear until the last line of the story. From the beginning, however, many readers have an impression that the speaker in the story is a woman. Of the twenty people to read the first line of the story, seven mentioned that they thought that it was a woman speaking. In none of my other stories did people spontaneously assign a sex to the speaker after only reading the first sentence. Apparently a number of the readers interpret the pattern of speech here to be typically feminine. This is illustrative of the subtlety of the kinds of clues readers pick up on and that authors count on.

Perhaps the most interesting response was that which subjects made to the WHAT questions. Here we get the clearest picture of their overall assessment of what the story is about. There were six categories of responses given by our subjects. These were:

1. *Clothing*—they thought the woman was talking about a hat or some jewelry.
2. *Fur*—they thought the woman was talking about a fur.
3. *Letter*—they thought someone was writing a letter.
4. *Pet*—they thought the story was about a pet.
5. *Stimulation*—they thought the story was about sexual stimulation.
6. *Toy*—they thought the story was about a stuffed animal or doll.

Figure 3 shows the pattern of hypotheses held by the ten people who read this version of the story. After the opening line, "Dear little thing," people were about evenly split between the possibility that it was about a pet or letter writing. The second line, "It was nice to feel it again," discouraged all but one of the letter writing hypotheses. Some of these decided that the story was about a toy or stuffed animal. Others assumed it was about sexual stimulation or had no clear idea. The third line moved almost everyone who didn't think it was a pet to the view it was a toy. The fourth line offered no new information and people held onto their previous hypotheses. The fifth line, "She put it on," was difficult to assimilate with any of the hypotheses and, as is evident from the figure, nearly everyone switched to the view that it was either a piece of clothing or jewelry or that it was a fur piece. The seventh line strengthened the FUR hypothesis and the eighth line clinched it for everyone.

The figure clearly shows the critical nature of the fifth sentence. We can see subjects, on the basis of such bottom-up information as the use of the word *dear*, determine that it might be a letter or a diminutive reference to a pet. Then, once finding a satisfactory hypothesis, subjects maintain and refine it until disconfirming information is made available. When disconfirmation occurs, subjects search out a new workable hypothesis.

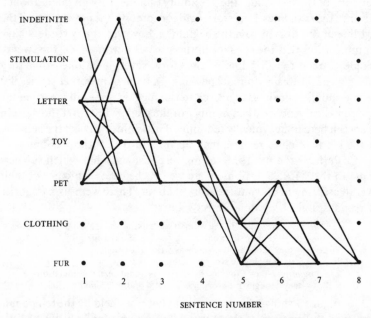

Figure 3. Set of paths through the hypothesis space for the question of WHAT in the "Dear Little Thing" story.

Clearly, in this case, my subjects are behaving according to the hypothesis evaluation mode that I have suggested. But is this the normal way of processing? Doesn't the procedure force them to respond in this way? These are serious questions. Indeed, I believe there is an effect of the procedure. However, I believe it is better categorized as making subjects read more carefully than at modifying the basic procedure. One bit of evidence for this view is that over all of the stories, subjects who interpreted the stories a line at a time more often agreed with one another (and with the experimenters) about the interpretation of the story than subjects who gave an interpretation only after having read the whole story. In addition, a second experiment was carried out to try to get an alternative measure of on-line processing. In this experiment, the subjects were not asked to make any interpretations of the story. Rather, they were presented the story one word at a time and asked to press a button after they read each word to get the next word. The time to read each word was recorded. We can then compare different versions of the same story, one in which we know from the interpretation experiments requires a rather dramatic shift in hypotheses, and another which requires no such shift or a shift at a different place. The "Dear Little Thing" story offers an ideal example. The alternative version of this story differed in three words. Sentence 5 was "She put it down" rather than "She put it on." Sentence 6 ended "by her left ankle" rather than "by her left ear," and sentence 8 ended "take her pet along" rather than "take her fur along." Thus, for the FUR version, subjects probably had to shift hypotheses after line 5. For the PET version, subjects probably already had the correct hypothesis by line 5. Thus, the two stories were identical for the first 49 words and differed in only 3 of the final 38 words.

Since we know from the interpretation experiment that a good deal of reevaluation occurs in the FUR form of the story after line 5 and that a large number of subjects have the PET hypothesis well before line 5, it is reasonable that people would read the last 38 words of the story more slowly in the FUR version. Table 1 shows the average reading time per word for the first 49 and last 38 words for the two versions of the story. The expected difference is apparent in the table. The average reading time for the first half of the story is about the same for the two groups. Those with the FUR version were about 200 milliseconds slower over the last half of the story. Unfortunately, the magnitudes in the table are probably somewhat misleading. There is an average difference of some 20 milliseconds between the groups for the first half of the story. In fact, this average is a mixture of some early slow responses and some later fast responses for the PET group. A better estimate for the difference between the two groups' base line reading speed is 125 milliseconds per word. Thus, the apparent 200 milliseconds per word differences evident in the table is probably closer to a 75 millisecond difference per word. Nevertheless, even with this conservative estimate of the difference between the base reading rate of the two groups, the 75 millisecond per word figure over the 38 words amounts to an average difference of almost 3 seconds longer for the FUR group. Thus, in spite of some difficulties with the data here, it would appear that we have been able to see, in slower reading times, the same hypothesis reevaluation our subjects in the interpretation experiment told us about.

TABLE 1

Mean Reading Time Per Word in Milliseconds

Story Version	First 49 Words	Last 38 Words
FUR	886	1011
PET	864	801

A closer look at the data appears to confirm this conclusion. Much of this effect is already evident on the reading of the last word of line 5. Figure 4 shows the reading times for each word in the line. The most obvious characteristic of these curves is the increased reaction time for the last word of the sentence for both versions of the story. This upswing on the last word of a sentence is normal in all experiments of this sort. It appears to represent some sort of "consolidation" phase of the reading process. More important to the present discussion, however, is the difference in response time between those subjects who heard the word "on" and those who heard the word "down" as the last word of the sentence. Upon hearing on the PET and TOY hypotheses are disconfirmed and subjects are forced to begin to reevaluate their hypotheses. This reevaluation apparently takes time. Indeed, as Figure 5 indicates, many of the subjects are apparently still formulating more hypotheses through the following sentence. Notice the time required by the subjects with the FUR version compared with those with the PET version for the word tail. Presumably those with the PET version have already hit upon the pet hypothesis and thus the word tail fits nicely into their existing interpretation. Many of those in the FUR version have probably chosen the hypothesis that the story is about a piece of clothing or jewelry and thus are not able to integrate "tail" into their existing interpretation—similarly, for the last word of the sentence. The subjects with the PET version have little or no trouble with the pet being near the woman's ankle. The FUR subjects find it difficult to reconcile something with a tail being near the woman's ear.

Overall, in spite of the unfortunate baseline differences between the two groups, the reading time results do appear to confirm the view that a very different method of gaining access to on-line processing leads to a generally congruent pattern of results.

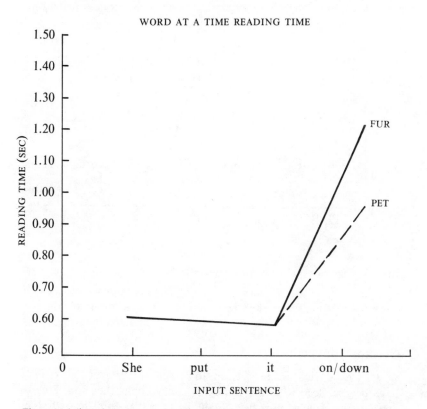

Figure 4. Adjusted word by word reading times for the two versions of line 5 of the "Dear Little Thing" story. Due to overall differences in the reading rates of the two groups, the times for the FUR group were adjusted downward by subtracting 125 msec for each point. This value was chosen so that the two groups showed about the same level of performance over the three words before the two stories diverge.

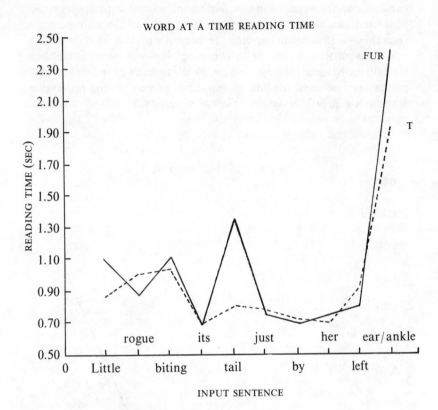

Figure 5. Adjusted word by word reading times for the two versions of line 6 of the "Dear Little Thing" story. Again the times for the PET data represent raw data while the FUR curve has been adjusted downward by 125 msec to adjust for overall differences in reading time between the two groups which was evident before the stories diverged.

General Comments

I have tried, in this section, to present a flavor of the results I have been collecting in the context of story comprehension. Due to limitations of space I have been unable to present a complete analysis of all of my data. Nevertheless, these examples should serve to illustrate the major points. When asked to generate interpretations of stories while reading through a story line-by-line, subjects generate hypotheses about the possible contents of the story and evaluate them against the sentences as they read them. If they find the new information confirmatory they maintain and further elaborate their hypotheses. If they find the new information disconfirmatory they eliminate the hypothesis and construct another consistent with the input data. This process seems to involve both top-down and bottom-up processes. Certain words and phrases appear to suggest, from the bottom-up, certain frameworks of interpretation such as the INTERROGATION framework in the first example. Once a particular interpretation has received a moderate degree of support, it can come to guide the processing and interpretation of future inputs. Subjects find it natural to go beyond the specifics of what the input sentences actually say. Their interpretations contain material about aspects of the situation which are totally unaddressed in the input text.

To what degree is this a natural process, as the schema theory sketched in the first section suggests, and to what degree does the procedure force the subjects to behave as the theory suggests they would? This is a difficult question for this approach. It is extraordinarily difficult to get data which bear on this issue. Three approaches have been tried:

1. I have collected word-by-word reading times for subjects not instructed to generate interpretations and have looked for correlations between points in the story where we believe subjects to be evaluating new hypotheses and those where we observe elevated response times. By and large, as the examples presented earlier illustrate, these two measures correlate.

2. I have collected interpretations of subjects after they read the whole story and compared them with those of subjects who read the stories a line at a time. The results showed that subjects who interpreted a line at a time nearly always generated the same interpretations as those who gave us an after-the-fact interpretation. The only discernable difference was that those who gave an interpretation only at the end showed somewhat more variability in their interpretations. It appears that this results from more careless reading on the part of the subjects offering an interpretation only at the end.

3. I have asked a few subjects for retrospective analyses of the processes they went through while reading the stories immediately after reading the stories. Although such subjects mention fewer hypothesis changes than those giving on-line interpretations, the overall structure of their reports seems to parallel those of the on-line subjects.

None of these methods is really totally convincing in and of itself. Nevertheless, the combination of the fact that the response times seem to follow the hypothesis interpretations, the fact that the interpretation paradigm doesn't seem to affect the final interpretations subjects generate, and the fact that in informal observations subjects' retrospective reports seem very similar to the line-at-a-time results points strongly to the view that the general pattern of hypothesis generation observed in our experiments is present in normal reading.

On Understanding and Misunderstanding

Before concluding, it is useful to consider the application of this general theory to the notion of misunderstanding. On the present account, understanding is the process of finding a configuration of schemata which offers an adequate account of a passage or situation. The analysis given illustrates how such a process is supposed to operate. Clues from the story suggest possible instantiations of schemata which are then evaluated against the successive sentences of the story until finally a consistent interpretation is discovered. Sometimes, a reader fails to correctly understand a passage. There are at least three reasons implicit in schema theory as to why this might occur.

1. Readers may not have the appropriate schemata. In this case they simply cannot understand the concept being communicated.
2. Readers may have the appropriate schemata, but the clues provided by the author may be insufficient to suggest them. Here again readers will not understand the text but, with appropriate additional clues may come to understand.
3. Readers may find a consistent interpretation of the text, but may not find the one intended by the author. In this case, readers will understand the text, but will misunderstand the author.

There are many examples of these three phenomena in the literature. Perhaps the most interesting set of studies along these lines were carried out by Bransford and Johnson (1973). They studied the comprehension of texts in which subjects lacked the appropriate schemata, ones in which the schemata were potentially available, but there were not sufficient clues to suggest the correct ones as well as ones in which subjects were led to choose a wrong interpretation. Consider the following paragraph used in one of their studies.

The procedure is actually quite simple. First you arrange things into different groups. Of course, one pile may be sufficient depending on how much there is to do. If you have to go somewhere else due to lack of facilities that is the next step, otherwise you are pretty well set. It is important not to overdo things. That is, it is better to do too few things at once than too many. In the short run this may not seem important but complications can easily arise. A mistake can be expensive as well. At first the whole procedure will seem complicated. Soon, however, it will become just another facet of life. It is difficult to foresee any end to the necessity for this task in the immediate future, but then one can never tell. After the procedure is completed one arranges the materials into different groups again. Then they can be put into their appropriate places. Eventually they will be used once more and the whole cycle will then have to be repeated. However, that is part of life. [p. 400]

Most readers find this passage, as written, extremely difficult to understand. However, once they are told that it is about washing clothes, they are able to bring their clothes-washing schema to the fore and make sense out of the story. The difficulty with this passage is not that readers don't have the appropriate schemata; rather, it stems from the fact that the clues in the story never seem to *suggest* the appropriate schemata in the first place. The bottom-up information is inadequate to initiate the comprehension process appropriately. Once the appropriate schemata are suggested, most people have no trouble understanding the text.

Although most readers simply find the passage incomprehensible, some find alternative schemata to account for it and thus render it comprehensible. Perhaps the most interesting interpretation I have collected was from a Washington bureaucrat who had no difficulty with the passage. He was able to interpret the passage as a clear description of his job. He was, in fact, surprised to find that it was supposed to be about "washing clothes" and not about "pushing papers." Here we have an example of the third kind of comprehension failure, "understanding the story but misunderstanding the author."

Conclusion

At this point, it might be useful to put this comprehension theory in the context of a theory of communication. I find it useful to think of the general view of comprehension put forth here as suggesting that the problem facing a comprehender is analogous to the problem that a detective faces when trying to solve a crime. In both cases there is a set of clues. The listeners' or readers' job is to find a consistent interpretation of these clues. In so doing, listeners use their own prior experiences and knowledge of the speaker to create a most plausible possibility. Just as the meaning of a particular clue that a detective might find cannot be determined except in relation to the way it fits into the whole situation so, too, the meaning of a particular word, phrase, or even sentence cannot be interpreted except in relation to the way it fits into the whole of the story. Similarly, speakers or writers are to leave trails of clues which, in the opinion of the speakers, will lead readers to make the inferences the speakers wish to communicate. Thus, speakers must use their knowledge of the listener, or at least of the cultural expectations of the listener, to create the set of clues which most reliably and economically leads the listener to the desired hypotheses.

Thus, authors of short stories do not need to spell out every detail. Instead, they provide the reader with subtle clues which they can expect the reader will pick up on. Thus, in the example of the INTERROGATION scene, by subtle use of the passive and the mention of bright lights and a white room, the author has generated in the reader a full-blown image of an entire INTERROGATION scene. The remainder of the story can then play off of these subtle clues and needn't waste time or words setting the scene. Similarly, in the "Dear Little Thing" story, in a single phrase the author has suggested to many that a woman is speaking. I suspect these stories are not at all unusual and that in general all of the inferences we wish to communicate never can be spelled out, and that we must always depend on our ability to draw forth the appropriate schemata in the listener through a large variety of clues.

Finally, let me comment on the direction I wish to push the sort of work I have discussed here. For the past several years, I have been attempting to create a computer simulation system capable of comprehending language according to the kinds of principles just described. I have taken as an empirical goal the attempt to create a program capable of mimicking the experimental results from the interpretation experiments. Obviously, a detailed account of the comprehension process requires a detailed description of the schemata readers have available, as well as an account of the conditions under which certain of these schemata are activated. There is a startling amount of knowledge brought to bear on even the simplest story comprehension task. Nevertheless, I believe that data of the sort I have described will provide a useful data base against which to evaluate models of comprehension.

Baker and Brown present concise definitions of metacognition, cognitive monitoring, and comprehension monitoring. They extensively review the emerging body of literature on monitoring and conclude that novice readers are less likely to take charge of their own cognitive processing while reading. The mature, competent reader is able to activate and use prior knowledge during reading, whereas the novice reader is developing in the ability to attend to the complex, simultaneously assaulting, demands of reading.

Cognitive Monitoring in Reading

Linda Baker
Ann L. Brown
University of Illinois

It is becoming increasingly rare to find discussions of reading comprehension that do not include the terms metacognition, cognitive monitoring, or comprehension monitoring. The proliferation of this terminology is largely attributable to the influence of cognitive science on the field of reading research and is apparent in many current volumes dealing with reading (Just & Carpenter, 1977; LaBerge & Samuels, 1977; Pearson, in press; Spiro, Bruce, & Brewer, 1980; Waller & MacKinnon, in press). It is the aim of this chapter to facilitate understanding of these terms, which are often used interchangeably, and to illustrate why they have come to play such an important role in research and theory on reading comprehension.

We will begin by defining the terms and tracing the historical antecedents. Next, we will consider in some detail the major methods of studying cognitive monitoring in reading. All of the following methods (and more) have been attempted: 1) asking readers to imagine a hypothetical reading situation and how they would perform in it, 2) asking readers to report what they are doing while actually reading, and 3) assessing readers' ongoing comprehension monitoring processes by a variety of performance measures. Any method has its own set of problems and we would like to begin by sensitizing the reader to the difficulties of interpretation attendant upon any particular method. In the third section we will give the highlights of the extensive literature now emerging, with comparisons between children and adults whenever possible.

Some Definitions

Metacognition, cognitive monitoring, and comprehension monitoring are hierarchically related concepts. Comprehension monitoring is one type of cognitive monitoring, and cognitive monitoring is a component of metacognition. The term metacognition was introduced by developmental psychologists to refer to the knowledge and control children have over their own thinking and learning activities (Brown, 1978, 1980; Flavell, 1978). Metacognition involves at least two separate components: 1) an awareness of what skills, strategies, and resources are needed to perform a task effectively; and 2) the ability to use self-regulatory mechanisms to ensure the successful completion of the task, such as *checking* the outcome of any attempt to solve the problem, *planning* one's next move, *evaluating* the effectiveness of any attempted action, *testing*, and *revising* one's strategies for learning, and *remediating* any difficulties encountered by using compensatory strategies (Baker & Brown, in press). The use of these self-regulatory mechanisms is known as cognitive monitoring (Flavell, in press). Since most of the cognitive activities involved in reading have as their goal successful comprehension, a large part of cognitive monitoring in reading is actually comprehension monitoring. Comprehension monitoring entails keeping track of the success with which one's comprehension is proceeding, ensuring that the process continues smoothly, and taking remedial action if necessary (Baker, 1979).

Few readers of this chapter would disagree with the claim that effective readers must have some awareness and control of the cognitive activities they engage in as they read. In fact, since the turn of the century, educators (Dewey, 1910; Huey, 1908; Thorndike, 1917) have recognized that reading involves the planning, checking, and evaluating activities subsumed here under the heading of metacognition.

In this chapter, we will summarize findings from a variety of different sources which implicate the importance of metacognition in reading. Our primary emphasis will be on research dealing with the self-regulatory cluster of metacognitive activities, especially those concerned with monitoring comprehension. Though researchers have also investigated cognitive monitoring in reading for remembering (studying), we will restrict ourselves here to reading for meaning (comprehending). (See Baker & Brown, in press, and Brown, 1980, for reviews of the studying research.)

Methods of Studying Cognitive Monitoring in Reading

We devote a separate section to methods that have been used to study cognitive monitoring in reading because there are nontrivial problems associated with each method and adequate interpretation of the data demands a careful consideration of the constraints under which those data were obtained. How disruptive of the normal reading process was the method of obtaining data? Is there convergent evidence for the inferences made about the comprehension process?

One of the most frequent criticisms leveled against research on comprehension is that it typically uses product rather than process measures; that is, it relies on measures obtained after reading, which are dependent on memory, to make inferences about processes that occurred during reading (Baker & Stein, 1981; Ryan, in press; Simons, 1971). This problem becomes acute if we wish to study readers' control over the activities involved in comprehending. Do we wish to ask them what they would do in a hypothetical situation? Do we wish to ask them to report what activities they were engaging in as they were reading? Should we devise other performance tests that will tap whether they were monitoring their ongoing activities? All of these techniques have been attempted but all are subject to problems of interpretation because of fallible memory or inadequate verbal abilities.

Recent advances in research technology are making it easier to obtain information about the actual processing characteristics of reading. In particular, eye movement research has contributed much to our understanding of the cognitive processes involved in reading (Just & Carpenter, 1980; McConkie, 1976; Rayner, 1978). In addition, interactive computer programs allow individuals to control the amount of time they spend on various segments of text and to reread sections at will (Mitchell & Green, 1978; Rothkopf & Billington, 1979). This on-line research can provide us with information about the comprehension monitoring that occurs during reading, at the same time it provides information about comprehension. For example, a demonstration that readers spend more time on difficult sections of text indicates that they are, to some extent, monitoring the success of their ongoing efforts to understand.

The on-line measures can be criticized, however, because they do not assess comprehension; did the particular behaviors the reader engaged in actually result in comprehension of the text? In order to

116253   23

provide an unambiguous interpretation, the on-line measures must be supplemented with performance measures. In short, the importance of obtaining converging evidence becomes more crucial as the cognitive activity of interest becomes more complex and more remote from directly observable events. We now consider how several of these research techniques have been implemented in studies of cognitive monitoring.

Verbal Reports

The interview technique used by Myers and Paris (1978), Garner and Kraus (1980), and Canney and Winograd (1979), consists of asking children a standard set of questions assessing their knowledge about various aspects of reading. Typical questions include "What does a person have to do to be a good reader?" and "What would you do if you came to a word you didn't know?" Such questions tap the knowledge component of metacognition as opposed to the ongoing self-regulartory functions, and we must not assume that what children know or say they would do is the same as what they would actually do while reading (Brown, 1978, 1980). Nevertheless, the interview studies tend to produce a consistent pattern of results, revealing both developmental differences and differences between children who vary in reading ability.

A related approach to studying cognitive monitoring is to ask readers to comment on their thoughts and behaviors while they are reading. Such self-reports are sometimes collected as running commentaries, or think-aloud protocols (Olshavsky, 1976-1977, 1978; Olson, Duffy, & Mack, 1978) or they may be retrospective reports provided after a reader has finished reading (Collins, Brown, & Larkin, 1980; Fareed, 1971; Ngandu, 1978; Smith, 1967; Strang & Rogers, 1965). Some researchers have also used more direct questioning to elicit comments about reactions to specific sections of text (Anderson, 1979; Baker, 1979). Though one may question the accuracy of these self-reports, they highlight the complexity, variety, and flexibility of the strategies readers may use as they attempt to comprehend.

On-line Processing Measures

Studies in which on-line measures of reading behavior are collected provide evidence of cognitive monitoring, regardless of whether they were specifically designed for such purposes. Interestingly, many of the earliest studies on the psychology of reading used eye movement recordings, and many of the findings (despite poor technology) have held up in more recent, carefully controlled experiments (Huey, 1908; Judd & Buswell, 1922).

Information about ongoing reading behavior also has been obtained through observation. For example, Paris and Myers (1980) observed children as they were reading a text and recorded the number of times they used such external study aids as looking words up in a dictionary or underlining. Wellman, Rysberg, and Suttler (1980) and Brown and Smiley (1978) observed children's reading and study behaviors as they prepared for a subsequent test on the material. In related experiments on comprehension monitoring during listening, children were videotaped as they listened to messages and later the tapes were analyzed for facial or behavioral signs of noncomprehension (Flavell, et al., in press; Patterson, Cosgrove, & O'Brien, 1980). The advantage of the observation technique is that it can provide evidence of comprehension monitoring in situations where verbal difficulties or memory limitations might otherwise yield negative results. Nevertheless, observations are limited by the reliability of the records and by the fact that many monitoring activities cannot be observed overtly.

Another source of evidence for ongoing comprehension monitoring is provided by analysis of oral reading errors (Beebe, 1980; Clay, 1973; Fairbanks, 1937; Isakson & Miller, 1976; Miller & Isakson, 1978; Paris & Myers, 1980; Weber, 1970). Of interest here is whether oral reading errors are sensitive to contextual constraints; that is, whether they are semantically acceptable substitutions given the surrounding context or whether they are both syntactically and semantically out of place. The extent to which unacceptable errors are spontaneously corrected provides an index of on-line monitoring of one's comprehension. One may argue that oral reading poses different constraints on a reader than silent reading and so the conclusions are not generalizable, though Beebe (1980) argues to the contrary.

Comprehension Questions

Several studies use as their main index of cognitive monitoring measures taken after reading has been completed. For example, one measure is provided by analysis of responses readers make to comprehension questions based on the text. Thorndike (1917) has argued persuasively (much as has Piaget, 1926), that errors in responding are at least as informative in revealing one's cognitive processes as are correct responses. Many researchers have made inferences about metacognitive aspects of reading based on responses to comprehension questions (Baker, 1979; Kavale & Schreiner, 1979; Paige & Simon, 1966; Sullivan, 1978; Thorndike, 1917; Whimbey, 1975). The major limitation to this approach is that the reader's memory may not be accurate.

Measures of Felt Understanding

One way of assessing feelings of understanding is to ask people to rate their certainty that they have answered a comprehension question correctly or incorrectly. Readers are considered good comprehension monitors if they indicate they are sure their answers are correct when in fact they are, or if they indicate that their answers are wrong when they are incorrect. On the other hand, readers are considered poor comprehension monitors if there is a mismatch between their confidence ratings and the correctness of their answers (Forrest & Waller, 1979). A limitation with the technique is that it tests one's ability to judge the correctness of an answer given *after* reading, rather than assessing one's feelings of understanding or misunderstanding *during* reading.

Another approach that has been used to assess reader's abilities to gauge their levels of comprehension is to ask them to study material until they are sure they comprehend it and then to administer a comprehension test (Wellman, et al., 1980). If they do not perform the task successfully, they are considered deficient at monitoring their understanding. The problem with this reasoning is that the paradigm requires memory for the passage; if the readers did not comprehend the material they would not be successful on the test. However, the reverse is not true; if they did comprehend, they may or may not be successful, depending on their memory monitoring ability.

Cloze Techniques

Cognitive monitoring has also been investigated using a cloze technique. In a cloze test, people are presented with passages containing word deletions and are asked to supply the missing words. This technique assesses a reader's ability to make efficient use of contextual information (DiVesta, Hayward, & Orlando, 1979; Neville & Pugh, 1976-1977). Cloze tests are somewhat removed from the normal reading situation, however, so strategies adopted in this task may not be the same as those typically used.

Baker and Brown

Text Disruption Techniques

In most of the approaches discussed above, readers are presented with short passages appropriate to their grade level and one or more measures of reading behavior are collected. Since there is no control over which specific sections of text might be found confusing, it is difficult to draw conclusions about the effectiveness of one's comprehension monitoring. In order to be able to make specific predictions as to when and where readers should experience difficulty if they are evaluating their understanding, several experimenters have manipulated the comprehensibility of the text itself. A favorite ploy is to introduce confusing elements into a text and then to examine the effects of such confusions on processing behavior and on the reader's subsequent ability to report that problems were present. For example, students are presented with a passage containing an inconsistency, ambiguity, or nonsense word and are not told in advance that a problem is present. After they have finished reading or listening to the passage, they are asked to indicate whether the passage made sense and was comprehensible (Baker, 1979; Garner, 1980; Markham, 1977, 1979; Pace, 1980; Winograd & Johnston, 1980). The ability to report the intended problem is taken as evidence of comprehension monitoring.

Unfortunately, failures to report message inadequacies may occasionally be due to factors other than poor comprehension monitoring (Baker, 1979; 1979a, 1979b; Brown, 1980; Winograd & Johnston, 1980). Perhaps the students believed they understood the message (i.e., they evaluated their understanding and found it adequate), but their interpretation did not match the author's interpretation. It is also possible that they made inferences to resolve any potential sources of confusion and, for reasons of verbal ability or memory, were unable to convey this when questioned. Students, especially children, also may be unwilling to point out problems in messages or to say they don't understand, despite efforts to make them feel comfortable doing so. Because of these alternative interpretations, it is important to supplement the error detection data with additional measures, such as reading times (Baker & Anderson, 1980); patterns of oral reading (Paris & Myers, 1980); recall questions and retrospective reports (Baker, 1979); and observations of the subjects while reading or listening (Flavell, et al., in press; Paris & Myers, 1980).

One criticism that may be levelled at the disruption technique is that it lacks "ecological validity;" readers do not typically encounter confusing elements in their reading material. We would argue against this position. Newspaper articles often appear with missing words or scrambled paragraphs; textbooks are published routinely that contain sections which can be only described as poorly organized, ambiguous, and inconsistent. Sensitivity to such problems is an important component of comprehension and of critical reading (Robinson, 1964; Torrance, 1967). The goal of researchers using artificially disrupted materials, however, is not to train people to detect confusions but to obtain information about readers' ability to evaluate their understanding, a skill of everyday reading if ever there was one.

Cognitive Monitoring in Selected Reading Activities

We turn now to a consideration of the research that either directly or indirectly reveals cognitive monitoring (or lack thereof) during reading. The review will be organized around nine activities that are crucial to good comprehension: 1) establishing the purposes for reading; 2) modifying reading rates and strategies in accordance with different purposes; 3) identifying the important elements of the passage; 4) capitalizing on the logical structure inherent in the material; 5) using prior knowledge to interpret new information; 6) showing sensitivity to contextual constraints; 7) evaluating the text for clarity, completeness, and consistency; 8) dealing with failures to comprehend; and 9) selecting appropriate standards for assessing one's level of comprehension. The data to be presented under each of these headings have been obtained by using a variety of research techniques and the reader should bear in mind the general limitations of the various approaches just discussed. Whenever possible, we will examine the metacognitive skills exhibited by children of differing ages and reading abilities, as well as by mature readers (i.e., college students).

Establishing the Purposes for Reading

This particular activity can be considered from two perspectives. The first perspective is concerned with beginning readers' conceptions of reading, its purpose, and methods. The second perspective is concerned with more advanced readers' understanding of the demands of a specific task and the knowledge that different purposes require different approaches.

A number of investigators have explored young children's conceptions of reading before they have received formal training and in the early phases of instruction. In addition, several researchers have compared good and poor readers' conceptions of reading. Most of these studies have used interview techniques. One much replicated finding is that younger and poorer readers have little awareness that they must attempt to make sense of text; they focus on reading as a decoding process rather than as a meaning-getting activity (Canney & Winograd, 1979; Clay, 1973; Denny & Weintraub, 1963, 1966; Garner & Kraus, 1980; Johns & Ellis, 1976; Myers & Paris, 1978; Reid, 1966). Although this outcome might be expected of children just learning to read, when decoding often is the primary focus of instruction, it is striking to note that some of the children who consider accurate decoding to be the primary goal of reading are twelve or thirteen years old (Canney & Winograd, 1979; Garner & Kraus, 1980).

It follows that if children believe the purpose of reading is to say all the words correctly, then their text processing should reflect this. Instead of organizing text into larger segments of meaning, the children would process in a word by word manner and hence would have difficulty in comprehending. A large number of studies, reviewed by Golinkoff (1976) and Ryan (in press), have shown that this does occur. To give an example, Canney and Winograd (1979) have demonstrated that children whose interview responses indicated a focus on decoding also claim that passages composed of semantically and syntactically unrelated words could be read and understood as easily as an intact passage. If the purpose is to decode, this is fine. If, however, the aim of reading is understanding, these children will be in trouble.

Younger and poorer readers seem to be unaware that they must expend additional cognitive effort to make sense of the words they have decoded. They seem to be relatively insensitive to the demands of reading for meaning. Myers and Paris (1978) examined children's knowledge about the influence of different variables involved in reading. Children's answers to a series of interview questions revealed many developmental differences in their understanding of purposes and strategies. For example, sixth graders understood that the purpose of skimming was to pick out the informative words, while second graders said they would skim by reading the easy words. These different skimming strategies reflect conceptions of reading as meaning-getting and as word-decoding, respectively.

Modifications in Reading Due to Variations in Purpose

A number of studies have examined readers' abilities to modify their behaviors in response to instructions to read for different purposes. Although children in the interview studies (Myers & Paris, 1978) sometimes indicated they would adapt their behaviors for different purposes, what they say they would do and what they actually do may be two separate phenomena. One might expect that metacognitive knowledge would precede metacognitive regulation, but this is not always the case. For example, Kobasigawa, Ransom, and Holland (1979) found that it was not until eighth grade that the majority of children could describe "how to skim," although from fourth grade on, approximately half the children made a reasonable attempt at skimming.

Before children can modify their reading rate appropriately, they must know how the modifications will affect the achievement goals. They must know that they should slow down when material is difficult, when they are looking for specific bits of information, and when they are experiencing difficulty grasping a point. They must know that they should increase reading rate when attempting to get an overview and when skimming. Children have difficulty with these task demands. For example, Forrest and Waller (1979) asked children in third and sixth grades to read passages for four different purposes: for fun, to make up a title, to skim, and to study. Not surprisingly, the older and better readers were more likely to adjust their reading strategies in response to the task instructions, as reflected by their performance on subsequent comprehension tests.

Smith (1967) reported that good readers at the high school level adjusted their reading behaviors depending on whether they were reading for details or general impressions, while poor readers used the same behaviors for both purposes. In addition, the poor readers were less able to report the procedures they used. Interestingly, Smith found that neither good nor poor readers remembered being taught how to read for different purposes; it seems this is a skill good readers develop on their own.

By the time many people reach adulthood, they exhibit flexibility in their reading rate. They modify their eye movements when faced with instructions for reading, such as reading for the general idea vs. reading to obtain a detailed understanding (Anderson, 1937; Gray, 1917; Judd & Buswell, 1922). Even within a specific passage, they slow down to allocate extra attention to goal-relevant information (Rothkopf & Billington, 1979). Nevertheless, there are students at the college level who still fail to set their own purposes, reading everything at the same rate, regardless of its difficulty or their reasons for reading (Bond & Tinker, 1973).

Identifying Important Ideas

Children are commonly exhorted to concentrate on the main ideas when reading, but in order to be responsive to this suggestion, they must be aware of what the main points of a passage are. But this is a gradually developing skill and although children as young as six can often indicate the main character and sequence of events in a simple narrative, they often experience difficulty isolating central issues in more complex prose (Brown & Smiley, 1977; Smiley, et al., 1977). For example, grade school children who were perfectly able to recall the main theme of folk stories after they had read them had much more difficulty rating sections of the stories in terms of their importance to the time before reading (Brown & Smiley, 1977; Brown, Smiley, & Lawton, 1978). When children are provided with a perspective within which to interpret the passage, they are better able to judge what is important (Pichert, 1979). It is not that children lack the ability to identify what is important; rather, they need help in focusing their attention on the relevant information. Not only do children become better at identifying important ideas as they grow older, they also exhibit changes in their conceptions of what is important and what is not (Stein & Glenn, 1979; Yussen, et al., 1980).

The research on important judgments sheds some light on the relationship between metacognitive knowledge and cognitive processing. Although young children have difficulty stating what is important, they are perfectly capable of recalling the most important information and their patterns of recall tend to be very similar to those of adults. The relationship between what one knows with respect to a particular task and how one performs is not a simple causal one (Flavell & Wellman, 1977; Markham, in press).

Making Use of Logical Structure

In addition to extracting main ideas from a passage, an important element of comprehension is understanding how and why the ideas are interconnected. In addition, efforts to learn the material will be aided if one is able to recognize and capitalize on any structure in the text. But young children have some difficulty detecting even gross violations of logical structure. For example, Danner (1976) presented children in grades two, four, and six with short expository passages that were either organized around a central theme or had the sentences randomly arranged. The children were asked to recall the passages and then asked which passage type was more difficult to learn and to justify their answers. The younger children showed similar recall patterns to the older children, in that organized passages were better recalled than disorganized ones. However, the younger children had less awareness of the cause of the differences in difficulty. All children reported that the disorganized passages were more difficult, but only the older children could explain how the two passages differed. A similar lack of awareness of the conventions of paragraph writing was observed by Myers and Paris (1978).

Good and poor students also differ considerably in their knowledge about logical relationships. Owings, et al. (1980) presented fifth graders with short stories which differed in the extent to which descriptions of characters were logically related to their behaviors. The children were tested for memory of the stories and were then asked which type was harder to learn and to justify their responses. Though all children had better memory for the logically related passages, only the better students consistently recognized that the less logical passages were more difficult and justified their answers appropriately. In addition, the better students spent more time studying the less logical passages, while the study times of the poorer students did not differ across the two passage types. These results show clear differences in the metacognitive knowledge brought to bear on the task.

Subsequent work by these investigators (cited in Bransford, 1979) revealed that poorer students were quite capable of evaluating whether the passages made sense when they were asked to evaluate them with respect to their own experiences. After experiences relating the passages to their prior knowledge in this way, the poorer students also showed differential study time for the two passage types. This finding has particularly important educational implications: Although poor students do not spontaneously monitor their understanding and mastery of prose material, they are capable of doing so with relevant instruction.

Activating Prior Knowledge

The ability to grasp the logical organization of a text is firmly rooted in one's prior knowledge of the world. If one does not have the relevant background information it may be difficult, if not impossible, to detect logical organization. Obviously, as children mature, their knowledge of the world expands through both formal instruction and day-by-day experience. As a consequence, many of the skills necessary for logical analysis of prose simply develop over time. Nevertheless, given equal levels of background knowledge, children differ in the extent to which they use it during comprehension (Spiro, 1979). Do some children simply not know that they should consider new information with respect to what they already know?

Two recent studies examined children's propensity to evaluate passages in terms of what they know about the world. Both of these experiments used variations of the "disruption" technique. In one study, Pace (1980) had kindergartners listen to short passages describing common daily events. One element in the passage was substituted so that it was not consistent with the event (e.g., having peanut butter and ice cream sandwiches for lunch). When questioned later, the children did not appear to notice anything abnormal with the passage. However, Pace later showed that kindergartners could notice violations that were more blatant if they were warned to be on the alert for them.

Winograd and Johnston (1980) examined the likelihood that sixth graders would notice the presence of contextually inappropriate sentences in passages describing familiar events such as a baseball game. Though better readers were more likely to report the problem than poorer readers, the probability was quite low, a finding that typically occurs in research using an error detection paradigm. Moreover, even if subjects received an orienting task designed to activate the relevant background knowledge prior to reading, they were no more likely to detect the inappropriate sentences.

Sullivan (1978) has also reported that poor readers at the high school level have difficulty relating their past knowledge to what they are reading. In brief, it seems that many students lack the metacognitive awareness that one should interpret text with respect to what one knows. Unfortunately, this is not strictly a characteristic of young students; many college students exhibit a striking lack of transfer of knowledge gained from one source to other sources (Bransford, 1979).

A related aspect of this problem is the tendency for many readers to accept as given whatever information is presented in the text. They fail to consider that authors write for a variety of purposes, using various propaganda techniques to sway the reader to a particular point of view. Unless readers consider the reading material in light of what they already know, they may in fact be misled.

The knowledge that one should activate prior knowledge during reading, and the ability to do so, are important metacognitive components of critical reading and studying. Of course, there are occasions when the reader lacks the relevant prior knowledge. Such situations require the companion metacognitive skill of recognizing that there is a gap in one's knowledge and taking steps to remedy it.

Sensitivity to Contextual Constraints

Good comprehenders use context as much as possible in constructing a representation of the text. They use context to make predictions about subsequent information and to organize words into higher-order units. Because they are sensitive to the semantic and syntactic constraints of the language, they are quickly aware of contextual violations during reading.

Several studies of oral reading have revealed differences between good and poor readers in their sensitivity to contextual constraints. Clay (1973) found that beginning readers in the upper half of their class spontaneously corrected 33 percent of their errors, while beginners in the lower half corrected only 5 percent of their errors. Weber (1970) reported that good and poor readers in the first grade did not differ in the extent to which they corrected errors that were grammatically acceptable to the sentence context, but that good readers were twice as likely to correct errors that were grammatically inappropriate. Beebe (1980) found that among fourth grade boys, those identified as poor readers were less likely to correct their unacceptable substitutions than good readers. The same pattern has been obtained for poorer readers in seventh grade (Kavale & Schreiner, 1979) and college students (Fairbanks, 1937; Swanson, 1937).

One explanation for these differences between good and poor readers is that poor readers have difficulty decoding the words and so are unable to benefit from the contextual information that signals meaning distortions. However, when good and poor readers are matched on the ability to decode words in isolation, good readers still make fewer errors when reading in context (Isakson & Miller, 1976).

Sensitivity to contextual constraints also has been studied using the disruption paradigm in combination with oral reading measures. Miller and Isakson (1978) introduced pseudowords into passages that children in grades one to three were asked to read aloud. The youngest children showed no signs of disruption due to the pseudowords but the older children did. These investigators also found that fourth grade good readers were more likely to detect semantic and syntactic anomalies than were poor readers (Isakson & Miller, 1976). When the

Baker and Brown

good readers encountered an anomalous word, they frequently tried to "fix up" the resulting comprehension difficulty by substituting a more sensible word. Poor readers, on the other hand, read the anomalous words without apparent awareness of the problem.

Paris and Myers (1980) disrupted text comprehensibility by inserting nonsense words and by rearranging words within clauses so that the clauses were both syntactically and semantically anomalous. Fourth grade good and poor readers were audiotaped as they read the passages aloud and the tapes were analyzed for hesitations and substitutions. The flow of reading was more disrupted by the anomalous phrases than by the nonsense words, for both the good and poor readers. In fact, the good readers were no more likely to be affected by the nonsense words than the poor readers.

Though these failures to notice nonwords suggest that even the good readers did not evaluate their understanding carefully, an alternate explanation is possible. Since the nonwords were pronounceable, the children may have assumed they were simply words whose meanings they did not know. Reluctant to admit their ignorance, they decoded and read the words without hesitation. This interpretation received support in a second task in Paris and Myers' study (1980), in which children were instructed to underline words or phrases they did not understand as they were reading. Again, neither good nor poor readers underlined many nonsense words, but good readers were twice as likely to recognize anomalous phrases as the poor readers.

The knowledge that context can be used to figure out words one does not know is an important metacognitive insight. Young children who are just beginning to read tend not to think of this as an option (Myers & Paris, 1978). Good readers are more likely to suggest using context than poor readers (Garner & Kraus, 1980). However, even poor readers recognize the utility of the strategy (Myers & Paris, 1980; Ngandu, 1977; Sullivan, 1978), but whether they actually use it is a different matter entirely. When fourth graders were provided with dictionaries in which to look up words they did not know, good readers were more likely to look up the words in the dictionary or ask an adult the meanings, while poor readers, if they even noticed the words, tended to ask for pronunciations (Paris & Myers, 1980). Garner (1980) introduced either difficult vocabulary items or contextual inconsistencies into passages and asked junior high students to rate the comprehensibility of the passages. Though the poor readers failed to mention the inconsistencies, they were apt to point out the difficult words. Although poor readers evaluate their understanding of individual words, they do not take remedial measures as often as do better readers.

This tendency to ignore word-level comprehension problems is not just a characteristic of immature readers (Anderson, 1979). Adults sometimes delay seeking outside help because of a strategic decision to avoid disrupting the smooth flow of reading. Only when the word is encountered several times or when it is clearly crucial to the passage does the mature reader decide that remedial action is necessary. It would be unwise to attribute such forethought to children who fail to look up words. The ability to make such decisions requires a variety of metacognitive skills, including identifying the important information and establishing criteria for assessing one's level of understanding.

Evaluating the Text for Clarity, Completeness, and Consistency

In this section, we will consider research on readers' sensitivity to text inadequacies; for example, knowing when a text is ambiguous, does not provide enough information, or contains ideas that conflict with one another. One source of evidence comes from research on children's oral communication and listening skills. Young elementary school children frequently indicate that they have understood a message even when it was ambiguous or incomplete (Ironsmith & Whitehurst, 1978; Karabenick & Miller, 1978). They often fail to question the speaker or seek additional information when their understanding is poor (Cosgrove & Patterson, 1978).

A recent study by Flavell, Speer, Green, and August (in press) provides a nice demonstration of children's difficulties monitoring their comprehension while listening. Kindergarten and second grade children were instructed to construct block buildings identical to those described on tape by a child. Some of the instructions contained ambiguities, unfamiliar words, insufficient information, or unattainable goals. Children were encouraged to replay the tape as often as necessary in order to construct the buildings. The children were videotaped as they attempted to carry out the instructions, and the videotapes were analyzed for nonverbal signs of problem detection, i.e., looking puzzled or replaying the tape. Later, the children were asked if they had succeeded in making a building exactly like the instructor's and whether they thought the instructor did a good job in conveying the instructions.

As expected, older children were more likely to notice the inadequacies in the message than were younger children. Even though both kindergartners and second graders showed nonverbal signs of puzzlement during the task, the kindergartners were less likely to report later that some of the messages were inadequate. This finding further attests to the importance of obtaining converging evidence in studies using the disruption paradigm (Brown, 1980; Winograd & Johnston, 1980). Several other investigators have also provided on-line evidence of problem detection in listening tasks despite failures to report the inadequacies verbally (Bearison & Levey, 1977; Lloyd & Pavlidis, 1978; Patterson, Cosgrove, & O'Brien, 1980).

Markman (1977) also examined children's ability to evaluate their understanding of oral messages. Children in first and third grades listened to simple instructions on how to play a game or perform a magic trick; crucial information was omitted. Third graders realized the instructions were incomplete much more readily than did the younger children. Often it was not until first graders actually tried to carry out the instructions that they realized they did not understand. Flavell, et al. also found that kindergartners typically did not detect message inadequacies until they tried to follow instructions, i.e., to construct block buildings.

In a related task, Kotsonis and Patterson (1980) found that learning disabled children were less able to judge when they had sufficient information to be able to play a game. Rules were given one at a time until the children indicated they knew how to play. Learning disabled children requested fewer rules than did nondisabled children.

It appears that many young children monitor their understanding of instructions by attempting to carry them out. Failure to achieve the desired goals indicates either 1) a failure to comprehend or 2) inadequate instructions. However, physical execution should not be the first test applied in evaluating comprehension of instructions; successful mental monitoring may prevent the unfortunate consequences that can occur if one attempts to carry out the specified steps without a thorough understanding of the entire operation. The studies summarized indicate that young children frequently do not engage in such mental monitoring.

In contrast to instructional prose, criteria for successful comprehension of expository prose are usually implicit. Readers must select their own standards for evaluation and develop their own technique for applying them. One strategy is to evaluate the text for internal consistency, checking to see that the ideas contained within the passage are consistent with one another. Successful use of the consistency standard develops slowly; in fact, many adults do not seem to use it (Baker, 1979).

Researchers have found developmental differences and differences due to reading ability in the application of the consistency standard. For example, Markman (1979) had children in third, fifth, and sixth grades listen to short essays containing inconsistent information and then probed the children for awareness of the inconsistencies. Some of the inconsistencies could be noticed only if the children made inferences, while others were quite explicit. Children in all grades tested were equally poor at reporting the inconsistencies, though they were somewhat more successful with the blatant problems. Markman also found that when children were specifically warned in advance that a problem might be present in the text, both third and sixth graders were more likely to report the implicit problems as the explicit when they were given this warning. Nevertheless, many children still failed to report the inconsistencies.

In a recent series of experiments, Garner and her colleagues (Garner, 1980, in press; Garner & Kraus, 1980; Garner & Taylor, 1980) have shown that junior high students, particularly those identified as poor readers, are also poor at evaluating text for internal consistency. The students were asked to rate brief passages for ease of understanding and to justify whatever low ratings they gave. Poor readers were less likely to rate inconsistent text as difficult to understand though good readers were by no means proficient at this task. The poor readers were better at identifying comprehension problems due to difficult vocabulary items than to inconsistencies (Garner, in press).

Garner and Taylor (1980) also found differences in the amount of assistance required to notice inconsistencies. After reading a brief passage, fourth, sixth, and eighth graders were provided with increasingly more specific hints as to the source of difficulty. Even after the experimenter underlined the two sentences that conflicted with one another and told the children they did not make sense, fourth graders and older poor readers were rarely able to report the exact nature of the problem. However, the intervention did increase the likelihood that better readers would notice the inconsistency.

In order to notice that information is inconsistent, it is necessary to compare the two pieces of inconsistent information. If one of the pieces is no longer in working memory, comparisons are difficult, especially in a listening task. In Markman's study, when inconsistent facts were in adjacent sentences, older children were more likely to report explicit inconsistencies than were younger children, but they still failed to make the necessary inferences to detect implicit inconsistencies. Garner and Kraus (1980) also examined whether the contiguity of inconsistent information would affect the likelihood of detection. Inconsistent facts were either placed four sentences apart or contained within a single (long) sentence. Good readers in junior high were more likely to report the inconsistencies when they were contained within a single sentence, but poor readers were not. These results suggest that one common shortcoming in children's comprehension monitoring is a failure to consider the relations across noncontiguous sentences in a text. Though they may be capable of evaluating their understanding of single sentences, they still need to develop the skills to integrate and evaluate information across larger segments of text. Even college students may have difficulty with the more demanding task (Baker, 1979).

One explanation for these failures to notice inconsistencies is that the children used a different standard for evaluating their understanding. Rather than focusing on the consistency of the facts *within* the text, they focused on an isolated fact and asked "Is it true?" (Osherson & Markman, 1975). In other words, they evaluated the information with respect to what they already knew, instead of comparing information within the passage. Markman (1979) suggested that several of her subjects used this standard, and Baker (1979) and Baker and Anderson (1980) observed that many college students who failed to report logical inconsistencies did report perceived violations with their prior knowledge. Earlier we argued that many readers fail to evaluate text for consistency with prior knowledge; here we see the other side of the problem; they fail to evaluate the text for internal consistency. A combination of internal and external consistency checks is necessary for effective comprehension monitoring. An overreliance on one or the other—or worse still, the absence of one or the other— would have deleterious consequences on the comprehension process.

The pattern that emerges from the studies by Markman and Garner is that less experienced and less proficient readers are quite poor at monitoring their comprehension. Failures to report a disruption, however, may be due to a number of factors other than poor comprehension monitoring. The nonverbal evidence of problem detection exhibited by 4 and 5 year olds (Flavell, et al., in press; Patterson, et. al., 1980) suggests caution with interpretations of data from error detection paradigms. Further reason for caution was provided by Baker (1979). College students were not likely to report problems such as inconsistencies, ambiguities, or inappropriate logical connectives. Even when specifically warned to look for inadequacies, the students reported but 38 percent of the problems. Retrospective reports and recall protocols, however, revealed that many failures to report confusions were not due to failures to monitor comprehension but to the use of strategies for resolving comprehension problems. (See Baker, 1979b for discussion of these strategies.) Students frequently made inferences to supplement the information explicitly presented in the text; they decided that some relevant information had been omitted and used their prior knowledge to bridge the gap. Some students reported using criteria for evaluating their understanding that precluded repair strategies; for example, they realized there was a problem but decided it was trivial and not worth attempting resolution. Moreover, some students occasionally failed to detect disruptions because they had assigned alternative interpretations to the text; they felt they understood but, in fact, did not get the intended meaning. Also, many students reported conflicts with prior knowledge rather than within the text itself.

The Baker (1979) study provides evidence of comprehension monitoring in the absence of confusion detection, but it requires inferences about processes occurring during reading. In order to obtain more conclusive evidence of comprehension monitoring during reading, Baker and Anderson (1980) presented college students with inconsistent passages, sentence by sentence. Students advanced to subsequent sentences at their own pace and were free to look back at previous sentences. A computer automatically recorded reading times on each exposure to a sentence and the pattern of movement through the text. After reading the passages, the students were asked to indicate which sentences, if any, contained inconsistencies. Half of the students were informed prior to reading that inconsistencies were present, while the remainder were told after reading.

As expected, students spent more time reading inconsistent passages than consistent passages, and they looked back at previous sentences more frequently when inconsistencies were present. Surprisingly, students who were explicitly instructed to monitor for inconsistencies during reading did not differ from noninstructed readers in either reading behavior or confusion detection. Our interpretation of this finding is that under favorable conditions, adults are able to monitor their comprehension effectively with or without specific instructions. Nevertheless, not all inconsistencies were caught by all students. In fact, less than 25 percent of the students noticed all intended confusions and the overall detection rate was only 67 percent. Again, we see that evaluating text for consistency is not a routine behavior even among college students who are expected to read texts critically and carefully in their courses.

Additional on-line evidence of comprehension monitoring has been provided in studies primarily concerned with the effects of text manipulations on comprehension. For example, readers return to previously read information and make regressive eye movements when they encounter pronouns whose referents are unclear (Carpenter & Just, 1977; Garrod & Sanford, 1977), and they require more time to read paragraphs which violate conventional organizational structure (Greeno & Noreen, 1974; Kieras, 1978).

Dealing with Failures to Understand

Realizing that one has failed to understand is only a part of comprehension monitoring; one must also know what to do when comprehension failures occur. Several important strategic decisions may be required. The first decision is whether remedial action is even necessary, a decision that will depend largely on the purposes for reading (Alessi, Anderson, & Goetz, 1979). If readers decide to take strategic action, a number of options are available. They may store the confusion in memory as a pending question (Anderson, 1980), in hopes the author will soon provide clarification. Or readers may decide to take action immediately and so reread, look ahead in the text, or consult outside sources.

We have already discussed research on children's knowledge and use of strategies to resolve word comprehension failures. Even elementary school children are likely to say that consulting a dictionary, using contextual cues, and asking other people for help are good strategies for dealing with unknown words (Ngandu, 1978; Olshavsky, 1976-1977). However, poorer readers are less likely to use these strategies when opportunities are provided to apply them (Paris & Myers, 1980; Strang & Rogers, 1965). Children apparently are sensitive to failures to understand words before they effectively remediate their failures.

One of the simplest strategies to use when experiencing difficulty in comprehending is to reread the previous segment of text in search of clarification. The evidence is conflicting concerning immature readers' knowledge about such strategies. Baker & Anderson (1980) found that college students reread texts when they encounter inconsistent information but immature readers may not be so strategic. Garner and Kraus (1980) found that poor readers in junior high were not likely to suggest using such a rereading strategy, but Olshavsky (1976-1977) found no differences between good and poor junior high school readers in the extent to which they suggested rereading. In addition, Pace (1980) found that even kindergartners understand relistening in that they suggested listening to a story for a second time to help them answer questions they had failed to answer correctly. Flavell, et al. (in press) observed many second graders and even some kindergartners replaying a taped message when they encountered difficulties in understanding. The inconsistency in the data may be due to the complexity of the situation in which the skills are tested. In particular, children may experience difficulty transferring skills they use for oral comprehension to the task of evaluating reading comprehension.

A second strategy that may be used when comprehension falters is to continue reading, seeking clarification in subsequent sections of the text. Many college students report using such a strategy (Baker, 1979). However, knowledge that this is a useful activity seems to be late developing (DiVesta, Hayward, & Orlando, 1979). Perhaps young children believe that failures to understand must be due to failures within themselves, that problems would not be inherent in the text. To date, we have no empirical evidence revealing what readers do when, after reading ahead, they are unable to derive a satisfactory interpretation of the text.

Comprehension failures may be resolved using knowledge-based strategies. Here readers bridge the gap in their understanding by drawing on prior knowledge (Baker, 1979). This is usually an adaptive strategy, but readers who always resolve comprehension failures by drawing inferences may erroneously believe they comprehend when they do not.

Assessing One's Level of Comprehension

Readers are apt to select different criteria for deciding how well they have understood something depending on their goals for reading. If they are instructed to read the material carefully enough to be tested on its content, they ought to apply purposive action to ensure memorability as well as comprehension. On the other hand, if readers are attempting to comprehend in preparation for an "open-book" question, their strategy may be somewhat different. Engaging in self-questioning is a good way to assess the level of one's understanding as well as one's mastery of the material (Andre & Anderson, 1978-1979; Singer, 1978). The ability to ask the right questions is a crucial component of this technique. As Collins, Brown, and Larkin (1980) suggest, many failures of comprehension may be due to a failure to ask the right questions.

Young children and poor readers are less able to judge how well they have comprehended something or whether they are ready to take a test. Forrest and Waller (1979) found that fourth graders and poor readers in sixth grade were inaccurate at rating the correctness of their answers to comprehension questions. In other words, they did not always know when they did or did not understand. Similarly, Wellman, et al. (1980), and Brown, Campione, and Barclay (1979) found developmental differences in children's ability to judge when they had studied a passage sufficiently well to be tested on the information. These studies suggest that one of the metacognitive skills children must acquire is the ability to accurately gauge their level of understanding. For many children, this task is left to external agents such as teachers (Schallert & Kleiman, 1979) or, too late, to tests. Self-questioning and self-testing one's level of comprehension are crucial parts of comprehension monitoring and can and should be fostered by explicit training (Brown, Campione, & Barclay, 1979; Brown, Campione, & Day, 1981).

Summary and Conclusions

In this chapter, we reviewed evidence from a variety of situations to suggest that immature readers have difficulty taking charge of their own cognitive processes while reading. They are not as flexible as mature readers in adapting their level of processing for tasks that differ in the degree of understanding they demand. Attention to main points at the expense of trivia cannot automatically be expected of the young reader and the ability to estimate what are the important sections of text is fragile. Strategies for capitalizing on logical structures or contextual constraints inherent in texts may also be late developing.

Similarly, immature readers are less efficient at deliberately activating relevant prior knowledge in order to render texts more comprehensible. Detecting inconsistencies within texts may be routine for the proficient comprehension monitor but not for the novice reader.

In general, the ability to assess one's own level of understanding, or readiness to risk a test of one's knowledge, is fragile in young readers, as is the ability to use such information to direct remedial activities. Such remedial strategies might include self-questioning, other-questioning (seeking outside help from people or books), rereading or additional studying, inferential or plausible reasoning as the basis of incomplete knowledge, and a variety of "fix-up" ploys that form a reliable feature of the comprehension monitoring repertoire of the mature reader. While such activities might sometimes be practiced by younger and poorer readers, they are certainly not routine features of their comprehension processes.

The evidence is clear that less experienced and less successful readers tend not to engage in the cognitive monitoring activities characteristic of more proficient readers. Though it is tempting to conclude that ineffective monitoring of one's cognitive processes during reading is the cause of poor comprehension, we caution against such a precipitous conclusion. The majority of the studies have shown that ineffective monitoring is associated with poor comprehension, but not that it is the cause. It may be that poor comprehension reduces the ability to monitor one's ongoing activities; or perhaps a third factor, such as impoverished background knowledge, is responsible for both problems. Further research is needed to establish more clearly the nature of the link between cognitive monitoring and reading comprehension.

Although instruction aimed at instigating cognitive monitoring should not be regarded as a panacea for reading difficulties, the literature holds promising implications for those children whose difficulties can be traced to inefficient application of rules and strategies. For example, merely making children aware that they should continue studying and self-testing until ready for a test improves study performance in young children (Brown, Campione, & Barclay, 1979). Instructing students in efficient self-questioning techniques is also an effective training procedure (Andre & Anderson, 1978-1979). Sensitizing young readers to the logical structure of text and the inherent meaning in certain passages again helps the less able reader (Owings, et al., 1980). And instructing children to evaluate text for consistency and truthfulness increases the likelihood that they will do so (Markman, 1979).

DeBeaugrande discusses the controversial issue of modeling reading as a
linear phenomenon. In this article he notes seven principles that can operate
concurrently and interactively on all levels of reading: the core-and-adjunct
principle; the pause principle; the look-back principle; the look-ahead
principle; the heaviness principle; the disambiguation principle; the list
principle; and interactions among the principles. He notes that evidence
from both the experimental literature and from a specific test with a story is
inconclusive, but further research appears worthwhile because the seemingly
certain fact of linearity in reading is still in doubt.

The Linearity of Reading:
Fact, Fiction, or Frontier?

Robert de Beaugrande
University of Florida

1. Some Difficulties

Many aspects of reading traditionally taken for granted have recently
been placed in dispute. Perhaps the most secure fact about reading is its
linearity: the way words are read in a line moving straight across the
page. Experimental findings appear to support what we would be
inclined to consider a commonplace truth. For example, Rumelhart
(1977, p. 123) reports:

> Sentences are naturally processed in a word-by-word, left-to-right order. This
> meets our intuitions about how we process sentences and is generally consistent
> with evidence from studies of eye movements which generally indicate that with
> the exception of a small number of regressions the eye jumps from left to right
> across the page, stopping for a quarter of a second or so every one to five words.

Gough's investigations (1972) indicate that this linear motion is
extremely detailed, registering even the sequence of letters in words
(Gough & Cosky, 1975).

The security of this observed fact, however, may be deceptive. It
encourages a model of reading in which the reader perceives and
recognizes each word in turn, looking into a mental dictionary for the
meaning, and then going on. The difficulties inherent in such a model
were already acute in machine translation programs that worked in
precisely this fashion. Dictionary meanings are often diffuse and
noncommittal, yet the sense of a text being read is usually fairly specific
and clear. How can this simple difference be explained? How can the

mind pick out and assemble appropriate meanings if understanding has to move in a straight line?

I should like to explore some hidden complexities of the linearity in reading. This aspect, though neither fact nor fiction in any obvious sense, is undoubtedly still an unmapped frontier for all kinds of theories and models. I shall sketch two widespread approaches and their implications, and then propose an emerging model now being probed in my own research and compatible with a number of already well-documented findings in the psychology and linguistics of reading.

2. The Structuralist Analogy

Structuralist linguistics exercised a pervasive influence on early approaches to reading. The whole process was viewed as an analogy to structural analysis, e.g. as performed by professional linguists of the time. Though in many ways unsatisfying, this analogy was among the major assumptions of psycholinguistics in the 1960s (Clark & Clark, 1977; Levelt, 1978). The act of reading a stretch of text would thus be a series of analyses performed on steadily deeper levels one by one: print (graphemes); words (morphemes and lexemes); phrase structures (syntagmemes); and finally, meaning (semes, semantemes) [for example see, Gibson, 1971].[1] Holmes and Singer (1961) drew upon linguistics to suggest a model with a set of "substrata."

It is important to bear in mind that such a view is largely due to historical accident in the development of the discipline of linguistics. This progression of separate phases exactly mirrors the order in which American linguistics went about the study of language. Often, each level was analyzed in seeming independence from the others—a matter of scientific ethics for some researchers (Trager, 1950; Harris, 1951; Chomsky, 1957). The shallow levels were naturally explored before the deep ones.

A major weakness pervades all models designed on this analogy: a class we can call *sequential-stage relay models*, because stages are in a fixed sequence and only communicate with others by relaying a finished analysis. This weakness is that analysis of the earlier (or more shallow) stages often requires results that are supposed to be obtained later on. Consider these actually occurring samples from de Beaugrande and Dressler (1981, p. 41):

1. With a great roar and burst of flame the giant rocket rose.
2. It is not those great words or silences of love. (Jennings)
2a. It is not those great words or silences of smallest size.

Imagine now that our reader is working only on syntax before going on to meaning. Moving in a straight line from left to right, the reader must decide which modifiers should be attached to which heads. Experiments indicate that in (1)[2] and (2), *great* is routinely (though not infallibly) attached to both noun heads (roar/burst, words/silences), but in (2a) to only the first (*words*). The prepositional phrase introduced by "of" is attached to both heads in (2), but only to the nearest one in (1) and (2a).

It seems highly unlikely that these assignments can be made only by analyzing syntax from left to right. We could appeal to the indefinite article in (1) being shared by both heads, thus encouraging readers to make the same use of the modifier. But we would need a different rule for the plural version:

> 1a. With great roars and bursts of flame, the giant rocket rose.

It hardly seems reasonable to run such similar passages through different sets of rules. In (2) and (2a), the determiner *those* need not, as we can see, force a particular grouping of modifiers even though it clearly attaches to both heads.

An early solution to such matters was to try incorporating certain factors of semantics into the syntax as restrictions upon how items could occur together (Chomsky, 1957, 1965; Harris, 1951). We could assign features such as abstract/concrete or animate/inanimate to particular items (compare Katz & Fodor, 1963; Greimas, 1966; survey in Le Ny, 1979). However, this tactic won't help our reader here, because the heads are similar along most dimensions (roar/burst, words/silences).

The second solution would be to store all possible structural assignments in the syntax phase and relay them all to the semantic phase for sorting. Though feasible for samples like (1) and (2), this method would soon overload the reader's capacities for storage with needless, often pointless, alternatives. For instance, in this simple statement (Schank & Wilensky, 1977, p. 141):

> 3. Time flies like an arrow.

such alternative readings as an assertion that an odd species of flies is fond of arrows, or a command to record flying times of flies as if they were arrows, demand entirely different syntactic analysis than the obvious reading and yet are utterly unreasonable. Surely reading cannot become embroiled in this plainly wasteful baggage.

The real solution is intuitively apparent. Readers must be consulting not just a neat dictionary of word definitions, but their entire knowledge of how the world is or might be organized; and this activity must accompany, not follow, the immediate left-to-right movement through the text. Thus, a "burst" is more likely to have a substance "of flame" in (1) than is a sound like "roar." [3] This reasoning is more approximate than the simple opposition of meaning between "great" and "smallest size" that is crucial for (2a). Still more subtle is the assignment for (2), which is a line from a poem. "Words" and "silences" are opposed in meaning, yet it is most satisfying to assign the same modifiers to both of them, i.e., to superimpose equivalence upon difference. Phrases like "great words" and "silences of love," if taken to be independent, seem too diverse to justify appearing together in a list.[4] Of course, poetry as a text type is expected to exploit similarities and contrasts quite extensively.

Though transformational grammar offered a different method of structural analysis from that of descriptive linguistics, the analogy carrying over into models of reading was still not very helpful. The issues just raised with our samples are nowhere accounted for in any version of Chomsky's theory, which still insists upon a mechanical, naive concept of linearity (hence the importance of terms like "precedence," "left-branching," "right-branching," etc.).[5] We now turn to a more recent analogy which may be more promising.

3. The Computational Analogy

"Computation" is popularly linked with mathematical reckoning, but in a broader sense designates any operation carried out with specified steps to attain a particular result or goal. If computers perform numerical manipulations, they do so only because these tasks have been elaborated as sequences of elementary actions.[6] Thus, the computational analogy gaining ground in current models of reading (see my comparative overview in de Beaugrande, 1981) merely requires us to view reading as operations scheduled to run reliably in real time. This approach was applied to sequential-stage relay models of understanding, e.g. transformational grammar, with discouraging results. As we already saw, operations rapidly break down under an explosion of possible, but pointless alternatives (see Woods, 1970). Consequently, more recent models of reading are to some degree *parallel-stage interaction models*. They foresee operations on different language levels going on simultaneously and consulting each other's results, e.g. syntax and semantics (Marslen-Wilson, 1975; Schank, et al., 1975; Bobrow, 1978; Woods, 1978).

In this perspective, linearity becomes a different sort of problem. The earlier sequential approach relied merely on recognizing units or string of units on a single level, as ordered from left to right. Operations were thus straight-forward, though (as we noted) vastly cumbersome and inefficient. The parallel approach, in contrast, allows for continual consultation among levels and forces us to explore how, when, and where such consultations are actually done during reading. A total analysis of each expression, covering all levels, could not be done one by one. Ortony and Anderson (1975) were able to show experimentally that even pairs of simplistic assertions along these lines:

4a. I ate a bowl of oatmeal.
4b. I ate a bowl of potato chips.

project quite different versions of the "eating" action. "Oatmeal" is a fluid substance typically consumed in the morning without noise by means of a spoon, and normally mixed with cream and sweetening. "Potato chips" are separate particles typically consumed at evening parties with considerable noise by means of the hand, and normally dipped in a spicy mix. The understanding of "ate" is thus not secure until the whole sequence of words is read. Apparently, a reader first sets up an approximate pattern and then fills its detailed slots as the occasion arises.

One could object here that samples (4a/4b) are short enough that understanding could be postponed until the whole sentence had been worked over. Yet that objection gravely underestimates the reading of connected discourse. In our sample story (35) below, the word "house" appears in the opening sentence; only three sentences (and 49 words) later do we read of a "fire escape" whose presence signals an apartment: house was just a designation for any dwelling, rather than for an independent, one-family edifice. Clearly, no reader is going to postpone understanding over such a stretch of text; nor would the motive for doing so be evident at the moment of reading house.[7]

Finding referents for pronouns is a further illustration. In Susan Miller's (1976, p. 73) composition handbook, a paragraph begins:

5. Authors who support themselves by writing have the same reluctance about actually getting down to the words-on-paper stage that their students do, and overcome their hesitation by using these methods. They set aside a special period of the day for actual writing.

Experiments show that readers prefer to link a pronoun to the most recently mentioned candidate noun phrase allowed by gender and number (Springston, 1975). The "they" at the start of the second sentence in (5), however, looks back to the most distant referent "authors," rather than to "students" or "methods." Though "methods" is easy to eliminate as making poor sense, the rejection of "students" as an antecedent is more intricate. Readers must recognize that "authors" is still the subject of the verb "overcome," signaled most clearly by the comma after "do" (see 5A). The next action "set aside" then can be attached to the agent most recently *active in mental storage,* but not *mentioned in the surface text.* Also, "authors" is at the moment the center of attention, whereas "students" had already been discussed in the chapter; readers expect to be enlightened now about these newly introduced entities.[8]

Although the computational approach raises, as we see, a host of difficult issues, it is probably a more productive outlook on reading than the structural analysis approach. Plainly, the linearity of the text cannot dictate the order in which readers *must* perform the various steps and stages of understanding. There must also be highly elaborated strategies sensitive to such factors as word organization, mental imagery, memory capacity, attention focus, discourse situation, and so forth. These strategies would be so adaptive that they could scarcely be captured by "rules" in the sense of conventional linguistics (where language is studied independently of its operational use). But we might be able to identify their nature in terms of the *directionalities* and *controls* involved in their functions.

I shall sketch some of these strategies in the next sections. My presentation is highly provisional, because most recent models of reading or understanding have centered on issues like propositional content (survey in de Beaugrande, 1981). Linearity is either treated as straightforward (Clark & Clark, 1977; Rumelhart, 1977) or else altogether set aside pending future research (Kintsch & van Dijk, 1978, who already start off with a proposition list). At such a time, getting the surface text back into our improved reading model is particulary urgent.

4. General Requirements

On one plane of abstraction, the linear order of words is a concern of *serial behavior* at large (Lashley, 1951). Many psychological experiments have been constructed on the assumption that the mind can only do one thing at a time. Experimental design is vastly simplified in this way, but the data obtained may be very soft. A good portion of the activities of readers is done *automatically*, requiring no conscious *attention* (LaBerge & Samuels, 1974). By definition, processes that do not demand attention can be performed simultaneously with others (Keele, 1973). It follows that experiments with time on task as the conclusive variable might fail to yield a realistic picture of reading: the actual time used up would represent only the operations done with attention. To explore the other operations, we will have to design models whose verification (or falsification) depends on success in apportioning resources and computing the operations done on reading tasks. Considerations here include a) *storage*, holding materials in mind long enough to work with them; b) *search*, calling up needed materials not already in mind; c) *access*, getting materials assembled where they belong; d) *scheduling*, setting up operations in ordered sequences; e) *attention-sharing*, alloting one's attention to tasks by juggling their various requirements; f) *hypothesis-testing*, creating and trying out provisional notions of what is being read; g) *setting thresholds*, deciding how complete, thorough, or exact operations should be for current purposes; h) *problem solving*, overcoming any obstacles to progressive understanding; i) *scaling units*, determining the stretch of text which can best be read as an integral unit, given current loads on the reader's mind; and j) *weighing priorities*, deciding which operations should be preferred when all of them cannot be fully achieved.

In this view, a given text might well be read differently by various readers; indeed, the same reader might act differently according to the circumstances imposed upon any one act of reading. For example, a second reading would never be quite identical to the first, because certain variables have already been fixed, and the overall load on the mind is attenuated. This factor is enormously disturbing for the experimenter, who may see a host of variegated acts on each single occasion. The need for integrated, well-designed models is thereby all the more acute: without them, observable facts are hardly likely to fall into place. The principles proposed in the next section are accordingly correlated with a variety of findings in the experimental literature.

5. Seven Principles of Reading

We now look into some principles which should apply to reading on all *scales* and on all *levels* (graphemics, syntax/grammar, semantics, pragmatics) in steady, concerted interaction. Such general-purpose routines might accept and process diverse kinds of materials in a single run-through and yet suffer no undue chaos or overload. Moreover, results on different levels, e.g. syntax and semantics, would be continually integrated, precluding many fruitless alternatives such as those discussed in section 2. The specific operations done at any moment or at any point would be adapted to materials themselves and their contexts of use; but the principles as such would be the same.[9]

5A. The Core-and-Adjunct Principle

This principle surveys presented or expected materials to distinguish between *central* versus *peripheral* entities. The central ones are then delegated as *control centers* for operations like those enumerated in (a) through (j) in section 4. Core entities indicate the adjuncts they are likely to have, and vice versa.

In syntax, we have the familiar division between *content words* as cores and *function words* as adjuncts (Bolinger, 1975). In English, many function words appear before their head units, notably articles, prepositions, and auxiliary verbs. Readers can thereby predict what classes of content words should be forthcoming (Kimball, 1973). Conversely, content words suggest the function words, especially in spoken discourse when the latter are indistinct (Pollack & Pickett, 1964). The reality of the division between function vs. content words is further demonstrated by speech errors: a word of one class is almost always confused with another of the same class (Garrett, 1975).

Within phrases, we have *heads* vs. *modifiers*, e.g. nouns vs. adjectives, verbs vs. adverbs. As we saw in samples (1), (2), and (2a), the linear ordering of heads and modifiers can be elaborate, requiring consultation of nonsyntactic factors to find out what groupings are compatible. Within clauses, the core-unit is the subject and predicate, while everything else is adjunct. Within standard sentences, the core is the main (independent) subject-predicate unit, and dependent clauses are adjuncts. We see already the importance of *scaling*: what is a core on a small scale may be an adjunct on a large one; the principle itself remains constant.

Punctuation reflects the core-and-adjunct principle in several ways. The normal procedure is to punctuate the boundaries between two cores or between core and adjunct. The period is reserved mainly for the end point of a sequence with at least one main core of subject-predicate. The main clause is often separated from a dependent one by a comma. Conversely, commas are seldom used within the core, e.g. when a subject is linked to two predicates. Compare:

de Beaugrande

6a. While I read through the contract, I began to have my doubts.
6b. I read through the contract and began to have my doubts.
6c. We read through the contract, and I began to have my doubts.

However, this normal usage may be overridden by other principles, such as the listing principle (5G) that applies especially to sets of three or more.

6d. I read through the contract, estimated the costs, and began to have my doubts.

Such cases illustrate how the seven principles must be able to interact at all times. The order of their application, I would surmise, is not fixed, but is scheduled to meet the requirements of each context (cf. 5H).

In semantics, the cores would be *primary concepts* (objects, situations, events, and actions), and the adjuncts would be *secondary concepts* (states, locations, times, causes). de Beaugrande (1980, pp. 79ff) offers a typology. As in the case of content vs. function words, the cores and adjuncts mutually support and determine each other. In samples (4a) and (4b), the "eating" action makes readers predict some kind of foodstuffs as the entities affected by that action; the affected entities in turn signal the specifics of the "eating," e.g. instrument, time, and substance. One measure of how well readers understand an event or situation mentioned in the text is the extent to which they can predict and integrate attendant circumstances (Brachman, 1978; Fahlman, 1979; Norman & Rumelhart, 1975; Schank, et al., 1975).

Here again, *scales* can vary. There are large scale frameworks known in the literature as *frames* and *schemas* which the memory holds ready for organizing all kinds of understanding processes (see review in de Beaugrande, 1980, pp. 163-177). For example, we read accident reports in newspapers so easily because we know the typical components of such events: location, people involved, results caused (Cullingford, 1978). On the other hand, small scale frameworks can specify the typical nature of a single concept, e.g., "elephant" (Fahlman, 1979). The scale depends partly on the focus allotted to some concept, e.g., a general description of circus life would give much less attention to "elephants" than a treatise on that one species of animal. Similarly, readers' prestored frameworks would conform to the extent of their personal expertise.

In pragmatics, the core units would be the communicative participant's *goals* (desired future states), and the adjuncts the detailed plan steps leading to the goals. Readers may proceed quite differently according to the goals they set for themselves or attribute to others (Allen, 1979). A command like

7. Avoid eye contact.

would yield totally diverse readings on a bottle of enamel remover as opposed to a textbook on the strategies of nonverbal communication: the goal for the former case is to protect bodily health, in the latter to maintain detachment or the like. Once more, scale can change in context: a goal in one perspective may be a mere step within a larger plan in another perspective.

The placement of cores versus adjuncts, as we can see, has important effects on control operations. For instance, Fillmore (1977) notes the differences between much-discussed pairs of the type:

8a. I smeared the wall with paint.
8b. I smeared paint on the wall.

where the implication that the entire wall was covered is much stronger for (8a), even though the statements seem otherwise equivalent. The difference arises because the direct object is a core-unit slot (and thus in focus of attention) and the prepositional phrase is an adjunct (and thus less in focus). Readers naturally assume that the whole wall was affected in (8a), and more concerned with the paint in (8b). This issue is probed later on in terms of *heaviness* (see 5E).

Miscues demonstrate how readers can mistake core vs. adjunct units. In one series of experiments (de Beaugrande, 1980, pp.226), (9a) was read as (9b), such that an adjunct was converted into a core by copying a previous predicate:

9a. Two red flares rose as a signal.
9b. Two red flares rose as a signal rose.

Notice how this change brings the firing of the signal more into the center of attention, as if there were now a second "rising" event.

5B. The Pause Principle

Within the overall sequence of reading events, there must be junctures where readers slow down or stop the intake of words and bring ongoing tasks to some provisional accomplishment before going any further. The stretch of text that can be managed before pausing would depend upon how much the mind is loaded with tasks. Unfamiliar or difficult reading matter would demand pauses much more frequently than familiar. Still, the internal organization of discourse offers various units as useful "chunks" for reading. The sentence has been best explored in this role (Levelt, 1978), but it is probably only one of many units being used (O'Connell, 1977). Others might be the tone group in phonemics, the printed line in graphemics, the configuration of a concept and its components in semantics (the circumstances of an event), and the plan step in pragmatics (the parts of a promise-action). Obviously, these various units would not need to call for pauses at the same places in the text. So far, however, syntactic pauses have been the main object of research.

What really goes on during pauses is far from clear. We know that eye movements along the printed line are periodically interrupted (cf. Rumelhart quote in section 1). Two possible causes are readily evident. First, the *serial* load may reach a point of saturation simply because the number of words that can be perceived before organizing them is limited. For example, clause boundaries would be natural places to stop and do a syntactic analysis (Bever, 1970). Second, the *parallel* load may cause saturation when the number of tasks going forward concurrently becomes large enough. The latter condition would come about, for example, if a passage were genuinely and lastingly ambiguous. Bransford and Johnson (1973) deliberately designed texts lacking in cues needed to solve ambiguities; readers showed poor comprehension and recall, presumably because they couldn't locate intermediate points to integrate current materials.

The pause principle, more than any other, dominates the use of punctuation. Commas, parentheses, dashes, semicolons, and periods, respectively, signal pauses of steadily greater decisiveness. While periods are comparatively noncommittal, the other marks indicate that the materials before the pause are in some way related to those after it. For example, the content expressed by two main core-units connected with a semicolon should be semantically close. Dashes lead into similarly close materials, but without any promise to maintain a continuous or complete surface structure. Material in parentheses is close, but less important than the rest of the sentence. Such usage is at least standard for punctuating, though not obligatory (de Beaugrande, in preparation).

In syntax, the pause principle is generally the converse of the core-and-adjunct principle: pauses naturally fall at the boundaries between core and adjunct, or between two cores. As already noted, these points are often punctuated.[10] Intriguingly, however, people appear to be more certain about pause locations than about the standards of punctuation. Writers whose language experience has been mainly with speech can mark an unduly decisive pause with a period, not a comma, and create a sentence fragment; or, preferring a nondecisive pause, insert a comma for a period and create a comma splice. By the same token, readers may misjudge pauses: their miscues may then show rearrangements of syntax (see section 6). This sequence

10. The signal for launching blazed forth: two red flares. Amid a deafening roar
    [...].

was misread by one subject who suppressed the pause at the period and changed "amid a" to "aimed at"; he seems to have expected the noun phrase "two red flares" to be a subject of some predicate further on.

On a larger scale, paragraph boundaries signal pauses of semantic and pragmatic nature. Different readers can agree on where paragraphs should begin if an unmarked sample is presented, but the criteria whereby this task is done are far from obvious (Becker, 1965; Koen, Becker, & Young, 1969). Semantically, a shift of topic is routinely cued with a new paragraph: a shift from general to specific or vice versa is another occasion (Christensen, 1965; Rogers, 1966; Grady, 1971; D'Angelo, 1974). Pragmatically, a new paragraph can mark a transition from one plan step to the next, e.g. within the stages of an argument.[11]

The activities of the reader's mind during a pause ought to reflect these various kinds of motivations to integrate or sort materials on various levels. As indicated by the literature on eye movements, significant pauses are made in order to integrate central (core) information into the overall content or purpose of the discourse (Carpenter & Just, 1977; Just & Carpenter, 1979). If forced to read at high speed, people are still able to obtain the gist (Masson, 1979), but being unable to pause very often, they are poor on integrating local details.

5C. The Look-Back Principle

Look-back is often needed because a reader cannot anticipate all uses that might be made of materials just being encountered. Since backward eye movements are relatively uncommon, much look-back must be done in active memory storage. It would be rather inefficient if look-back were achieved by a simple reverse scanning of the word-for-word sequence just read. The punctuation of descriptive versus relative clauses offers a fairly simple illustration:

11a. He can't remember the weekend, which seems odd.
11b. He can't remember the weekend which seemed so odd at the time.

The comma before "which" invites a look-back to the subject-predicate core (the whole state of "not remembering" is "odd"), while the lack of comma invites a look-back only to the nearest noun-head (the "weekend" was "odd"). Kimball (1973) suggests that syntactic look-

de Beaugrande

back is routinely oriented toward the most recently presented constituent; Springston (1975) predicts the same for pronoun referents. However, we saw from sample (5) in section 3 that substantially more elaborate search can be required. It would hardly be sensible to run back word-for-word in such cases. More likely, certain points are designated as likely candidates for subsequent reuse—an instance of the look-ahead principle presented in 5D. In sample (5), "authors" is the topic currently in focus, and the pronoun "they" is preferentially attached despite its distance within the linear sequence.

Since syntax is not an independent goal of communication, but only a demand imposed by a linear medium, various strategies are used to streamline it. Two such strategies are *recurrence* (simply reusing the same expressions) and *parallelism* (reusing a syntactic format with different expressions) (de Beaugrande & Dressler, 1981, pp. 54ff.). In this George Burns (1976, p. 85) anecdote about Jack Benny playing dice, we see both devices skillfully deployed:

> 12. He held the dice for forty-five minutes. He finally threw them and rolled a crap. He lost five dollars and they had to hold *him* for forty-five minutes.

The reuse of expressions and patterns from the first sentence in the last frees the reader's attention and underscores the surprise of a reversal in content. Special effects can also be obtained when recurrence signals some disproportionate circumstance, as in (Burns, 1976, p. 175):

> 13. His mind was always on the script, whether he was sitting in a bar, driving his car, sitting in a bar, relaxing at home, sitting in a bar, eating at a pizzeria, or maybe even sitting in a bar.

Since readers expect a steady flow of new material, they will react to such repetition by making steadily stronger assumptions about the person's drinking habits.

In semantics, look-back figures prominently in *narratives*. When reading about some event in a story, we look back to find some earlier one that might be a plausible cause or reason (de Beaugrande & Colby, 1979; Stein & Glenn, 1979). In our sample story (35) in section 6, many events are easily understood as caused by the narrator's immoderate consumption of garlic. Here also, look-back works together with look-ahead; e.g. when reading about the garlic, we are already predicting that people will react with repulsion toward the narrator.

Semantic look-back has been explored under the notion of *inferencing* (Rieger, 1975; Warren, Nicholas, & Trabasso, 1979). This activity builds bridges between the content currently in focus and that already comprehended. In sample (12), readers easily infer that Jack

Benny, a notorious tightwad, was so upset at the loss of five dollars that he couldn't stand up and had to be "held" upright. Though inferencing as a mental process is still not well investigated, it is certainly pervasive and reliable. Writers speculate confidently that most readers will make the same inferences (Burns, 1976, pp. 86, 207):

14. A few months after we returned from London Lisa moved into my house. Now hold it, I know what you're thinking!
15. Ten minutes later the honeymoon couple next door started arguing about their wedding—they couldn't decide where to have it.

In (14), the inference is repudiated; in (15), the point of the gag is to overturn an inference readers are making about a "honeymoon couple."

Look-back shows up in miscues. A previous word may simply pop up again, as when a student read (16) aloud and replaced "teachers" with "parents":[12]

16. He was married and added five children to the population, which our Eugenist says was the right number for a parent of his generation. And our teachers report that he never interfered with their education (Auden).

Even this case may reveal more than mere return of words: the reader may be trying to predict the organization of situations and events, e.g. in (16), something like: "And our parents always followed the advice of the Eugenists." We return to this matter in the discourse of the sample story in section 6 (pp. 30ff.).

5D. The Look-Ahead Principle

This principle is the necessary converse and complement of look-back. Reading could not possibly be done effectively unless readers were able to anticipate upcoming occurrences. In 5A, I cited some literature on the role of function words as cues for anticipating specific classes of content words. Readers have rather detailed and accurate capacities for making syntactic predictions within sentences (Stevens & Rumelhart, 1975).

The most obvious punctuation mark for look-ahead is the colon, which usually announces a listing, elaboration, or justification of what has just been read. But other marks contribute as well. The dash announces a transition to some commentary. The left parenthesis suggests that the following material is subsidiary. The semicolon alerts the reader that the next core-unit is semantically related to its predecessor. The comma can clarify a point where the current unit might otherwise be extended, as in:

17a. I presented her my candy and my flowers.
17b. I presented her my candy, and my flowers were already on her table.

where the comma in (17b) looks ahead to a new subject-predicate core rather than to a second direct object of the previous core. We return to this matter in 5F.

Syntactic look-ahead is also demonstrated by *cataphora*: using a pro-noun (or other pro-form) before its antecedent (de Beaugrande & Dressler, 1981, pp. 61ff.):

18. Because they go into the blood directly instead of through ducts, hormones circulate all over the body.

This sentence, taken from a student composition, is clear in reference, whereas a reverse placement ("Because hormones go...through ducts, they circulate....") is subject to confusion over "ducts."

Junctives are linking words that indicate what relationship forthcoming materials hold to already stated ones. New materials are simply added by conjunction (and); disjunction (or) announces alteratives; contrajunction (but) foreshadows opposed or unexpected materials; and subordination (because) marks some relationship of contingency or dependence (de Beaugrande, 1980, pp. 159ff.).

Semantic look-ahead is supported by a process known as *spreading activation* (Collins & Loftus, 1975). An activated concept in working memory tends to "spread" its status to closely associated concepts. In sample (15), the mention of "honeymoon" primes us to read about a "wedding." Tests show that readers perform worse on question-answering if expectations raised by the opening sentence of a passage are violated in the continuation (Flood, 1978). Conversely, my test readers generally did well with the garlic story (35) examined below, because the events followed directly from an obvious premise.

The reality of look-ahead is evinced by many kinds of miscues, such as the syntactic changes on samples (9) and (10). On the semantic level, there are cases where spreading activation replaces text words with alternates that are both visually similar and conceptually connected to active materials:

19. Through dust where the blacksnake dies (Dickey) [was read: "dries"].
20. My crop of corn is but a field of tares,
And all my good is but vain hope of gain (Tichborne) [was read: "grain"].

Like look-back, look-ahead raises the question of range. Upon occasion, readers need to anticipate things that might not be mentioned until much later. Researchers have suggested that upon encountering some event or situation in a text, readers at once set up a framework of slots that henceforth watch for appropriate fillers (Schank, et al., 1975, 1978; Kintsch, 1977; Rumelhart, 1980).[13] Under proper conditions, these slots may survive a long time. In murder mysteries, for instance, the crime is mentioned early in the story, but the agent kept in concealment until the end. These slots are presumably specialized and react only when triggered by specific types of entries. Thus, look-ahead, like look-back, does not usually follow the linear order of words during its search, but scans only strategic points.

5E. The Heaviness Principle

"Heaviness" seems a helpful designation for such factors as informativity, importance, length, focus, emphasis, involvement, salience, and surprise. Obviously, not all items in a reading selection could be equally "heavy" along any of these dimensions. Listeners can rely on intonation contours (Brazil, 1975), but readers must consult more complex and diverse kinds of cues, among which italic or bold print are only the most superficial. As a general maxim, the heavier an item or passage, the more processing effort the reader will expend on it.

In punctuation, the exclamation mark indicates heaviness of various sorts: assertiveness, surprise, stress, and so on; the question mark indicates an uncertainty or an unwillingness to be assertive. These two marks are not very frequent, however, because their effects decline with overuse. The comma can signal heaviness by marking off items that might otherwise be subsumed into larger items, e.g.:

21a. Finally the rocket took off.
21b. Finally, the rocket took off.
21c. Finally the rocket took off and the dust cleared.
21d. Finally the rocket took off, and all the personnel at White Sands breathed a sigh of relief.

With the comma in (21b), "finally" becomes heavier (indicating impatience, for example) than without it in (21a). In (21d), the comma recognizes the greater involvement and length of the two core-unit stretches, as compared to (21c).

In syntax, each core-unit is normally expected to bring at least one stretch of heavy materials. Since it is strategic to allow readers to get oriented first, this stretch is typically in the latter part of the predicate—an issue explored as "functional sentence perspective" (review in de Beaugrande & Dressler, 1981, pp. 75ff.). For example, one George Burns (1976, p. 238) story begins:

22. One of my very close friends is Eddie Buzzell, who was one of our top motion picture directors. He directed many movies, including *Honolulu*, the last motion picture Gracie and I made.

The opening announces a "very close friend" who is identified at the end of the clause; a version like this would place the name in much weaker focus:

22a. Eddie Buzzell was one of my very close friends.

The predicate concludes with the heavy item "top motion picture directors," a superlative of sorts. The second sentence contains a subject-predicate core whose content is so predictable that the sentence could hardly stop there; instead, it goes on to appeal to the narrator's involvement and to mention another superlative ("last"). Note that the subject slot of the follow-up sentence is typically the item introduced as new information in its predecessor (see Firbas, 1966, for discussion).

For comparable motives, heaviness will be noticeable in the number of short, simple sentences or paragraphs. Materials presumed to be self-evident, familiar, predictable, or the like, can be formated into lengthy or complex sentences or paragraphs. A compromise is offered by constructions with a dummy-like opening, leaving a high-focus slot toward the end, e.g., the advertising slogan:

23. What we want is Watney's.

where the brand name is reserved until after the sequence, which arouses curiosity by withholding the "wanted" item.[14]

In semantics, heaviness is especially linked to what is considered typical knowledge about the world. The effectiveness of sample (15) in 5C hinges on knowing that a honeymoon couple in a hotel is typically already married, whereas this couple is still planning the event. Salience is important also, as in this section from a student composition:

24. It is important to be careful when the line is cast, as you may snag a person, or, as I experienced, you may follow through too much, and fall right in the water.

She ends up with the most salient event in her fishing lesson: "falling right in the water" is memorable even though it is a typical hazard of fishermen.[15]

The pragmatic aspect of heaviness is its close connection to the particular feelings, expectations, and beliefs of the writer and reader. These considerations are prominent in samples like (22) and (24). Yet heaviness is indecisive for the utilization of all language levels because it affects people's mental loads and resources for any kind of task. In poetry, readers expect bizarre or surprising occurrences, yet cannot suspend their normal predictive tendencies, so that miscues ensue. In (25), the reader changed "man" to "a man":

25. Step to me as man (Jarrell).

Conversely, a miscue may create a still more exotic statement fitting only for poetry:

26. And cocktail smells in bars (Eliot) [was read: "barns"].

Research on the question of what is the best degree of heaviness for general readers is still sparse.[16] Certainly, many school readers err by supposing that heaviness should be avoided. Children are especially attuned to creativity.

5F. The Disambiguation Principle

Linguists have been quite attentive to ambiguous sentences such as:

27. Visiting relatives can be tiresome.

The usual recourse is to suggest a "transformation" or "derivation" which yields a syntactically non-ambiguous phrasing. But readers encountering such sentences more probably work in terms of differently organized events, asking what would make the best sense in the current context. There is no cognitive motive for postulating an additional level of "deep syntax" for such matters.

Though careful analysis can uncover legions of possible ambiguities, readers probably preclude many right away. In sample (3) from section 2, only one reading is at all convincing—the others demand intense focus and searching to even be noticed. Look-back and look-ahead also keep down the number of ambiguities. Even if read aloud, (28) would not be ambiguous (Miller, 1976, p. 3):

28. Anyone who has listened to politicians field questions in press conferences realizes the difference.

because "politicians" at "press conferences" give answers, not "field questions," so that "field" must be a verb rather than part of a noun compound.

Pronouns are not always near their antecedents and yet are usually not ambiguous. In sample (5), "authors" is the topic and the heaviest item, thereby offering itself at once as the antecedent for "they" later on. In a story beginning like this (Wilensky, 1980, p. 28):

29. John wanted Bill's bicycle. He walked over to Bill and asked him if he would give it to him. Bill refused. Then John told Bill he would give him five dollars for it.

readers know how bargaining situations are organized and have no difficulty in sorting out the referents for the frequent pronouns "he" and "him."

The conclusion here is that readers eliminate most ambiguities automatically. Perhaps they would notice more if they read slowly and meticulously. Experiments in which ambiguous samples disturb test persons on tasks like inventing a continuation (MacKay, 1966) might encourage precisely this atypically high expenditure. On the other hand, some ambiguities present a real impediment. My test subjects had great difficulty punctuating (30), but not (31):

30. Whether or not we win the game will be more exciting than last week's was.
31. While my girlfriend was dusting her brother and his pals walked in.

A comma after "win" is thus much more essential for reading than after "dusting." However, even improbable alternatives, as in (31), are disturbing and may distract from accomplishing a writer's goals.

The question of how genuine ambiguities are treated by readers is far from settled (survey in Clark & Clark, 1977, pp. 80ff.). Most experiments used single sentences out of context, magnifying the difficulties of resolution. But even efficient use of the principles of core-adjunct, look-back, look-ahead, and heaviness could not eliminate all ambiguities; otherwise, good readers should always be exactly in tune with the text and would make no miscues. There may be a threshold at which readers simply pass over ambiguities as nonessential for overall comprehension. Only beyond that threshold do they deploy conscious searching and problem-solving to reach a fully determinate meaning. The threshold itself should fluctuate with the time and resources available for the reading.

5G. The List Principle

This principle encompasses all means whereby a set of related elements is enumerated in sequence. The subsuming notion for the list is often announced, as in this passage from a student composition:

32. Checking the lobby consists of changing the garbage bags, wiping off the tables, sweeping the floor, changing ash trays, and cleaning the spice area.

In sample (13) in 5C, the listing contained the typical activities of George Burn's scriptwriter; the repetition of one list item ("sitting in a bar") draws attention (is "heavy") because each item is normally listed only once.

The lists in (13) and (32) are *non-ordered*: the items could be moved around without consequences. But lists may be *ordered*, e.g. in a time progression:

33. At the counter, the employee waits on customers, prepares coffee, tea, and milkshakes, and packs the orders to take out.

Note the inclusion of a non-ordered list ("coffee, tea, or milkshakes") that resembles a familiar cliché for airline stewardesses (with "milk" as its last item); but the list of the "employee's" activities is in a natural order.

The reading of a list can be facilitated if the list status is clearly signalled. In punctuation, the colon can be used, e.g. inserted after "consists of" in (32). Commas usually separate list members, and "and" or "or" looks ahead to the final item.[17] If list items contain commas within them, semicolons can demarcate their boundaries. In syntax, parallelism emphasizes a list, as we can observe in the present participle plus prepositional phrase of (13), or present participle plus direct object in (32). Each list item may fill a whole sentence, possibly preceded by cues like first, second, etc., as in my own second paragraph under 5B—where recurrence of words (load, may, saturation, number of) and parallelism are also deployed. Elaborated items may fill a whole paragraph each.

The crucial aspect of reading lists is to recognize the criteria that make the items comparable.[18] Readers can then set up a conceptual framework into which each incoming item is integrated in turn. This procedure should work best if the list progresses from the least heavy item toward the heaviest, allowing readers to work forward to the most difficult or salient materials, e.g.:

> 34. Possible options include diplomatic protest, economic sanction, military pressure, or openly declared war.

Such cases as (34) are also controlled by being normal chains of causality and temporal sequence, thus encouraging look-back and look-ahead.

5H. *Interactions among the Principles*

The seven reading principles outlined should be construed as high-powered operation types that perform many kinds of detailed tasks. They are not themselves chunks of content, and should not require attention and memory space; rather, they *organize* and *shape* the capacities of attention and memory space. Presumably, they do not run in a standard sequence, but are always ready to be triggered by any appropriate occasion. They certainly must interact with each other to be useful.

For example, the core-and-adjunct principle mutually influences and is influenced by the pause principle as an indicator of unit

de Beaugrande

boundaries. Look-back and look-ahead must continually prime each other. Heaviness affects the formatting of cores vs. adjuncts and the placement of pauses. Pauses can be essential for disambiguation, a process which in turn cooperates with look-back and look-ahead. Listing allows for efficient look-ahead, and often implies a steady rise in heaviness; the heavier the list items, the more likely they are to receive core formats and have pauses between them.

I have tried to show that these seven principles apply to all language levels: graphemics (notably punctuation), syntax, semantics, and pragmatics. Readers can thereby correlate the ongoing require- ments of these levels and select only those occurrences that are directly helpful for managing the current context. Increased limitationsof time and mental resources would dictate a higher degree of approximation without endangering the recovery of the gist.[19]

In this view, the linearity of reading in fact emerges as a constant juggling of mental tasks whose organization is certainly not linear much of the time. The mind is predisposed to zero in on certain points and patterns within the line of words and to send the findings to the proper mental "addresses." The uncertain, flexible nature of this predisposition is demonstrated by miscues. Even so, the success with which readers achieve a workable understanding of a text, despite the complex operations involved, remains somewhat astonishing.

6. A Sample Story

To conclude, let us glance at the reading of a simple story in terms of the principles sketched above. At the age of thirteen, George Burns heard that the tenor Caruso ate six cloves of garlic a day. Burns adopted the same tactic in hopes of improving his voice, though the impact on his personal life was ominous. The following anecdote covers only the behavior of his family at the time, and is situated among other anecdotes on the same topic (Burns, 1976, p. 151):

35.1. I came from a big family, seven sisters and five brothers, and during my garlic period whenever I'd come into the house I'd get a standing ovation—35.2. they all not only got up but they left the room. 35.3. But it did help my sleeping. 35.4. I shared a small bed with my brother Sammy and my brother Willy. 35.5. The minute I'd get into bed they'd go out the window and sleep on the fire escape and I had the whole bed to myself.

35.6. But my mother was smart. 35.7. She knew how to take advantage of my pungent personality. 35.8. Whenever a bill collector came to the door she'd have me answer it. 35.9. I'd open the door and say, "What do you want?" 35.10. and the guy would reel back, gasp "Forget it!" and run down the hall.

Though fairly self-contained, the story requires pragmatic knowledge about the writer as a show business personality and comedian. Readers must also apply world-knowledge about garlic, e.g.: "If X eats garlic, predict that X will be avoided by other people because of the resulting odor." Such knowledge yields a schema which is applied three times within the story (see 5A). Each application may be designated a story episode.

The garlic consumption is the main topic within each anecdote has its own subtopic: in (35), the family scene. It is strategic, though not compulsory, to announce the topic right away and thereby trigger look-ahead: "I came from a big family" is the opener (35.1). As we can see from Figure 1, a substantial amount of look-ahead and look-back hinges on this opener. There is the listing of the many siblings immediately afterward (35.1), specified later with two brothers (35.4); and the "mother" can appear in the subject slot in (35.6) as a predictable part of the "family." There is the mention of "the house" (definite article) as a typical location for a family. The various parts of the "house" can be cited with the definite article also: "the room" (35.2); "the window" and the "fire escape" (35.5); "the door" (35.8-9); and "the hall" (35.10). The "house" is thus specified to be an apartment by virtue of having a "fire escape" outside the "window" and a "hall" outside the "door." One of my test readers reported envisioning a "small house" that became "two stories" to accomodate the "fire escape" and was given a "larger foyer" to supply the "hall." This reader recalled the first episode like this: "When he came in, his parents ran upstairs." We see how minor misreadings can restructure the world of a text in order to preserve coherence in the face of difficulties.

The "bigness" of the family sets up another track of expectations that it might be economically deprived under the strain of twelve children. Such events as "sharing a small bed" (35.4) and fending off the bill collector (35.8ff.) are thus eminently reasonable. The "poverty" topic is left unstated, but is readily supplied by readers. One reader, asked why the bill collector ran away, reasoned: "Because they wouldn't pay him."

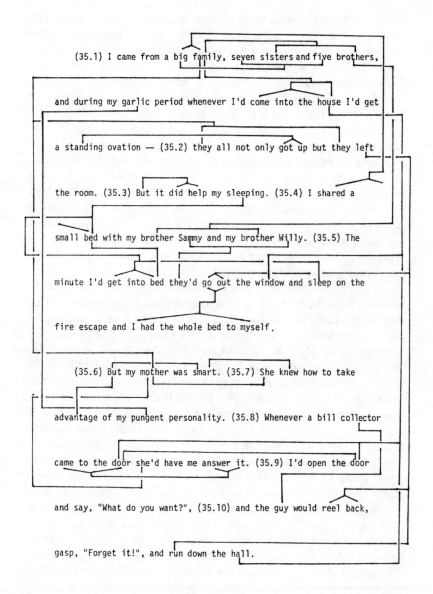

Figure 1. Semantic look-back and look-ahead. Slanted brackets are used to encompass more than one word in sequence.

Look-back and look-ahead operate on a more local scale as well. Having a "family" suggests coming home to confront them; three readers miscued by reading, "whenever I'd come home" (35.1). "Standing" looks ahead to "got up" (35.1-2). "Sleeping" anticipates three mentions of "bed" in (35.4-5), and of course the recurrence "sleep"; the withdrawal of the two brothers prepares us for reading: "I had the whole bed to myself." The mother's "smartness" foreshadows her "knowing how to take advantage" of a situation that brought disadvantages to the two brothers. Notice the use of "but" to start off each episode (35.3, 5) as a signal that, despite the negative effects just recounted, there was a positive side to it all as well. The emphatic verb format "it did help" rather than "it helped" in (35.3.) has the same motivation. The announcement of an "advantage" is similarly supportive in the final episode. A "bill collector" is often unwelcome, but this method of defeating him is novel. Observe how the otherwise everyday actions in "I'd open the door and say, 'What do you want?'" (35.9) thus gain special heaviness in the context.

My experiment with twenty freshman-age readers bore out the role of look-back and look-ahead. Ten readers were told in advance that they would read a George Burns story about a time when, to improve his voice in emulation of Caruso, he ate six cloves of garlic a day. The others were simply told, "Please read this story aloud to me." The "garlic period" is mentioned here only in a non-focused adjunct slot (35.1), rather than as a subject-predicate core (e.g. "and at the time I was eating lots of garlic"), because it is known from previous anecdotes in that chapter. The first group, thanks to my introductory remarks, all comprehended the story in terms of this key concept, reporting "bad breath," "bad smell," and the like—except for one reader apparently striving so hard to read perfectly that he had no attention left to make sense of the story and could report nothing. In contrast, the second group was often at a loss. Only four readers could retell the story in relation to the "garlic period"; one said the phrase "threw her," and she couldn't fit it into the story. The other five readers missed the point entirely, either saying they "didn't know" why the narrator's presence was avoided, or else speculating about a disagreeable personality, e.g.: "No one liked her, everyone knew what she was like and used her in different ways." (These five readers were also uncertain about the narrator's gender: two make him a "girl" and three said "he or she," "someone," or "they.") Two of these readers couldn't even find the cause when I gave them the story to read over. They either missed the reference to the "garlic period" or couldn't rebuild their mental representations around it (compare similar findings in Kay, 1955). Unlike the first group, the second lacked a crucial *control center* that would attach the relevant entries in the story line.

Efficient reading of the story hinges upon setting up a schema for the first episode and reusing it for the other two (see above). We have an *initial state* ("a big family," "sharing a bed," and the "mother being smart"), a *problem event* ("I'd come into the house," "I'd get into bed," and "a bill collector came"), and a *resolution event* for the problem ("left the room," "go out the window," and "run down the hall") (de Beaugrande & Colby, 1979). The problem is in each case an arrival, and its solution involves a departure.

Superimposed on this recurring schema is a steady increase in heaviness. Each time, the solution is more radical: just leaving the room, then going to sleep in a dangerous place, and finally, abandoning one's professional duties. The narrative becomes steadily more detailed, and the mental images elicited become more grotesque. The third episode is further marked as heavy by being assigned a separate paragraph. Obviously, this rise in heaviness is much more strategic than a drop. These episodes really wouldn't work in any other sequence, though they would still make sense.

However, my readers' retellings indicate that such a schema often was not properly applied. Very few could reproduce all three episodes, even though they were recalling immediately after their reading.[20] Despite its *recency*, the third episode proved hardest to recount, presumably because of its heaviness. Readers changed the antagonist to a "tax collector," or attributed the speech "Forget it!" to mistaken or unidentified speakers ("the family," "somebody"). Nearly half of the readers generalized on the first two episodes (e.g., "He was avoided by his family") and omitted the third entirely.

Heaviness also emerges in the use of the core-and-adjunct principle. The first episode is all one long sentence, though the dash is an important pause. The opening stretch presents known or predictable materials (the family and its "house," the "garlic period") and ends with the unexpected "standing ovation" (a reference to the narrator's show business personality, as remarked above). The stretch after the dash moves from the normal action of "getting up" for the "ovation" to the abnormal one, "leaving the room." Notice that all the heavy materials here are main core-predicate sequences toward the end of a stretch.

The second episode has three sentences of increasing length. The first and shortest presents a new subtopic ("sleeping"), so that the other sentences can be longer in developing the subtopic. The "bed-sharing" is also predictable from the "big family." The results of "getting into bed" are partly expected, but the location "fire escape" (mentioned at the end of the first main subject-predicate core) is surprising. "Having the whole bed" is by now foreseeable, but still deserves final position and a main core format because it is the point of the gag.

The third episode also has three sentences of increasing length. Again, the first and shortest sets the stage for the second, and the second for the third and longest. As already remarked, opening the door and saying "What do you want?" are commonplace acts and thus they ought to be mentioned before the bill collector's uncommon reactions, giving us the sequence of the final sentence.

If pauses indicate processing load, their positioning should be revealing. I studied the tapes of the test readers and found that they all routinely paused at commas, periods, and the dash. However, they also paused at many non-punctuated points. Figure 2 shows in square brackets the number of readers who paused at those points. Notice that the long sentences were often broken down, but not necessarily at major boundaries of phrases and clauses. Often, the pause came after the reader had already launched into the new phrase or clause, e.g. in (35.3, 5, and 8). In each case, the end of the phrase/clause is not predictable from its beginning. Apparently, readers would pause to consider their predictions, or would become disoriented by glancing ahead and slow down for adjustments. A special case is "pungent," a hard word for most of my freshmen: six paused before, and four after the word, signalling that disturbances may be optionally met with either look-ahead or look-back. Interestingly, five readers miscued with "pugnant," defining it later in such a way that they must have had "repugnant" in mind—a perfectly reasonable change that could be left standing without impeding comprehension. They disambiguated an unfamiliar expression by using context.

Otherwise, little disambiguation is needed, thanks to carefully planned formatting. The "standing ovation" is immediately reinterpreted from approval into dismay (35.1-2). "They all" (35.2) can only refer to "sisters" and "brothers" (35.1), "all" precluding any singling out. The "it" (35.3) gathers the whole situation of the "garlic period" as a prelude to a new episode; "room" is easily rejected though, as the many pauses before the predicate suggest, the identity of the subject hangs in suspension for a moment (see Figure 2). The "it" of (35.8) goes right

de Beaugrande

(35.1) I came from a big family, seven sisters [1] and five brothers,

and during my [1] garlic [2] period [5] whenever [3] I'd [2] come [2] into

the house [3] I'd [1] get [2] a standing ovation — (35.2) they [1] all [1]

not only got up [5] but they left the room. (35.3) But [1] it did [5] help [1]

my sleeping. (35.4) I shared a small bed with my [1] brother Sammy [4] and

my brother Willy. (35.5) The minute I'd get [1] into bed [4] they'd go out

[5] the window [4] and sleep [1] on the fire escape [5] and [3] I had [1]

the [1] whole bed to myself.

(35.6) But my mother was smart. (35.7) She [1] knew how to take advantage

[1] of my [6] pungent [4] personality. (35.8) Whenever a [1] bill collector

came to the door [6] she'd [3] have [2] me [1] answer it. (35.9) I'd open

the door and say "What do you want?", and the guy [2] would [2] reel back,

gasp, "Forget it!", and run down the hall.

Figure 2. Numbers in square brackets show how many readers paused. There was a total of twenty readers.

back to "door," and that of (35.10) is part of a standing expression, referring at best to "whatever we're talking about just now." Note that the narrator often assists the reader by repeating words that could safely yield to pronouns, e.g. the last "bed" in (35.5) and the "door" in (35.9) [both could be "it"]. This technique frees attention for appreciating the gag delivered in that same sentence.

The listing principle operates here on various scales. The entire story is a list of three related episodes in the order of increasing heaviness (see 5G), but not of any time sequence—the "whenevers" (35.1, 8) and the verb forms, e.g. "I'd come" (35.1), "I'd get" (35.5), "I'd open" (35.9) show that these encounters were periodically repeated. We have the smaller lists as well: the members of the big family (35.1), the two brothers (35.4), and the three reactions of the bill collector (35.10). Only the last-named is in a fixed (temporal) order.

Figure 3 shows the miscues made by my readers. I have already cited some of them as evidence of the seven principles at work. Look-back and look-ahead are especially prominent. In syntax, we have an inserted recurrence: "I'd come" was aligned with the previous "I came" (35.1); use of common phrases: "I'd get in" (35.2), "help with" (35.3), and "I'd get up" (35.5); and possibly an alignment of tenses when "I got" was read to match "I shared," "they left," etc. (35.2-5).[21] In semantics, we have the insertion of "home" for the "family" (35.1), the "little brother" for the "small bed" (35.4), and perhaps the "gave" as a usual response to a "bill collector" (35.8). One reader also inserted negatives ("didn't," "never") into (35.3) and (35.7), apparently assuming that all effects of the "garlic" would be equally negative for everybody.

The misjudging of cores and adjuncts could be responsible for the omission of "they" in (35.2), and in the insertion of "and" in (35.1). Both miscues eliminate one main core subject-predicate, either by merging it with its predecessor (35.1) or including it in a set of dependent cores (35.1). This result ignores the writer's intentional assignment of heaviness as I explored it already. The listing principle seems to be the culprit when the "and" was removed or displaced in the series of events mentioned in the last sentence (35.10): the placing of an "and" decisively affects the inner organization of the listing. In the original, we have a list of two actions by the narrator (no comma before the internal "and"), then an "and" with comma leading to a list of three actions by the bill collector (with "and" plus comma to announce the final item). Any reorganizing affects the status of these connections. Note also "then" being added to clarify the temporal order of the second list.

(35.1) I came from a big family, seven sisters and five brothers, and

during my garlic period whenever ⎡*I came* / *I'd come home* {*3, 1c*} / I'd come ⎤ into the ⎡*house and* / house ⎤ I'd

⎡*get in* {*c*} / get ⎤ a standing ovation — (35.2) they all not only got up ⎡*but left* / but they left ⎤

the room. (35.3) ⎡*Boy did it* / *But I did* {*c*} / *But did it* {*c*} / But it did ⎤ ⎡*help me* / *help with my* / help my ⎤ sleeping. (35.4) I shared a

small bed with my brother Sammy and ⎡*my little* {*c*} / my ⎤ brother Willy. (35.5) The

minute ⎡*I got up* {*c*} / *I'd gotten into* / I'd get into ⎤ ⎡*my bed* / bed ⎤ they'd go ⎡*through* / out ⎤ the window and sleep on

the fire escape and I had ⎡*that* / the ⎤ whole bed to myself.

(35.6) But my mother was smart. (35.7) She ⎡*never knew* / knew ⎤ how to ⎡*get* / take ⎤

advantage of my ⎡*pugnant* / *pungant* {*2*} / pungent ⎤ ⎡*purge* {*c*} / personality. (35.8) Whenever ⎡*the bill* / *a - a bill* / a bill ⎤

collector came to the door ⎡*she gave* {*2c*} / she'd have ⎤ me answer it. (35.9) I'd open the

door and say, "What do you want?", ⎡*the guy* / and the guy would reel back, ⎤ ⎡*and gasp,* / gasp ⎤

"Forget it!', and ⎡*then run* / run ⎤ down the hall.

Figure 3. Miscues are in italics. Numbers in curly brackets are used where a miscue was made by more than one reader; c = miscue corrected by the reader before moving on.

Notes

[1]The designation "deeper" applies to the language levels further removed from the "surface" text of words manifested in sound or print (discussion in de Beaugrande, 1981). Unit names ending in "-eme" were coined for each level (Pike, 1967; Koch, 1971), apparently with little concern for the very different status of the units, e.g. of sound vs. meaning.

[2]For example, readers would report a "loud roar" and "a giant flame." However, many omitted the sound and concentrated on the flame, which is treated more fully in the text. For discussion, see de Beaugrande, 1980, sections VI. 3 and VIII.3. On the definite article, readers sometimes miscued: "a great roar and a burst of flame."

[3]Test readers would recall more obvious modifiers, e.g. a "loud roar," or a "thunderous roar." Compare note 2.

[4]On the need for list items to be comparable among themselves, see 5G.

[5]The latest version (Chomsky, 1976), despite its claim for "universal" validity is, if anything, more centered on linearity than earlier ones.

[6]Computers work so much arithmetic because humans are poor on accuracy. In principle, however, computers can complement the human mind in many other ways.

[7]See discussion in section 6.

[8]In 5C, this example is depicted as an interaction of "look-back" with "heaviness."

[9]Perhaps these seven principles apply to *all* linear activities of the mind, not just to reading, but evidence for such a claim would demand complicated experiments. On their application to writing, see de Beaugrande (in preparation).

[10]When reading aloud, people pause not only at punctuation, but also at points where they are predicting or integrating the sequence. See section 6.

[11]Filling a separate paragraph can be a sign of heaviness also.

[12]These miscues with poems were observed under a special condition: my students were reading texts they had thoroughly studied and analyzed *in advance*. Familiarity with the material is no protection against on-line miscuing.

[13]On these frameworks and their various designations ("frame," "schema") see de Beaugrande (1980), Ch. 6. We examine a "story schema" in section 6.

[14]As Halliday (1967, p. 224) notes, this phrasing has been more successful and enduring than the company's original slogan "We want Watney's."

[15]The writer reported that she placed the comma before "and fall" expressly to emphasize this last-named event. Compare examples (21a-d).

[16]Measurements of "information" on statistical grounds, as proposed by Shannon and Weaver (1949), disregard both context and participant knowledge. For a different approach to "informativity," cf. de Beaugrande (1980, Ch. 4).

[17]Though omitted by many writers, the comma before the final "and" is essential to distinguish simple list items from compound ones. Compare note 15.

[18]Compare note 4.

[19]The term "graceful degradation" has been proposed for the mode in which the mind adjusts its performance to limitations and obstacles (Norman, 1979). A parallel-stage interaction model should account for this phenomenon much more easily than a sequential-stage relay model; the latter should simply break down before any "deeper" levels could be reached (e.g. no gist should be obtainable).

[20]Similarities among story episodes can invite conflation in memory (compare de Beaugrande & Miller, 1980).

[21]The appearance of "got up" in (35.2) may have also been influential; but the current context was probably more decisive.

In this paper, Spiro notes a rebirth of interest among psychologists in the mental processes associated with prior knowledge and individual experience. However, he points to the curious lack of research in the qualitative nature of subjective experience and the role of varying qualities of consciousness on ordinary cognitive processing. As a rationale for future experimental work in affective consciousness, Spiro focuses on five major observations: 1) there is a unity of consciousness and it has residual traces of memory, 2) there is mood-based cohesion in memory and recall, 3) individuals' feelings of consciousness help them to index memories for retrieval, 4) immersion may result in heightened recall, 5) it may be useful to stimulate actual subjective experiences when reading texts.

Consciousness and Reading Comprehension[1]

Rand J. Spiro
University of Illinois

The past twenty years in psychology have seen a rebirth of interest in mental activities, following the long antimentalistic reign of behaviorism. Among the fruits of this development are the recent advances in our understanding of the representation of knowledge and the role of prior knowledge in comprehension, often referred to as schema theory (Anderson, 1977; Bransford & McCarrell, 1974; Spiro, 1980). It is somewhat surprising, however, that the cognitive revolution has not addressed itself more to the most basic and directly accessible of mental phenomena, our subjective consciousness. There has been some concern for the necessity of conscious awareness in certain processing situations and the benefits of overcoming that necessity (see LaBerge & Samuels, 1974, on the role of automaticity in reading). More positively, investigation of the role of metacognitive awareness of the adequacy of understanding has recently become a productive line of inquiry (Brown, 1980; Collins, Brown, & Larkin, 1980).

However, there has been little concern for the qualitative nature of our subjective experience and whatever role these varying qualities of consciousness may have in ordinary cognitive processing. The one exception of note is the recent work on state dependent processing, which has demonstrated a facilitative effect of recalling information in the same emotional mood (induced by hypnosis) as when the information was initially encountered, with some interference when in a different mood at recall (Bower, 1980).

Consciousness was once a primary concern of those interested in the functioning of the mind. James (1890), among many others, made it the focal point of his investigations. (See Blumenthall, 1970, for discussions of others such as Herbert, Wundt, & Buhler who were directly concerned with the role of consciousness in cognition and also see Mandler, 1975, for a review of psychological work on consciousness and emotion.) Why, then, has this concern not been revived as part of the current cognitive revolution? One important reason is the resistance of subjective experience to systematic treatment—it cannot be precisely described (except metaphorically), much less formally modeled. Furthermore, psychologists, neuroscientists, and philosophers continue to be stymied in their attempts to find a basis for the existence of consciousness, becoming mired in the ancient antinomies and paradoxes of the various mind-body dualisms. However, we all know that our own individual subjective mental world does exist. If we accept this premise, it then becomes meaningful to inquire as to the functions that the ongoing experiential aspect of mental functioning might serve. That is my intention in this paper.

I will highlight five issues related to the nature of our conscious experience that might have important implications for reading comprehension and its development. The format of my discussion will be speculative, although I believe all the issues are empirical ones and experiments are in progress to test most of the hypotheses presented (see Spiro, in preparation). Accordingly, it should be kept in mind that the point of view offered is a preliminary one and should not at this point influence instructional decisions.[2]

The Unity of Consciousness and Its Residual Traces in Memory

First, let us identify some commonly observed characteristics of consciousness. One of the most ubiquitous metaphors for our subjective experience is its stream-like nature. Consciousness seems to have a continuity over time, especially for local regions. Because we always experience through our own minds, there appears to be at least local homogeneity of mental "mood." Furthermore, at any moment this mental mood is experienced in an all-at-once gestalt fashion. It also seems reasonable to assume that we have some memory for what our experience felt like. Phenomenological support comes from Bartlett's discussion (1932) of what he called "attitude" in the anecdotal reports of his memory subjects, to be discussed. It would also make sense from an evolutionary perspective that we would have rapid and accurate access to the way we felt in a given context in the past so that we could avoid situations that have unpleasant or, especially in our species' distant past, dangerous connotations.

Given, then, that our conscious experience has a continuity and all-at-once unity that is felt as a mental mood and has some representation in memory, what might the implications be for text processing? I will suggest several potential involvements. Relevant to all of them would be the fact that our conscious experience is usually a free byproduct of our biological existence; we do not always (or ever) need to expend mental energy to experience our living (although mental effort is required to try to conceptualize that experience or to put it into words). As such, it would not require much additional processing capacity to utilize. I see it as analogous to handwriting, where a handwriting expert can detect the mood of the writer of a particular sample, a mood that was unintentionally and effortlessly represented in the sample. Similarly, I think there is a "mental handwriting" (to be taken very figuratively). When something is represented in memory, it automatically contains information about the mental mood at the time of encoding or activation. I will argue that this gestalt mood information functions to enhance the cohesion of event representation (and to reduce memorial disintegration over time); to distinguish different events in memory that have conceptual commonalities and, therefore, might be assimilated with loss of particular identity; and as "signatures" that help to index and retrieve events from memory, as well as to rationalize the generative aspect of event reconstruction.

Mood Based Cohesion

One characteristic of long term memory representation is that it seems to be characterized over time by a movement away from the episodic particulars of events toward a reductive conceptual common denominator (Bartlett, 1932; Schank, 1979; Spiro, 1977). We all have been to restaurants many times and the particulars of early visits helped us to build our generic knowledge about what tends to happen in restaurants. However, a consequence of this abstractive process is that individual trips that are not especially exciting or unusual begin to lose their particular identity and, therefore, their distinguishability from one another. Sometimes this matters and sometimes it does not (it matters if you are a lawyer maintaining the particular identity of specific related cases, but not if you are a high school student who has read about World

War I in different places and cannot remember what was read where). When it does matter, the fact that one event which might otherwise be assimilated to related ones had its own characteristic mental mood "handwriting" may help it to retain its particular identity. Thus, aspects of different events are less likely to be confused. Looked at another way, event representations are less likely to disintegrate, with some parts of the event recallable in one retrieval context and other parts recallable only in a different context. This kind of cohesion produced by mental mood homogeneity would augment the more conventional kinds of semantic and syntactic cohesion conventionally addressed (Halliday & Hassan, 1976). In this case, it is more a coincidental cohesion due to common roots in a shared frame of mind.

Signature Feelings, Retrieval Indexing, and Reconstruction

Another possibility is that the representations of our feelings of consciousness help us to index our memories for retrieval purposes. We are currently developing a model that would operate in the following manner. Information in a retrieval context would elicit a partial and tentative feeling or mood. Memory would then be searched in the vicinity of the particulars of the retrieval context with a rough preliminary first scan. This first pass would not be at the level of particulars (the specific content of the mental representation), but would be for approximate matches of the retrieval context's tentative mood and the"signature feelings" of the long term memory representation. By calling them signature feelings, we are suggesting that particular events in memory, especially if they were initially very meaningful, will not be just hodgepodge collections of feelings but, instead, will have some *dominant* quality or signature. The idea is that "mental handwriting" can be "seen" from a greater psychological distance and, therefore, is amenable to a more rapid heuristic search. This process would err in the direction of producing too many erroneous retrievals, so a second stage of more analytic testing of the candidate retrievals would be required (this one has a fairly close mood but does not make sense as a candidate). The process also would contain a progressive refinement aspect. With each successive heuristic pass through memory, locations tested for feeling would become more local and specific, and the target feeling searched for would become more highly specified.

Once a retrieval location is accepted as appropriate, other memories that share the same mental handwriting would be located (as in the discussion of mood based cohesion above). However, the remembering process does not stop there. It seems likely that our explicit memory representations are usually incomplete. Not only is there forgetting of some information, but much information probably never receives any explicit representation. In particular, information that appears to be derivable from other already represented information or preexisting world knowledge may be superficially processed at input and left to be derived later if needed (Spiro & Esposito, in press). Part of the remembering process then involves reconstructing the whole of a past event from the partial memories of it that remain—figuring out how the past must have been based on partial data in the present (Bartlett, 1932). Bartlett observed a pervasive tendency for his subjects to report that the first thing that came to their minds when recalling stories was a vague, general impression of the stories (rather than specific details from them), which he called an "attitude." This attitude seems to be very like the signature feelings we have been discussing. He concluded that reconstructions tended to be constrained by these attitudes. In other words, when inferring the missing element from a past event, one test applied to candidates is whether they fit the mood associated with that event. If there is no fit, the candidates might be rejected. The mood might also guide the generation of candidates.

Thus, aspects of long term memory representations related to subjective experience may help in keeping memories together; help in finding them; and once found, help in inferentially elaborating them.

The Role of Immersion

We are now ready to explore the reason why immersion might be helpful. Most people would agree that things go better when we lose ourselves in an activity (shooting a basketball, reading a book) such that we are not aware of *what* we are doing, but are just doing it (with some awareness of the products of the activity). For example, when reading a story we may forget that we are reading and instead "live" imaginatively in the world of the story, vividly empathizing with characters with whom we identify. Why might reading in an immersed mode be advantageous? First, it must be acknowledged that the immersion itself may not be what is producing any advantage but, rather, the skill in processing and the availability of relevant background knowledge that are the enabling preconditions for immersion to occur. However, it seems there are likely to be advantages specifically attributable to immersion itself. Most prominent, in the context of the previous discussion, is the likelihood that the dominant mood of our subjective experience will be related more to the content of the story than to the feeling of our processing activities or our coincidental moods of the moment unrelated to the story. For example, if we are thinking about our reading, our experience is likely to include our feelings about how the process is going. One might feel confusion, interest in some syntactic construction or choice of words, or concern over the time being spent reading. Or one might be angry or depressed from the day's activities. Such feelings will detract from the possibility of extensive representation of *content related* experiential qualities. The consequence would be a decrement in the quality of the various processes related to cohesion, retrieval, and reconstruction discussed earlier.

Instruction Implications

We have focused on only a few of the possible roles our subjective experience of consciousness may have in the understanding process. Spiro (in preparation) discusses these in greater detail as well as implicating felt experience in a number of other processing activities (e.g., decisions made when studying and problem solving). Should the various hypotheses offered in this paper receive empirical support, what would that suggest for reading comprehension research and classroom instruction in reading comprehension? To take just the most obvious implication, it may prove productive to encourage children to simulate actual experience whenever possible in their reading. What this means is fairly clear in narrative texts, but is somewhat less clear in the more abstract subject areas. Here we believe there is also a role of our subjective experience, but it is of a different sort. We are developing the notion, following the work of Dewey (1887) and James (1890), that even the most intellectual and analytic of activities are felt or experienced. For example, James has argued persuasively that there are experiences of *relationships* between entities. Some of these intellectual feelings would be more salient than others (for reasons too detailed to go into here). These more salient feelings would then provide "regional experiential landmarks" guiding reconstruction of parts of content area materials' memory representations in ways similar to those described with respect to stories.

In sum, it seems possible that the felt aspect of consciousness might play a very important role in cognitive processing. If so, for how much longer can we afford to neglect that role just because it is difficult to study?

Notes

¹This work was supported in part by Contract No. US-NIE-C-76-40016. Helpful discussions with Avon Crismore and Gerald DeJong are gratefully acknowledged.

²"Consciousness" is a term that has been used in many ways. In this paper I am using it to refer to the felt quality of mental activity or, as it is sometimes called, subjective experience. It is important to note that emotions are part of subjective experience, but far from the only part.

Dehn notes that the field of Artificial Intelligence (or AI) has not been directly concerned with the teaching of reading, but there has been considerable work in AI in developing computer programs that can themselves read and that can paraphrase, translate, and answer questions about what they read. In constructing these process models, she suggests that AI theorists have been developing theories of reading comprehension that may shed light on why and where human poor readers have difficulty in understanding what they read and/or in demonstrating their understanding.

An AI Perspective on Reading Comprehension

Natalie Dehn
Yale University

1. An AI Approach to the Study of Reading Comprehension

There is more than one way of studying human cognitive capabilities such as reading comprehension. One can, of course, take the psychology approach of observing humans with that capability, but another option is to take the Artificial Intelligence approach of constructing computer programs with that capability. This chapter will consider the Artificial Intelligence (henceforth AI) approach. Before we can seriously consider what AI has to offer, however, three questions need to be cleared up:

1. Is it possible for such programs to be written? Could a computer, a machine, ever really read and understand something?
2. Even if such programs could be written, what could they tell us about the way humans read? After all, computers do scientific calculations, payrolls, and airline reservations but such programs bear little relation to, and tell us little about, how people do these tasks.
3. Why go to all the work of building computer programs that read when there are already lots of human subjects available?

Let us consider these questions in turn.

Q1: *Is it possible for such programs to be written?*

A: Yes. In fact, several such programs already exist.[1] None has truly general reading capabilities—each program is being developed as a means of studying a particular aspect of the reading comprehension problem, so each can only read certain classes of text with certain degrees of comprehension; a great deal of further work remains to be done. However, both collectively and individually these programs can clarify many issues involved in human story comprehension, including what is meant by comprehension and what is required for comprehension.

To those who are used to thinking of reading as a uniquely human activity, it may seem unclear as to what it would mean for a computer program to read. The beauty is that it means exactly the same for a computer program to read as it does for a human to read! This is true both in a theoretic and in a pragmatic sense.

It is true theoretically in the sense that the very question of whether computers can read "too" is premised on an undue distinction between humans and computer programs. This is not to claim that humans are "just machines," but rather that the physical characteristics of humans and computers (which are, admittedly, extremely different) are irrelevant to the question we are concerned with, namely that of reading comprehension. Reading is a cognitive process, and computer programs are perfectly capable of being *process models* of human cognitive processes.

Pragmatically, "reading comprehension" means the same thing in reference to computer programs as in reference to humans because we can examine a computer program's understanding in any of the ways we normally examine a human's understanding.

For instance, let us consider the following little story:

STORY 1:

John wanted money.
He got a gun and walked into a liquor store.
He told the owner he wanted some money.
The owner gave John the money and John left.

This is one of the stories read by a program called PAM (Wilensky, 1978, 1980; Schank & Abelson, 1977). One may, of course, question whether PAM actually did understand the story, or if it just looked at all the words and then declared itself done. One way of satisfying ourselves on this issue is the same as we do with children: by giving it a comprehension test. Below are some of the questions about the story and the responses PAM gave:

Why did John get a gun?
Because John wanted to rob the liquor store.

Why did John threaten the shopkeeper?
Because John needed to get some money.

Why did the shopkeeper give John the money?
Because the shopkeeper didn't want to get hurt.

Why did John leave?
Because John didn't want to get caught.

PAM's understanding was further probed by asking it to retell the story from John's point of view and from the store owner's point of view. Below are the two paraphrases the program made up:

PAM'S PARAPHRASE FROM JOHN'S PERSPECTIVE:

> I needed to get some dough. So I got myself this gun, and I walked down to the liquor store. I told the shopkeeper that if he didn't let me have the money then I would shoot him. So he handed it over. Then I left.

PAM'S PARAPHRASE FROM SHOPKEEPER'S PERSPECTIVE:

> I was minding the store when a man entered. He threatened me with a gun and demanded all the cash receipts. Well, I didn't want to get hurt, so I gave him the money. Then he escaped.

Q2: *Even if such programs could be written, what could they tell us about the way humans read?*

A: As a model of human reading comprehension, a great deal. Record-keeping or computational programs in use commercially are a bad analogy to reading programs developed as part of AI research because the former aren't even attempting to model humans—they are just intended to get a task done. That for some simple tasks performed by humans there are alternative (and sometimes superior) methods available to computers has no bearing on reading programs built to help the researcher to better understand understanding. The only difference between the computer and human instantiation of a particular cognitive process that is significant is that we can manipulate the computer version in ways that we couldn't or wouldn't the human, and can hence use it to learn a lot about how reading works and where it can fail.

Q3: *Why go to all the work of building computer programs that read, given the availability of human subjects?*

A: Program-building is important and useful methodological-ly, as a scientific tool for the refinement and debugging of theories of comprehension. More specifically:

1. The very writing of the program reveals hidden assumptions and lack of clarity in the underlying theory, and makes it clearer where further thought is needed. Thus writing AI programs can both help detect and help correct inadequacies in theories of comprehension.
2. The program, once written, can serve as experimental apparatus. One can thus "try the theory out," exploring what it does and does not account for. What is learned from such experimentation can help the researcher greatly in better understanding the phenomena under study. Programs serving as experimental apparatus are, of course, based on existing theories of the phenomena under study, and hence are almost invariably "wrong." Frequently a researcher can be aware that a theory is wrong before the

program is even written—but will write it anyway because such a computer program can show where the theory is wrong, how it is inadequate, what is irrelevant, and what else is needed.

3. The program, once written and tested, can serve as a demonstration of the theory it embodies, as an aid to the communication and explanation of that theory.

The power of program writing and testing in deriving theory development is far greater than might at first seem apparent. As each cycle of writing and testing a program points out more and more about what is and is not significant about a phenomenon, the initial theory wanes in significance. Many AI research efforts have used extremely naive theories as a way to get started. But an initially simple theory can evolve into a theory that is more complete. This evolution is made possible by applying what is learned from each successive cycle of program development (see, for instance, Schank, 1978).

The clarity gained by computer process models such as PAM should not be underestimated. For instance, any theory of, or technique for teaching, reading comprehension has to be concerned with the meaning of the text that the student is expected to arrive at—but what is it we mean by "meaning"? A common way of talking about the meaning of a text is with a paraphrase of the text. This is clearly inadequate, however, because though the ability to generate a paraphrase is a sign of understanding, and though paraphrasing a text for someone may help clear up that person's misunderstanding of the original text, the paraphrase is not itself the meaning of the original text. The paraphrase, like the original text, is itself a text which needs to be understood!

AI has give us a way of getting at understanding itself. AI theories of comprehension are detailed and explicit process models of human understanding. AI programs give us a way of watching the understanding process, and of examining the knowledge and memory representations that mediate between them.

2. The Reading Comprehension Problem

A major problem in understanding reading comprehension is in recognizing what the reading comprehension problem is. For instance, story 1 may have seemed pretty explicit. But let us consider two "variants" of this story.

STORY 2:

Mary wanted some diamonds.
She got a grenade and walked into a socialite's home.

She told the owner that she wanted some diamonds.
The owner gave Mary the diamonds and Mary left.

STORY 3:

Harold wanted a bagel.
He got some lox and walked into a bagel bakery.
He told the owner he wanted some bagels.
The owner gave Harold the bagels and Harold left.

Story 2 is, in fact, rather like the original story, while story 3 bears almost no resemblance. That the textual similarities are equivalent is simply irrelevant. What does matter is that stories 1 and 2 are about robberies and threats of violence, while story 3 is merely about someone gathering his brunch (i.e., there are underlying conceptual structures such as *holdup* or *shopping* that we understand a story in terms of).

But as it never says so explicitly, how do we decide that in story 1 and story 2 the protagonist was making a threat, while in story 3 he was not? We infer it. *Making inferences* is an essential aspect of reading (or, indeed, of any form of understanding); anyone "reading" story 1 or 2, for instance, without inferring the threat simply hasn't understood what was read.

With this perspective, if we return to the comprehension questions PAM was asked about story 1, we notice that at least part of what they were testing was whether the reader made some of the inferences s/he would have to have made to genuinely understand the story. (Poor readers and poor theories of reading comprehension share the characteristics of undue concern with the text itself—with paragraphs, sentences, and words—rather than with the meaning conveyed by the text.)

The problem of reading comprehension, therefore, is one of constructing an internal conceptual representation of the story, of recognizing how the story being read relates to prior concepts and mental structures. Understanding story 1 requires, for instance, seeing the situation as a holdup, with John as thief, the liquor store owner as victim, and the money as loot.

Even highly literate adults, however, do not always understand the same story in the same way, i.e., in terms of the same set of prior concepts and structures. A child failing to answer a comprehension question "correctly" (such as, "Who was the victim?") could be reflecting a different cultural bias (socialites are evil, worthless exploiters), a dearth of conceptual understanding (under what circumstances does someone give someone else her diamonds—suppose, for instance, Mary had asked the socialite for a cigarette?), or a genuine inability to read. While there may be disagreement about how it is most appropriate to respond to a student in each of these three cases, most people would agree that a different teacher response is warranted in each of these circumstances. (In fact, for a child with relevantly different conceptual structures, the "right" answers to comprehension questions can sometimes diagnose reading difficulties.)

Restricting our attention to problems of literacy, our goals for a poor reader might be that he be able to understand a story presented as written text as the same as that story presented as a puppet show. AI research in understanding, however, sheds light on all three types of comprehension "problems," as discussed in the sections that follow.

3. What Reading Comprehension Requires

Other than language and vision skills, what prior abilities and background does a reader bring to a story in reading and understanding it? This question, which is important in determining where (human) poor readers are having difficulty and what can be done to help them, is also one that has to be dealt with in building computer programs that read, because any such abilities and background have to be explicitly built in by the programer.

3.1. Making Inferences

We have already seen that understanding a text requires making inferences. For instance, any good reader reading the liquor store story will understand that John used the gun to threaten the shopkeeper and that it was out of fear of being hurt or killed that the shopkeeper gave him the money. Any reader, in contrast, who legalistically insists that the only thing known about John and the gun is that he "got" it before going to the liquor store, is not being careful but rather illiterate! Understanding stories absolutely depends on making such inferences.

Good readers make most appropriate inferences so automatically that it is very difficult for them to even be aware that they are making them. Computer modelling, therefore, plays a valuable role in helping make explicit what these inferences are. TALESPIN (Meehan, 1976), for instance, is an AI program that makes up Aesop-like stories, and whose development furthered our sensitivity to inferencing necessary to story comprehension. (Making up a story, of course, requires story comprehension capabilities, just as reading one does.) The TAILSPIN program was given all the inference rules it seemed it would need for understanding situations that could arise in such stories. Nonetheless, several important rules, it turned out, were initially omitted because they were so "obvious" as to be virtually invisible. Running the program, however, pointed out several such inadequacies, via "mis-spun tales" it produced. Here are two examples of stories resulting from incomplete inference rules; both the examples and their analyses are excerpted from the original thesis (Meehan, 1976).

> One day Joe Bear was hungry. He asked his friend Irving Bird where some honey was. Irving told him there was a beehive in the oak tree. Joe threatened to hit Irving if he didn't tell him where some honey was.

> Joe has not understood that Irving really has answered his question, albeit indirectly. Lesson: answers to questions can take more than one form. You've got to know about beehives in order to understand that the answer is acceptable. Also, it's polite to give some details when you answer a question. ("Do you know what time it is?" "Yes.") So now Irving says that there's honey in the hive and that so-and-so (a bee) owns the honey.

> One day Joe Bear was hungry. He asked his friend Irving Bird where some honey was. Irving told him there was a beehive in the oak tree. Joe walked to the oak tree. He ate the beehive.

A further refinement is to unscramble an acceptable answer in the proper fashion, remembering a little better what the original question was.

As a further taste of the pervasiveness of inferencing, the following is a classification (Rieger, 1975) of general classes of inferences that could be made from a single conceptualization (the meaning of a sentence):

1. Specification Inferences
   example: John picked up a rock.
   He hit Bill.
   JOHN HIT BILL WITH THE ROCK.

2. Causative Inferences
   example: John hit Mary with a rock.
   JOHN WAS PROBABLY MAD AT MARY.

3. Resultative Inferences
   example: Mary gave John a car.
   JOHN HAS THE CAR.

4. Motivational Inferences
   example: John hit Mary.
   JOHN PROBABLY WANTED MARY TO BE HURT.

5. Enablement Inferences
   example: Pete went to Europe.
   WHERE DID HE GET THE MONEY?

6. Function Inferences
   example: John wants the book.
   JOHN PROBABLY WANTS TO READ IT.

7. Enablement-Prediction Inferences
   example: Dick looked in his cookbook to find out how to make a roux.
   DICK WILL NOW BEGIN TO MAKE A ROUX.

8. Missing Enablement Inferences
   example: Mary couldn't see the horses finish.
   She cursed the man in front of her.
   THE MAN BLOCKED HER VISION.

9. Intervention Inferences
   example: The baby ran into the street.
   Mary ran after him.
   MARY WANTS TO PREVENT
   THE BABY FROM GETTING
   HURT.

10. Action Prediction Inferences
    example: John wanted some nails.
    HE WENT TO THE HARDWARE
    STORE.

11. Knowledge-Propagation Inferences
    example: Pete told Bill that Mary hit
    John with a bat.
    BILL KNEW THAT JOHN HAD
    BEEN HURT.

12. Normative Inferences
    example: John saw Mary at the beach
    Tuesday morning.
    WHY WASN'T SHE AT WORK?

13. State Duration Inferences
    example: John handed a book to
    Mary yesterday.
    Is Mary still holding it?
    PROBABLY NOT.

14. Feature Inferences
    example: Andy's diaper is wet.
    ANDY IS PROBABLY A BABY.

15. Situation Inferences
    example: Mary is going to a
    masquerade.
    SHE WILL PROBABLY WEAR A
    COSTUME.

16. Utterance-Intent Inferences
    example: Mary couldn't jump the
    fence.
    WHY DID SHE WANT TO?

Making inferences, in turn, requires prior general knowledge.

3.1.1. Prior Domain Knowledge

It may be relatively easy to see the knowledge of chemistry needed to understand chemistry papers, but it may, at first, seem that there is not very much prior knowledge needed to understand the liquor store story. Nonetheless, for a computer program (or person) to understand it, substantial prior knowledge is needed. It is this knowledge that enables us to understand the bagel bakery story as a radically different story than the liquor store story, and the socialite's diamonds story as basically the same story.

Let us take a look at some of the prior knowledge needed to understand these stories:

- The normal reason to go to a store is to buy something carried by the store. In particular,
- The normal reason to go to a liquor store is to buy liquor.
- The normal reason to go to a bagel bakery is to buy bagels.

- Guns are frequently used to kill people.
- Guns are frequently used to injure people.
- Guns are frequently used to terrorize people.
- Bagels are something to eat.
- Lox is something to eat.
- Bagels are frequently eaten with lox.
- If someone goes out of his way to obtain an object, it is probably because he intends to use it.

- People normally don't like to give up their property.
- People normally don't like to be killed.
- People normally care more about their personal safety than about the safety of their possessions.

This list could be extended for pages; but let us rather consider the *types* of prior knowledge needed for understanding stories. This is a question that has been central in attempts to build programs that understand what they read.

One of the simplest types is the script (Schank & Abelson, 1977). A script is a way of capturing knowledge about conventions, knowledge about what normally happens in common activities. SAM (Cullingford, 1978) is a program that was developed to explore scriptal knowledge needed in story comprehension. Consider, for instance, a story SAM read, and a few of the questions it answered about it.

STORY 4:

John went to New York by bus. On the bus he talked to an old lady. When he left the bus, he thanked the driver. He took the subway to Leone's. On the subway his pocket was picked. He got off the train and entered Leone's. He had some lasagna. When the check came, he discovered he couldn't pay. The management told him he would have to wash dishes. When he left, he caught a bus to New Haven.

Why did John take the subway from Leone's?
So John could take a bus to New Haven.

How could John take the subway from Leone's?
Probably John had a token.

Did anything unusual happen on the bus?
I don't remember anything.

Did anything unusual happen on the subway?
A thief picked John's pocket.

Did anything unusual happen at the restaurant?
John discovered that he couldn't pay the check and so he had to wash dishes.

The most intelligent and fluent readers couldn't answer "How could John take the subway from Leone's?" without prior knowledge about subways, nor could they answer "Did anything unusual happen on the subway?" because, although they would know that John's pocket was picked there, they wouldn't know whether that was unusual. It is not significant that John talked to an old lady on the bus, even though such an event was explicitly mentioned, but it would be if old ladies were rarely to be found on buses, or if there were a rigidly enforced taboo against talking in a bus, or if conversations between men and old ladies were viewed as particularly bizarre.

Thus scripts, in the sense of knowledge about human institutions and conventions, are one kind of prior domain knowledge a reader needs to understand stories. Let us consider a few others.

Closely related to scriptal knowledge is knowledge of *role themes*, or how a person is likely to behave in a societally-defined role, such as that of waitress or customer.

Understanding stories also requires knowledge of the physical world. Consider, for instance, the following two sentences.

1. John threw an egg at the wall.
2. John threw a rock at Mary.

"Common sense" knowledge of physical properties is needed to realize that in the first sentence, it is the egg that will be physically damaged and the wall will merely get messed; in the second sentence, it is Mary who will be physically damaged while the rock will merely get messed.

Yet another kind of prior knowledge needed is that of human nature. One such kind of knowledge is what Schank and Abelson called interpersonal themes. Consider, for instance, the following two stories (Wilensky, 1978).

STORY 5:

John loved Mary. One day, John saw a truck coming down the street towards Mary. John ran up behind Mary and gave her a shove.

STORY 6:

John hated Mary. One day, John saw a truck coming down the street towards Mary. John ran up behind Mary and gave her a shove.

To understand that in story 5 John was trying to save Mary while in story 6 John was trying to kill her, the reader needs to know about love and hate and the goals they give rise to—that people will try to protect those they love and hurt those they hate.

Goals, and plans for achieving goals, are yet further examples of what people need prior knowledge of. This includes knowledge of what goals a person is likely to have (in any given set of circumstances), what he or she is likely to do to achieve that goal, and of how goals can interact (conflict, compete, subsume one another, etc.) (Carbonell, 1979; Schank & Abelson, 1977; Wilensky, 1978). Without such knowledge, story 5 could barely be distinguished from story 6, and certainly would not be understood. Recognizing and tracking character goals and plans, and the interpersonal and role themes that give rise to them, is central to understanding most stories, and requires a substantial amount of prior knowledge.

Children can apparently understand script-based actions at quite an early age (Schank & Abelson, 1977), but do not develop the ability to track goals and plans until several years later (Schank, in press b). Children are also greatly lacking in thematic knowledge. Schank (in press b) illustrates this point with the following story which, though within the reading aloud capabilities of a third grader, is well beyond such a child's understanding.

> John hated his boss. He went to the bank and got twenty dollars. He bought a gun. The next day at work he decided to ask his boss for a raise. But John was so upset by his own plan that he told his boss he was sick and went home and cried.

As Schank points out, a third grader is not likely to have a sufficient understanding of hate nor of "fear of being an outcast, immoral person, or a criminal, all of which the child can imagine to be something going through John's mind." With insufficient knowledge of plans and goals, one cannot even infer the causal connections between the events mentioned.

Thus "domain knowledge" for general reading such as stories is quite substantial, encompassing common-sense knowledge of physical causality, human intentionality, and societal norms. Lack of such knowledge makes a story as incomprehensible as a technical paper is to a nonspecialist. Most people, of course, have an advantage over current computer programs in that they can pick up most such general knowledge effortlessly in their daily interactions and experiences, but particular holes in their experience may be distorted into an apparent inability to read. While there has long been concern about cultural bias in reading instruction, AI models of reading comprehension can greatly clarify both the problem and the solution. When the problem is lack of prior knowledge, simplification of vocabulary or style won't help.

Such domain knowledge is needed for any form of understanding, be it of written text, spoken language, or of a directly experienced situation.

3.1.2. Expectations

An important aspect of the inferencing process is the forming of expectations.

Suppose, for instance, someone was just given the first two lines of the story:

> John wanted money.
> He got a gun and walked into a liquor store.

After reading thus far, it should already be obvious what is going to happen. One already has the expectation that John is going to "hold up" the liquor store, using the gun to threaten, physically disable, or kill whoever is there. This, in fact, answers the question that arose earlier, of how we knew that "He told the owner he wanted some money" was a threat.

A reader who, midstory, has insufficient or inappropriate expectations, has not understood the story thus far and will have difficulty processing the remainder of the story.

Expectations is a large part of what makes reading something in context so much easier than reading the same thing out of context. For instance, an unfamiliar word, like "abutment," can be adequately understood in the context of a newspaper account of a car accident in which a car skids into an abutment, killing the driver.[2] We saw earlier that inferences in general can be wrong, but that they are important to make nonetheless. Expectations can, of course, be violated. For instance, the liquor store story could have continued as follows:

> John wanted money.
> He got a gun and walked into the liquor store.
> He offered to sell it to the owner for $25.
> The owner gave John the money and John left.

Violated expectations can play an important role in story comprehension.[3] Violated expectations frequently leave ghost paths (Lehnert, 1978), as is reflected in the reader's ability to say why something didn't happen in the story. Further, authors frequently deliberately mislead the reader (Granger, 1980), setting up expectations so that they can be violated. Anyone reading a detective story or thriller who doesn't fall into such traps is missing much of the fun and even more of the meaning.

A usefully violated expectation demands explanation, and in forcing the reader to construct such an explanation usefully directs processing towards better understanding of what did happen.

3.2. Controlling Inferences

Computer modelling revealed the extensiveness of inferencing, but in doing so, highlighted yet another problem: the need to control the inferencing process. If a story understander made every applicable Rieger inference to each conceptualization, things would quickly get out of hand. Not making any inferences at all excluded the possibility of understanding, but attempting to make all possible inferences would lead to exponential explosion.

Further, making an inference just because it was possible to, could lead one greatly astray. One should not, in reading the first sentence of the liquor store story ("John wanted some money"), be lead into musings on the nature of economics.

3.2.1. Variable Depth Processing

Reading is not a uniform process. Sometimes one reads carefully, aiming for depth of understanding (BORIS, [Lehnert, et al., 1980]); sometimes one skims, just looking for the major points (FRUMP, [DeJong, 1979]). Even within a given text, however, there are aspects that one will find more interesting than others. By doing *variable depth processing* (Schank, 1978), the slighting of material that seems less important or interesting allows one to pay more attention, and process more deeply, material which warrants it. Really understanding anything to any reasonable depth requires that one ignore a good deal else; hence, variable depth processing is essential to reading comprehension.

This process is somewhat modelled by IPP (Lebowitz, 1980), a news story reading program which is interested in international terrorism, which ignores or pays minimal attention to things that it finds uninteresting, focusing on what it thinks matters.

3.2.2. Beliefs

One of the factors greatly affecting how much attention one pays to various aspects of a story is one's prior *beliefs*. This was explored by the development of a program called POLITICS (Carbonell, 1979) which read stories with political implications. The program could assume the political beliefs of either an American conservative or liberal, about the goals of the United States, Russia, and third world nations, and about the relative priority of the goals of each.

The effects of beliefs on story understanding were explored by giving each political variant of the program the same stories to read, and then probing the understanding of each with a series of questions.

Following are dialogues illustrating two perspectives.

DIALOGUE WITH CONSERVATIVE:

Russia massed troops on the Czech border.

Q: Why did Russia do this?
A: Because Russia thought that it could take political control of Czechoslovakia by sending troops.
Q: What should the United States do?
A: The United States should intervene militarily.

DIALOGUE WITH LIBERAL:

Russia massed troops on the Czech border.

Q: Why did Russia do this?
A: Because Russia wanted to increase its political influence over Czechoslovakia.
Q: What should the United States do?
A: The United States should denounce the Russian action in the United Nations.

DIALOGUE WITH CONSERVATIVE:

The US Congress is expected to approve the Panama Canal Treaty.

Q: Should the US approve the treaty?
A: No, the treaty is bad for the United States.
Q: Why is the treaty bad for the US?
A: The United States would lose the Canal to Panama and the United States would be weaker.
Q: What might happen if the United States loses the Canal?
A: Russia will try to control the Canal.
Q: Why would Russia try to take over the Canal?
A: Russia wants to expand its military control. The Panama Canal has high military value.
Q: How might this happen?
A: The United States may not be able to stop anyone taking over the Panama Canal. Torrijos is a communist. Torrijos will let Russia control the Canal.
Q: Why should the US worry about Russia taking over the Canal?
A: Because Russia wants to control the world.
Q: What should the US do to stop Russia from taking over the Canal?
A: Congress should vote against the Panama Canal Treaty?

DIALOGUE WITH LIBERAL:

The US Congress is expected to approve the Panama Canal Treaty.

Q: Should the US approve the treaty?
A: Yes, the Panama Canal Treaty is good for the United States.
Q: Why is the treaty good for the US?
A: The Panama Canal Treaty improves relations with Latin American Countries.
Q: What happens if the US keeps the Canal?
A: This will cause discontent and conflict in Panama and Latin America.
Q: Why would this lead to conflict?
A: The Canal Zone is a United States colony. Latin America does not like colonialism. The United States would maintain colonialism.
Q: What if Russia tries to take over the Canal?
A: Russia does not want conflict with the US. Russia will stay out of the Canal if the United States defends it. The United States defending the Canal is part of the treaty.

Although both variants of the program were equally good readers, most people are tempted to believe, on the basis of the answers given to comprehension questions, that one understands the stories better than the other.

All this is related, of course, to the culture controversy. Children with beliefs differing from their teacher's may have perfectly adequate reading comprehension skills, yet score poorly on comprehension tests. The lack of an assumed belief, like the lack of assumed knowledge, can make them miss something "perfectly obvious"; different beliefs are likely to lead to inferences that the teacher may grossly misinterpret.

3.2.3. *Memory Organization*

Poor readers frequently "have" the knowledge they need to understand a text, but don't use it; i.e., if they are asked about it in the right (Socratic) way, they will be able to recall it, but they don't recall it spontaneously when they should in reading a text assuming such knowledge.

Similarly, they may "know" the answer to a reading comprehension question if the question is couched the right way (prepared for by an appropriate prior sequence of questions), but be unable to anwer it otherwise.

Both of these phenomena are due to the fact that not everything in one's memory is equally accessible at all times (Kolodner, 1980). If it were, we would be overwhelmed by the quantity.

Although such problems reveal themselves as retrieval difficulties, the real source of the problem is at the point where the person is noticing the fact and storing it away, because that determines how it can later be found and used.

How one has one's knowledge and beliefs organized will affect what one pays attention to in reading, hence how one understands what one reads and how one remembers it (Schank, 1979; in press, a). At any intermediate point in the story understanding process, structures that are being accessed will determine what, of what's coming up, one believes is most important to pay attention to, and how one believes it will fit in. Thus, not only prior knowledge, but also prior memory organization, limit what a reader is currently capable of understanding.

4. Testing Reading Comprehension

Not only can AI programs tell us about how people read, they can also tell us about the testing of reading comprehension. Though computer programs have the advantage that we can "look inside their heads" before and after reading a passage, and thus "really see" to what degree they understood what they read, they generally are also required to prove themselves by the more traditional means of answering comprehension questions and retelling what they read in their own words. We have already seen some examples of each of these activities; this section discusses what we have learned about such tasks from building such programs.

It should be realized that, for humans as well as for programs, understanding is captured by the reader's memory. It is this that allows the reader to do the tasks (spontaneously or under examination), and it is this that comprehension tests should actually be aiming to probe.

4.1. Comprehension Questions

There are two ways a comprehension question can fail to test comprehension: it can be too hard, or it can be too easy. It can be too easy by not requiring comprehension of the text in order to be answered; it can be too hard by requiring, in addition to comprehension of the text, other skills or achievements which the testee is lacking and which are not the point of the question.

One thing that is alwasys required in answering a reading comprehension question, in addition to the understanding of the original text, is understanding of the question itself. Understanding questions is a more complex activity than it may appear at first. The understanding (and answering) of questions is considered at length in Lehnert (1978).

Sometimes understanding a question about a story one has read is virtually all the work required for answering the question (Dyer & Lehnert, 1980). For instance if asked, after reading a story involving such an event, who John lent money to, one's understanding of the question might be a reference to the event being referred to, from which it would be trivial to extract the recipient of the loan.

In other cases, even after understanding what is really being asked, "retrieving" the answer from one's memory is a complex, reconstructive process. A model of reconstructive recall in question answering is presented in Kolodner (1980).

Questions can be quite effective at testing comprehension when they reveal inferences made (or not made) and memory organization. Thus, returning to story 1, "Who got a gun?" does not necessarily test comprehension, whereas "Why did John get a gun?" does.

4.2. Paraphrase

Paraphrases can reveal many of the inferences the reader has made, and also the structures in terms of which the reader understood the story. Let us, therefore, look again at SAM's understanding of story 4, this time as revealed through the paraphrase it produced when instructed to retell the story in detail.

Original Story:

John went to New York by bus. On the bus he talked to an old lady. When he left the bus, he thanked the driver. He took the subway to Leone's. On the subway his pocket was picked. He got off the train and entered Leone's. He had some lasagna. When the check came, he discovered he couldn't pay. The management told him he would have to wash dishes. When he left, he caught a bus to New Haven.

Computer Paraphrase:

John went to a bus stop. He waited at it a few minutes. He entered a bus. The driver got the ticket from John. He went to a seat. He sat down in it. While John was on the bus an old lady and John talked. The driver took John to New York. He went to the driver. When getting off the bus John thanked the driver. John got off it.

He entered a station. He put a token into the turnstile. He went to the platform. He waited at it a few minutes. He entered a subway car. A thief went to John. The thief picked John's pocket. He went. John went to the seat. He sat down in it. The driver took John to Leone's.

He entered Leone's. He looked around inside it. He saw he could go to a table. He went to it. He sat down in the seat. He ordered some lasagna. The waiter indicated to the chef John would like him to prepare something. The chef prepared the lasagna. The waiter got it from the chef. The waiter went to the table. He served the lasagna to John. He became full.

He asked the waiter for the check. John got it from the waiter. John discovered he was unable to pay the check. The management told John he would have to wash the dishes. He entered the kitchen. He washed the dishes. He left Leone's.

He went to the bus stop. He waited at it a few minutes. He entered the bus. The driver got the ticket from John. He went to the seat. He sat down in it. The driver took John to New Haven. He got off the bus. (Cullingford, 1978)

A deeper level of understanding (displaying greater intelligence) is recognizing what the point of a story is, and is thus demonstrated in being able to give a short but apt paraphrase. This reflects yet a different kind of inference—inferring the significance. Such understanding is demonstrated by a program called FRUMP (Dejong, 1979), which skimmed the following UPI news story and produced the following summary.

Original Story:

The United States welcomed Soviet Foreign Minister Andrei Gromyko Thursday with a statement it will continue to abide by the expiring strategic arms accord so long as Russia also observes its provisions.

The Administration told Congress in a letter it will issue a "unilateral statement" pledging the United States to observe the 1972 SALT I agreement even after its Oct. 3 expiration date.

The decision was conveyed to Sen. John Sparkman, D-Ala., Chairman of the Senate Foreign Relations Committee, diplomatic sources said. It sparked immediate concern among some senators, including Sen. Henry Jackson, D-Wash.

At the State Department, Secretary of State Cyrus Vance began a first round of talks with Gromyko in an effort to break the current stalemate in U.S./Soviet strategic arms limitation talks and open the way to a new accord.

Gromyko was scheduled to meet President Carter Friday. The Soviet official said on arrival Wednesday progress would require movement by both sides. But U.S. officials said they anticipated no major Soviet concessions.

Computer Paraphrase:

Cyrus Vance met with Andrei Gromyko in the United States about the SALT agreement.

It is interesting to note that translation of texts by recent reading programs (such as SAM, PAM, and FRUMP) has been basically the same process as paraphrase generation. Once the original test is understood, it has conceptual representation in memory. Given this, and the ability to generate in the target language, the problem of getting the story back into words does not depend on the source language. "Paraphrase," then, can be viewed as translation in which the source and target language happen to be the same.

Conclusions

In the development of programs that can understand written language, research in Artificial Intelligence has given us a much more concrete sense of what the requirements, processes, and results of reading comprehension are, and hence has implications for the teaching and testing of reading comprehension. A detailed process model of reading comprehension can help in the teaching of reading comprehension by clarifying:

1. what readers need to know in order to understand what they are reading,
2. what can be lacking in readers that would hinder comprehension, and
3. what can be interfering with comprehension (or masking otherwise adequate capabilities).

A detailed process model of reading comprehension can help in the testing of reading comprehension by clarifying:

1. what one actually wants to measure,
2. where things can go wrong (and, therefore, what to check for), and
3. to what degree particular probes actually test that which one is trying to test.

Detailed process models of question answering and paraphrase generation can test theories of how these tasks reflect understanding and what else these tasks depend on.

The AI process models are still a long way from being complete, but existing partial models have already told us a great deal about how prior knowledge and memory organization affect what and how we understand, how understanding alters our knowledge and memory organization, and the role of making inferences and predictions in the process of comprehension. They thus help us to better understand both understanding and misunderstanding.

Notes

[1] See, for instance, BORIS (Dyer and Lehnert, 1980); (Lehnert, et al., 1980), IPP (Lebowitz, 1980), ARTHUR (Granger, 1980), FRUMP (Dejong, 1979), POLITICS (Carbonell, 1979, 1981), PAM (Wilensky, 1978, 1981), SAM (Cullingford, 1978, 1981), Ms. Malaprop (Charniak, 1977), and unnamed (Charniak, 1972).

[2] This example was one actually encountered and handled by a program called FOUL-UP (Granger, 1977). If given a story identical except that the car skids into an elm, where the program has never heard of elms, it will build the same working definition—which is actually quite appropriate, given that that is all one knows about elms.

[3] It is important, though, to distinguish between appropriate expectations that are nonetheless violated, and expectations that are inappropriate ever to have formed. The former both reflects and aids in comprehension, while the latter reflects misunderstanding and hinders further comprehension even if (or perhaps even especially if) they happen to be fulfilled.

Dehn

PART TWO   Focus: Language

Menyuk poses the question: "How can one read what one does not know in oral language?" She notes that researchers in the fields of language and cognition have become increasingly uncomfortable with the simplistic notion that written language processing is wholly dependent on oral language knowledge. She extensively reviews the literature on this topic, presenting a sound theoretical explanation of the areas in which we know written language development to be dependent upon oral language development. She presents some detailed speculations about the relations between oral and written language development. Her speculations are supported by recently completed studies. Finally, she presents possible implications for instruction from her studies.

Language Development and Reading

Paula Menyuk
Boston University

Introduction

In a paper concerning the use of language to control and plan motor behaviors, Wozniak (1972) presents the following paradox: How can we tell ourselves something we don't already know? In this statement, Wozniak is presenting the dilemma of researchers who attempt to explore the relation between "cognition" and "language." Although, in general (there are exceptions), the child doesn't talk about things she doesn't know about, it is clear that talking about what one knows about, either to oneself or aloud, modifies what is known. It has become evident to researchers in this area that simple-minded notions about dependency relations between nonlinguistic cognitive development and linguistic cognitive development do not provide adequate explanations of development in either domain or developments that depend on interaction of the two domains (Menyuk, 1980).

"How can one read what one does not know in oral language?" would be the statement of a paradox similar to the one cited above concerning the relation between cognition and language. Researchers who are concerned with the relation between oral and written language development have become increasingly uncomfortable with the simplistic notion that written language processing is wholly dependent on oral language knowledge. The reading researcher is interested in obtaining a detailed description of the relations between oral and written language development, just as the development researcher is interested in determining, in detail, the relations between the nonlinguistic and linguistic domains of development.

In this paper I will present some notions about possible relations between developments in the two domains of oral and written language. I will do this by first discussing the findings of studies of oral language development that seem germane to the issue. Some hypotheses concerning the relation between the two domains of development and some data directly assessing the proposed relation will then be reviewed. Finally, some conclusions will be drawn about possible relations. These will, of necessity, be highly tentative conclusions since detailed exploration of relations between the domains of development is still in its infancy stage.

Oral Language Development

The latest (over the past ten years) studies of oral language development have seriously challenged the notion that the child knows most of what she has to learn about the structure and use of oral language by the age of five or six years. Previously, it was thought that "almost" adult competence in, at least, phonological and syntactic knowledge was achieved by that age (McNeill, 1970). More recent studies indicate that developmental changes in knowledge of syntactic and morphophonological rules continue to occur after age five and, indeed, throughout the school years. Therefore, it is not the case that the child on entrance to school has a fully mature grammar of the language which might then be available for processing all types of written material presented. There are areas of structural knowledge which remain to be acquired.

Despite the above statements, the normally developing child does know a great deal about the language on entrance to school and has been communicating effectively with others in her environment for a number of years. This substantial knowledge exists in all aspects of language: pragmatics, semantics, syntax, and morphophonology (Menyuk, 1977). Further, this competence in communication has been achieved by all normally developing children *in their native language* regardless of socioeconomic status (Ervin-Tripp, 1971). Emphasis has been placed on the term "in their native language" since varying degrees of competence are to be expected in use of a second language.

The questions that arise, then, are: What do most children know about language at age 5 and what are they yet to learn over the school years? and, What differences in language knowledge exist among normally developing children that may affect acquisition of written language? The remainder of this section will attempt to deal with these questions.

It was stated above that normally developing children at age 5 have acquired substantial knowledge of all aspects of language. What children appear to know in each of these aspects will be discussed separately since, it will be argued, each aspect of oral language knowledge plays a differing role in the acquisition of written language knowledge.

The pragmatic rules of a language are concerned with how to convey the purpose of the utterance; that is, to assert, command, request, question, negate. These purposes have been termed "speech acts" (Clark & Clark, 1977). Another aspect of pragmatic competence is knowledge of how to engage in conversation: how to take a turn, how to initiate and respond appropriately in a conversation. This latter requires the ability to keep track of what is being said and has been said in the conversation as well as physical parameters that are crucial to clarity of communication. Cultural rules of how to say what to whom under what circumstances (for example, rules of politeness) must also be learned.

Pragmatic competence, then, involves both knowledge of structural rules and rules of use of language that require both ongoing memorial abilities (keeping track in conversation) and, in some instances, retrieval from memory of past experiences. In addition, particular cultural rules for exchange must be kept in mind and these require both situational and addressee appraisal for appropriate communication. A great deal of what makes for pragmatic competence depends on inferencing abilities (for example, interpretation of paralinguistic cues of intonation, stress, and gesture and keeping in mind referents or deducing referents from situational cues) rather than merely understanding the utterances produced.

Although the child at age 5 communicates very effectively with members of her own linguistic community and knows how to generate the speech acts listed, there are any number of communicative situations the child has yet to learn about (for example, how to converse with a teacher), a number of domains of discourse the child has relative unfamiliarity with (for example, formal mathematical and scientific notions), and a number of speech acts that the child has yet to engage in (for example, commissives or argumentation based on causal, conditional, or hypothetical physical conditions). Development of these abilities is highly dependent on further experience. The domains of discourse in the home and classroom and the written materials children are exposed to are the experiences which will broaden pragmatic competence. Domains of discourse are also a critical source for acquisition of word knowledge.

Semantic and syntactic knowledge is knowledge of word meanings in the context of varying structures. For example, comprehension of the sentence "The boy kissed the girl." requires knowledge of the meaning of each morpheme in the sentence (boy, kiss, ed, girl) and the relation between morphemes (*the* modifies boy and girl; the boy is the actor and the girl the object; *ed* modifies kiss).

By the time the child enters school she has acquired a vocabulary of some two to three thousand words and is using these words in structurally complete utterances. The child's acquisition of word knowledge is derived initially from physical contextual information and then from the linguistic contexts in which words are used. An unfamiliar word such as "avocado" might be, at least, partially identified in a context such as "He likes avocados in his salad." The two areas of development, semantic and syntactic, are mutually interdependent. In addition to the child having acquired a sizable lexicon by the time she enters school, she is also able to understand a number of structurally different types of utterances which allows further interpretation of old lexical items and interpretation of new lexical items. These new lexical items allow, in turn, acquisition of knowledge of still other syntactic structures. It should be stressed that comprehension of the meaning of utterances is dependent on both lexical and syntactic knowledge.

The further developments of word knowledge that occur after entering school are, obviously, an increase in the size of the available lexicon and, less obviously, changes in the meanings of the words in the lexicon. This developmental change takes place in two ways. One way is an increased hierarchical organization of words which provides connections between words. For example, red, white, and blue are organized into the category of color and have the same privileges of occurrence in sentences; man, woman, boy, girl are humans; plants, animals, humans are living things; run and jump are action verbs. A second direction in which word knowledge grows is the understanding that words can have more than one meaning and play different roles in sentences.

Knowledge of the syntactic possibilities in the language also grows. Knowledge is acquired of types of structures; further, just as in semantic development, not only is further knowledge acquired but the depth of knowledge changes as well. The child becomes aware of structural paraphrase possibilities in the language (there is more than one way to say the same thing) and, therefore, connections between structures. The child also becomes aware of ambiguities (a sentence can have more than one meaning). These developments continue over the school years and beyond.

By the time the child enters school she is able to discriminate between all the phonological segments in the language that are crucial for word identification and can accurately generate most of these segments with the possible exception of strident clusters (/str/, /spr/). In addition, the child is able to apply plural and tense markers appropriately, although she may still be having some difficulty with strong nouns (feet) and, more frequently, strong verbs (brought). Despite this clear ability to accurately perceive and produce phonological distinctions in the language, many children are unable to segment words into phonological components at this age. Others have difficulty in rhyming words (cat, hat, bat) or generating words that have the same initial sounds (bat, ball, boat). These abilities develop over the early school years and, as with other areas of development, are probably enhanced by engaging in the reading acquisition process. Thus, although children tend to group words on the basis of their surface structure (phonology) rather than meaning at four years of age (in the series cap, can, hat; cap and can are grouped and not cap and hat) and to provide "clang" responses to unknown words on a word association task, there does not appear to be a conscious awareness of phonological segments as belonging to a category among all children on entrance to school.

A further development that takes place over the school years in the morphophonological aspect of language is acquisition of knowledge of 1) rules of stress to create different syntactic categories (pérmit, permít) and to create nominal compounds (bírdhouse) and 2) rules of phonological change to create different syntactic categories (sane - sanity, discuss - discussion). These phonological developments are like developments in other aspects of language. Some of these developments require acquisition of new knowledge (derivational rules for complex words such as "indisputable") and other developments require reorganization of old knowledge; observation of similarities in sets of categories (segmental and syllabic paraphrases). Unlike category developments in other aspects of language many of the segmental and syllabic categorizations the child must make are unrelated to meaning. The categories /b/ or /t/, /ub/ or /ut/ carry no meaning.

The above findings indicate that, although the child at age five or six appears to be a highly competent speaker-listener of the language, further developments occur in all aspects of language over the school years and many of these developments, as I shall argue, seem particularly important for the reading acquisition process. Figure 1 presents a summary of these developments in each aspect of language. In all aspects of language, new categories of language knowledge are acquired and this knowledge is applied in new contextual and linguistic domains. For example, pragmatic discourse knowledge is applied to an increasing number of different situations; lexical knowledge is used in an increasing number of areas of inquiry; semantax knowledge is applied in increasingly different and abstract contexts; phonological knowledge is applied over increasingly longer and more complex words. In three aspects of language (lexicon, semantax, and phonology) relations between or paraphrase of categories is observed, in two (lexicon and semantax), multiple meanings are acquired.

The data illustrated address the first questions posed: What do children know about language on entrance to school and what are they yet to learn? The second question (what differences in language knowledge are there among normally developing children which may affect reading acquisition?) is a more difficult question to answer since it is not entirely clear exactly what children have to know about language to acquire reading. Theoretically, different children, aged five or six years, will bring to the reading acquisition process different sets of knowledge about the varying aspects of language. As I will argue below, these differences in sheer language knowledge might affect what

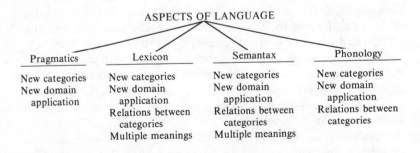

ASPECTS OF LANGUAGE			
Pragmatics	Lexicon	Semantax	Phonology
New categories	New categories	New categories	New categories
New domain application	New domain application	New domain application	New domain application
	Relations between categories	Relations between categories	Relations between categories
	Multiple meanings	Multiple meanings	

Figure 1. Developments over the school years.

material can be read and understood but it is not clear that such differences should affect the reading acquisition process per se when the material to be read is very simple structurally and lexically.

Another source of difference which might seriously affect the acquisition process itself is differences in the content and organization of a child's language knowledge. It has been argued that the orthography is indifferent to dialectal or native language variation (Menyuk, 1976). All readers are required to translate the orthography into their lexical-phonological representations to access word meaning. However, if a "double" translation is required (that is, from orthography to a second language and then to the native language), then the task may not only be more difficult but also will depend on the accessibility of such translations to the reading (Chu-Chang, 1979). The ease with which these latter children engage in the acquisition process may, therefore, be very dependent on the degree of familiarity these children have with the lexicon of the second language. The organization and content of their knowledge of other aspects of language will affect how they continue to read.

Possible Relations to Reading

It was stated above that sheer amount of knowledge about language as indicated in spontaneous language production does not appear to be the factor that crucially distinguishes between good, average, and poor readers who do not have a marked difficulty in oral language. Weak, although significant, correlations have been found between such measures as vocabulary and sentence length and reading performance at grades one and two (Bougere, 1969). It is, of course, during the early years of school (grades one through three) that reading materials are carefully controlled and do not seriously challenge the language knowledge acquired by most children at ages five through seven or eight. As discussed below, this does not continue to be the case throughout the school years. It was also stated that speakers of another native language might have difficulty in acquiring reading because of, possibly, being confronted with a double translation task.

The statements above are meant to suggest that the relation between oral language knowledge and reading differs depending on the nature of the reading task and over time. They are further meant to suggest that oral language knowledge differences between good, average, and poor readers may vary and that particular differences will affect the reading behavior of the individual child initially and over time.

What will be argued throughout this section is that different aspects of oral language knowledge and *state* of knowledge of these aspects are required in the processing of written material over time. It will also be argued that, with time or maturation, these relations undergo a change. That is, it will be suggested that Vygotsky was partially correct when he stated "Written language consists of a system of signs that designate the sounds and words of spoken language, which in turn are signs for real entities and relations. Gradually this intermediate link, spoken language, disappears and written language is converted into a system of signs that directly symbolize the entities and relations between them" (Vygotsky, 1978, p. 106). Vygotsky's statement implies that at the beginning of the reading acquisition process reference is always made to a linguistic representation of an orthographic category (letter, word, sentence). This requires bringing to conscious awareness these linguistic representations. But, as the process becomes mature, it no longer requires bringing to conscious awareness these linguistic representations. The process becomes automatic. My first statement implies, however, that if the orthography represents linguistic entities and relations that are not easily accessible to the reader then the process does require bringing these entities and relations to conscious awareness. Therefore, orthographic representations of well learned structures will be read automatically; representations of less well learned structures will require conscious awareness of their oral language representations; and representations of structures that have not yet been acquired will be incorrectly read because of approximations made to the text based on structures that are available (Menyuk, 1980, in press).

The three categories of reading tasks to be considered in this discussion are: acquisition, comprehending, and comprehension. The first and initial task, acquisition, has been viewed in two ways: as a decoding or word attack task, or as a procedure to discover how language is represented in orthography. Data collected by Goodman (1976) support the fact that children during the earliest and later stages of reading make guesses about the words they read based on the linguistic context of what they are reading and extralinguistic knowledge. Other data indicate that the first step in accessing the lexicon in reading is via translation of the orthography of the word into the phonological representation of that word. These latter data also suggest that the process of translating the orthography into a phonological representation requires bringing to conscious awareness this phonological representation by relating the letters of the words to sound segments and reconstituting them (Liberman, Liberman, Mattingly, & Shankweiler, 1978). These researchers find, for example, that there is a significant correlation between the ability of young children to count the number of segments in CVC (consonant-vowel-consonant) words and reading achievement during the early grades.

It is not clear that these two positions are mutually exclusive even at the beginning stages of reading, except when words are presented in isolation. Then accessing must be through phonological representation. But when the child is reading a sentence, the sentential context in conjunction with minimal orthographic-phonological cues may elicit guesses that are correct in terms of semantic field ("toy" for "train") or partially correct phonologically but incorrect semantically ("fort" for "fortune"). Taken from Goodman's article, these so-called miscues may be corrected by reference to both phonology and semantics. Since it seems to be the case that being taught to read helps to develop awareness of phonological segments and that, in fact, illiterate adults have difficulty in segmenting words (Liberman, et al., 1978), it may be the case, then, that semantic representations interact with phonological representations to store in memory relations between orthographic representations, phonological representations and meanings during the beginning of the reading process. When this does occur for a particular word then the reading of the word becomes automatic and no longer requires bringing to conscious awareness either the phonological or semantic representations of that word. A parallel processing procedure would be required initially in which both phonological and semantic representations must be brought to conscious awareness. At the beginning stages of reading a word, or in the process of reading acquisition, then, phonological segments and semantic features must be brought to conscious awareness. If the child has yet to achieve the ability of phonological segmentation and reference to orthography, then learning to read will be a difficult process. However, if the child is able to relate orthography and phonology but has no semantic representation for the product or has difficulty in accessing this representation, there would be equal difficulty in reading. There are two populations in whom this latter difficulty can be observed: children with so-called word retrieval problems (Wolf, in press) and children required to read a language with which they have little familiarity. Gleitman and Gleitman (1979) note that the difficulty in word segmentation and reconstruction continues to distinguish successful from unsuccessful readers through twelfth grade. They suggest that poor readers have acquired a logography, a set of memorized words, and that, therefore, as the list of words to be read rapidly exceeds this finite list the reader who is unable to apply word attack skills will flounder. It might be the case, however, that word attack skills, alone, are not the only requirement in comprehending written sentences. Further knowledge of other aspects of the language is required when the materials to be read are sentences and not simply words.

Listening to and comprehending sentences clearly require not only phonological accessing but, also, lexical, syntactic and pragmatic knowledge. For example, the listener, when attempting to understand a double function relative clause such as "The horse racing past the barn fell." needs to have knowledge of the syntactic possibilities of the language, the meanings of words, a strategy for determining clause boundaries (Bever, 1970), and the ability to keep in mind the whole sentence in order to comprehend it. One would assume that reading and comprehending sentences also calls upon each and every one of these aspects of linguistic knowledge and not simply translation of orthography into phonology. One can also assume that the child's knowledge of all these aspects of language changes with maturation.

At the beginning stages of reading acquisition, the materials that children are required to read are usually simple sentences that are well within the children's levels of syntactic and lexical knowledge. Additionally, the subject matter is usually within the child's experience. The beginning reader reads about topics and relations that she is familiar with and which, usually, meet her pragmatic expectations. Some examples, again taken from Goodman (1976), make the point clear. For the beginning reader the following is provided:

> Jimmy said, "Come here, Sue,
> look at my toy train.
> See it go."

For the older reader the following passage was read:

> So education it was! I opened the dictionary and picked out a word that sounded good.

The relative lexical and syntactic complexity of the two passages is evident. Further, in the first passage, how Jimmy is talking to Sue and what he is talking about seems reasonable if not an exact representation of what might be said. The assumption being made is that it is "easier" for the beginning reader to read language that is composed of linguistic categories and relations that the young child can easily process. Thus, at the beginning stages of reading the principal requirement is translation of word orthography into phonological and semantic representations.

However, after this task has been achieved (it is clearly not a minimal one for some beginning readers), the reference to lexical entries and sentence relations in the material are probably automatic since the words are well known and are in sentence structures that are well learned. Comprehending written sentences of these simple forms becomes an automatic process and does not require bringing to conscious awareness the relations being expressed.

Some children who learn how to read the materials presented to them in the first through third grades encounter difficulty in the fourth grade. This difficulty has been attributed to the sudden requirement to read materials that are no longer carefully controlled for vocabulary and structure. It is probable that the problem lies not in the nature of the reading material but, rather, in the reader since a large number of children do not find this change in the structure of material a source of difficulty. The problem may lie in the fact that while the child is learning more about the structure of language (and as I have indicated previously, the child learns a great deal more about language over the school years than she knew before) she is, simultaneously, being confronted with more complex written material. This material is more complex in all structural aspects of language (lexicon, syntax, and morphophonology) and is also less familiar in terms of topic.

A possible source of difficulty for some readers might then be in comprehending sentences that contain structures that are relatively unfamiliar. What appears to be universal in the reading process is that the process initially requires the ability to bring to conscious awareness the structural categories and relations in language and that, with time, the process becomes automatic. But automaticity requires easy availability of the structures being read. If these categories and relations are not easily accessible to the reader (be they morphophonological, lexical, or syntactic), the reader encounters difficulty in comprehending the sentences read.

Reading a passage or story requires still other linguistic skills. These latter skills are needed in comprehension of the content and interpretation of connected sentences. The ability to integrate information across sentences and retain (remember) crucial information is required. The task is somewhat similar to listening to and comprehending a story or oral lecture. In this latter task, verbatim recall of sentences becomes impossible and listeners, rather, attempt to select, integrate, and organize linguistic information across sentences (Clark & Clark, 1977). The reader also must select, integrate, and organize linguistic information. Varying descriptions of these abilities have been used. For example, some researchers have described organizational ability as employment of a story grammar (Stein & Glenn, 1979) when the context is a story. Other researchers have described selection and integration of materials as inferencing abilities (Fredericksen, 1976).

In summary, the processes employed by the reader depend on the structure of the material to be read. Reading of words engages different aspects of language knowledge from that of reading of sentences which, in turn, engages different aspects from that of reading of passages. The different types of knowledge required in reading are presented in Figure 2.

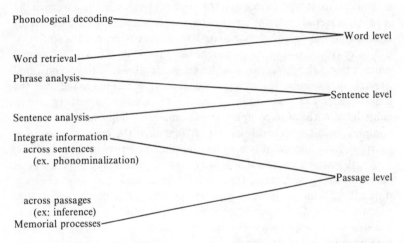

Figure 2. Levels of language required depending on reading task.

The highest level of processing (passage) requires some processing at all levels. The processing is parallel and, therefore, requires some information from all levels simultaneously but, just as in oral language processing, does not require complete information from all levels.

Further, the linguistic knowledge of the reader changes with development as does the material she is required to read. As the child's linguistic knowledge increases and as her linguistic processing abilities mature, the complexity of the materials to be read increases. In many instances, these two developments are congruous but in some instances they are not. Still further, a reciprocal arrangement appears to exist between having linguistic knowledge available, bringing it to conscious awareness, and reading. That is, the process of reading requires the intuitive language user to initially bring to conscious awareness the categories and relations in language and, therefore, learning how to read and reading provide new insights into the structure of language to the language user. However, and importantly, if readers do not have oral language knowledge of certain categories and relations available, they obviously cannot be brought to conscious awareness for the reading task. The most obvious level at which awareness is required is the morphophonological and lexical level. Indeed, it has been suggested that difficulty at this level alone can account for most of the difficulty of poor readers from childhood to adulthood (Gleitman & Gleitman, 1979). It has been suggested here that availability of categories and relations in all aspects of language contribute to comprehending and comprehension of written material.

The above statements are hypothetical. There is very little evidence available to support the above position. There is a wealth of direct evidence concerning the importance of phonological awareness in acquisition of reading. There is, however, also a wealth of evidence, based on miscues in reading, to support the notion that other aspects of language are actively used in the reading process. In the next section some additional evidence will be presented to support the notion that awareness of structural relations in sentences plays a role in the reading process.

Some Preliminary Data

There have been two studies which have, in differing ways, examined the relation between syntactic development and reading. Bowey (1980) found, upon examining the ability of third, fourth, and fifth grade readers to read differently structured sentences aloud, that significantly more errors occurred with complex sentences as compared to simple. For example, children had more difficulty with passive and relative clause sentences than they did with active and question sentences. Goldsmith (1977) found that children aged 9 to 11 years had greater difficulty in comprehending orally and in written form relative clause sentences as compared to conjoined sentences. The dyslexic children in this population had more difficulty with relative clause sentences than did the non-dyslexic children, but both groups of children had increasing difficulty with more complex types of relative clause sentences than with simpler types. For example, the children found sentences such as "The boy who kissed the girl ran away." easier to understand than sentences such as "The cat that the dog chased ran into the house."

These data indicate that relative unfamiliarity with structures leads to greater difficulty in reading them aloud and greater difficulty in comprehending these sentences in either oral or written form. It seems reasonable to suggest that the further syntactic developments that occur over the school years in oral language can account for the differences found in reading performance with different structures. These further developments are either more delayed in a dyslexic population (i.e. the more complex structures are simply not available at the same age) or the processing skills required for comprehending these more complex structures are not available to the dyslexic children. In either case, and with both normal and dyslexic readers, there seems to be a relation between syntactic oral language knowledge and reading performance.

Oppenheim (1981) examined the oral linguistic processing skills of average kindergarten children and their later reading performance. Two aspects of language processing were examined: phonological and syntactic. She found that the ability to segment words *and* the ability to comprehend sentences with embedded structures were significantly predictive of later reading performance. The two linguistic processing behaviors appeared to be related in that those children with better segmenting abilities were also those children who were better able to comprehend sentences with embedded structures. These latter findings may indicate that some of the processing abilities required at the word and sentence level are the same and that these same processing skills are required in reading as well as listening.

Two studies have examined the morphophonological processing of complex derived words. Myerson (1976) examined the ability of children aged 8 to 17 years to derive words from nonsense stems by the application of appropriate phonological rules (for example, "glanity" from "glane" using the model of "sane" - "sanity"). Myerson found that there were developmental changes in the ability of children over this age range to apply the appropriate rules and that some children, at age seventeen, could not apply all the rules required in the task. Myerson also found that there were significant differences between poor, average, and good readers in their ability to apply these rules.

Loritz (1981) studied third and fifth grade children's ability to read aloud real and nonsense polysyllabic words. The question being examined was the possible relation between the ability to decode polysyllabic words by application of appropriate stress rules and reading and spelling abilities. Loritz found developmental differences between the grades in application of simple (left-right) versus more advanced (right-left) application of rules. Among the fifth graders, also, there were differences in application of rules. Age alone did not determine ability to apply appropriate rules. Acquisition of advanced rules was found to be significantly correlated with standardized measures of vocabulary, spelling and reading.

Just as syntactic knowledge increases over the school years so does morphophonological knowledge. The decoding or word attack skills required with polysyllabic words which have undergone derivational changes from base stems demand more than the ability to segment base words and relate them to phonological representations. Both of the above studies provide evidence that those children who have acquired more advanced knowledge of morphophonological rules are also the more advanced readers for their age and/or grade.

Most of the studies discussed thus far indicate that *level* of phonological and syntactic knowledge affects how written linguistic structures are processed. However, it was previously suggested that it is not simply how much one intuitively knows about the differing aspects of language which predicts reading performance but, rather, that the degree of knowledge of any particular structure, as indicated by being able to bring it to conscious awareness, predicts how well that category or relation will be read. What has been found, developmentally, is that children appear to intuitively comprehend and produce linguistic structures before they achieve the ability to judge whether a sentence is correct or incorrect and they achieve this latter ability before they are able to correct incorrect forms. It has also been found that the most sophisticated behaviors (judgment and correction) occur with differing structures as the child matures. Intuitive knowledge of varying structures precedes conscious knowledge of these structures. The most sophisticated form of knowledge of structures is being able to bring this knowledge to conscious awareness. However, this ability does not appear for all structures at a particular period of development. The ability to bring differing structures to conscious awareness depends on how well the child has learned particular structures. For example, at the time when a child can bring to conscious awareness tense and plural markers she may still be unable to bring to conscious awareness the relations expressed in center-embedded relative clauses (Menyuk, 1977). As indicated previously, reading helps in bringing structures to conscious awareness but the structures must be there for reading to aid in awareness.

All of the oral language tasks and, by definition, the reading tasks described above required bringing to conscious awareness knowledge of varying syntactic and morphophonological structures. However, none of the above studies explicitly examined metalinguistic awareness of particular structures and the ability to read these same structures. A study undertaken by Flood and Menyuk (1979) indicated that ability to read structures might be dependent on awareness of structures. Developmental data from studies of oral language processing abilities had indicated that the ability to paraphrase occurs during the middle childhood years and that, further, the ability to paraphrase lexically occurs before the ability to paraphrase structurally. The same sequence of abilities appears when the task is one of detecting ambiguity in the lexical domain and the same sequence is observed in the structural domain. Using these data as a basis, Flood and Menyuk examined the ability of fourth grade average and above average readers to read and paraphrase lexically and structurally, to read and detect lexical and structural ambiguities, and to paraphrase the two (or more) underlying meanings of the ambiguous sentences. It was found that the ability to carry out the two types of tasks was significantly correlated with reading ability. It was further found that there were differences between average and above average readers in terms of the complexity of the structures they could paraphrase and the options for paraphrase they selected. The above average readers could more easily deal with structural paraphrase and more frequently selected to paraphrase by structural rather than lexical means than did the average readers. The data indicated developmental differences between average and good readers in metalinguistic awareness of the same structures.

To more directly test the hypothesis, rather than relying on the findings of other studies, a pilot study has been carried out to examine metalinguistic awareness of varying structures in oral language processing *and* written language processing (Menyuk & Flood, in preparation). Fourth, seventh, tenth grade and adult good and poor readers were asked to judge and correct non-grammatical and anomalous sentences and to paraphrase sentences and detect ambiguities in sentences in both the oral and written modes. The preliminary findings, in comparing good and poor readers, indicate that poor readers perform more poorly than good readers at all age/grade levels in *both* modes of processing. In fact, adult poor readers do worse than fourth grade good readers. There are developmental changes which occur in both modes of processing but much less marked developmental changes in the poor reading population. The order of difficulty of processing the varying structures is similar throughout the age range for both good and poor readers and across listening and reading tasks. The ability to paraphrase and to judge anomaly and non-grammaticality is consistently better than detection of ambiguity when the sentence is presented either orally or in written form. This is quite consistent with other developmental findings. The reading and listening behavior of good readers is quite similar, but there is a tendency for poor readers to do somewhat better in detection of ambiguity in the listening mode and somewhat better with paraphrase in the reading mode. This makes sense if the assumption is correct that well-learned structures (i.e., those easily available) can be processed more easily in the written than in the oral mode because the former mode places less constraint on memory (Menyuk, 1980).

These preliminary findings, that varying aspects of metalinguistic abilities continue to develop over the schools years in good readers and that these abilities are related in listening to and reading sentences, lend some support to the notion that oral language metaknowledge is related to reading throughout the school years. However, these preliminary studies still leave many questions about the details of the relation over time and, importantly, about what differences exist between good, average, and poor readers in metalinguistic abilities.

The issue of application of language knowledge to the reading of passages has not yet been addressed. Although it may be the case that comprehending written sentences is a prerequisite to comprehension of passages, such comprehension clearly demands more and something different than the comprehending of sentences. It was previously stated that selection, integration, organization, and recall are required in this task. There has been a great deal of research on children's early development of the ability to recall stories in terms of story grammar (Stein & Glenn, 1979), use of topical information to make inferences about references in stories (Brown, et al., 1977), and to infer, in general, from spoken language (Barclay & Reid, 1974). There has not been, however, a systematic examination of the developing child's ability to select, integrate, organize and recall the *same* material when presented orally and in written form. Until such comparisons take place we can simply point to some data which indicate that there is likely to be a relation between the two when recall constraints are similar in oral and written comprehension (i.e., when the written passage is not present for recall).

Two studies have been carried out with "special" populations that have some bearing on the issue. Wilson (1979) compared deaf and hearing children's ability to answer verbatim and inferential questions about short (4 sentences) stories presented through the air (orally and signed) and in written form. The children were reading at second, third, fourth, and fifth grade levels. In this study the children's ability to comprehend the sentences containing various structures was pretested. The deaf children showed a significant developmental trend in the acquisition of linguistic inference abilities, whereas no such trend was observed with hearing children; hearing children reading at second grade level were able to answer inferential questions almost as well as those reading at higher levels. There were remarkable differences between the two groups in their ability to answer literal questions. Very importantly, hearing subjects performed significantly better with spoken than with written presentation, whereas the inverse occurred with the deaf children. These data indicate the very early ability of hearing children to draw inferences from heard stories. These abilities are then applied to written stories. This ability, as stated previously, is an important one in comprehension and recall of passages.

Another study provides some evidence concerning the importance of inferential abilities in comprehension and recall of spoken stories. In this study (Graybeal, 1981), the ability of language disordered and normally developing children to recall orally presented stories was examined. In this study, sentence comprehending was also pretested. The principal difference between the groups was in amount of information recalled. There was no difference between groups in the components of story grammar recalled or in the order in which they were recalled. It was also found that after two types of treatment conditions (one in which verbatim questions were asked and one in which inferential questions were asked) that the amount of information recalled by the language disordered children was markedly improved after inferential questions were asked but not after verbatim questions were asked. No such effect was observed with normally developing children. They were performing very well to begin with. Although the written language processing of these children was not assessed, the findings of this and the previous study described lend some support to the notion that inferential abilities are important in passage comprehension and recall, be the passage written or oral, and that these abilities develop early and first in the domain of oral language processing and then are applied to the written language domain.

Conclusions

The argument has been presented that oral language development has an important and continuing effect on written language development. It has also been argued that oral language development cannot be simply viewed as an increasing amount of intuitive knowledge acquired but, also, as changing *state* of knowledge *and* developmental changes in how language is processed. If this argument has validity then one should be able to observe developmental changes in what is known intuitively about language, what is consciously known and in how oral language is processed. The interaction of these factors would predict what is comprehended and recalled in written language. There are also clear indications of a reverse effect; that is, the reading task per se changes the *state* of knowledge of oral language. Some examples of each of these arguments are presented below.

An obvious example of the effect of what is known about language on reading is lexical knowledge. If a lexical item is not in the vocabulary of a child then it cannot be comprehended in reading unless the context provides this information. A less obvious example would be the child's lack of comprehension of a syntactic structure as in "The boy who kissed the girl ran away." If the child doesn't understand this sentence orally she will not comprehend it in written form. Something further, however, is required when reading the word or sentence. In the first instance, the phonological representation of the word must be brought to conscious awareness; in the second instance the semantic/ syntactic relations in the sentence must be brought to conscious awareness. How available (that is, how well learned) a structure is will affect how easily it is brought to conscious awareness. This is what is meant by state of knowledge of a structure. Thus, there are some structures that will be very well learned when the reading process begins (simple morpheme structure rules and certain semantic/syntactic structures in sentences), others that will be less available, and still others that remain to be acquired. Those that are very well learned will be processed automatically without the requirement of their being brought to conscious awareness.

How oral language is processed will have an effect on what is known about oral language. If, for example, oral language is processed by a surface-structure strategy with heavy reliance on contextual information for comprehension then the child will not be ready to understand sentences in which this strategy does not lead to correct interpretation (as in the example sentence above). How the child represents information about linguistic categories and relations in memory will have an effect on what the child knows about language. For example, if the child relies on imaginal representations rather than linguistic representations for storage and recall of lexical meanings, a behavior that is observed during the early years of life (Conrad, 1972) and continues to store imaginally syntactic-semantic relations in the early stages of acquisition of new structures (Kosslyn & Bower, 1974), then, linguistic representations will not be available and, therefore, cannot be brought to conscious awareness in the reading process. A shift from imaginal to linguistic representations has, in general, been observed at about 5 to 7 years. But any particular child might yet be in the process of development of this shift during the early stages of reading acquisition.

The ability to draw inferences from the linguistic context and world knowledge appears to be crucial in the comprehension and recall of connected discourse. This ability is first exercised in the oral language domain and then applied to the written language domain. This seems to be a very early ability in the normally developing child but somewhat delayed in children with developmental problems. However, again, there may be developmental differences among children in the age at which this processing strategy is available and is used plus differences in experiences which will affect the presence of or nature of the inferences that can be made.

Figure 3 is a graphic presentation of the notions expressed above. It suggests that as the child matures changes take place in the strategies used to process language, the set of linguistic rules the child has intuitive knowledge of, the set of rules the child is able to bring to conscious awareness if required to do so, and the set of categories and relations which are automatically processed in reading.

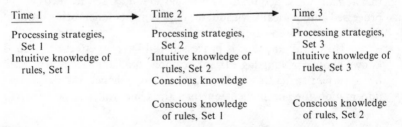

Figure 3. Developmental changes in processing strategies and state of knowledge of linguistic rules.

Menyuk

Particular linguistic experiences, particular social experiences, and possibly biological capacities can account for individual differences in the development of meta-awareness (conscious knowledge) of language categories and relations. These differences can account for individual differences in the development or rate of development of processing strategies and, therefore, in the development or rate of development of intuitive knowledge of categories and relations in the language as well as conscious knowledge of these categories and relations. Since conscious knowledge is dependent on intuitive knowledge then differing children will achieve differing sets of conscious knowledge and, as I have argued, this will affect what is comprehended in reading.

Salus and Salus note the shortcomings of the network models, the set-theoretic models and the feature-comparison models of semantic memory. They propose a richer model that accounts for nested and distributed approaches to human memory rather than hierarchic and localized approaches. They present implications of their model to reading comprehension.

Word Finding, Word Organizing, and Reading

Peter H. Salus
University of North Florida
Mary W. Salus
S. Allen Smith Speech Clinic
Jacksonville, Florida

Every act of reading is an act of translation, for the essence of reading is the transmodal process of gleaning information from visually presented verbal material. As this visually presented material takes the form of strings of words, the questions of word knowledge and word recognition (whether written or spoken) are important to our understanding of the reading process.[1]

Each of us carries about a word-hoard or mental lexicon which contains, among other things, the meanings, spellings, pronunciations, and grammatical classes of the "listed" words. Just how complex each "entry" in the mental lexicon is can be seen from the elaborate ways in which information can be retrieved.

In terms of the sound structure, we can find words that rhyme and alliterate, words with two or three syllables, words that are stressed in certain ways. In terms of spelling, we can find words that begin or end alike, words that are similar in some way, even words that are "anomalous" in terms of the standard spelling rules. In terms of meaning, we can find synonyms and antonyms, superordinates and subordinates, and—when we do crossword puzzles—we can cross or combine categories.

Thus, none of us has any trouble assembling arrays like *able*, *gable*, *stable*, and *table; aardvark, alligator,* and *armadillo; Blackfoot, breakfront* and *breakfast; April* and *September; spoon, pillow, grassy,* keep; sure and sugar; horse and steed; parent: mother and father; tree: oak, elm, pine, cedar, maple, hickory, cottonwood; or even a five letter metric measure beginning with "l" (liter).

There is, of course, much more that each of us can do with the words in our heads, in fact the mental lexicon must actually be much more like a mental encyclopedia. For we can find nineteenth century authors from New England with three names (like Louisa May Alcott, Ralph Waldo Emerson, Henry Wadsworth Longfellow, and Henry David Thoreau), or presidents with double initials (like Calvin Coolidge, Herbert Hoover, and Ronald Reagan), and what seems like an infinite amount of other information, all of it recognizable when heard or read and capable of being uttered or written. The questions we would like to treat here deal with how we acquire this information, how we store it, and how we access it.

The Acquisition of Words

The concept of "first word" is a familiar one and the first words of children have been written about at great length. Yet it must be obvious that not only are these words pronounced differently from the way that they are pronounced by adults, but also that these words do not mean the same things to the child that they mean to the adult. Not only is the acquisition of lexical items an exfoliating process, but the assignment of meaning to those items is a matter of both elaboration and refinement as well. Much of the most interesting work on the development of the vocabulary and the assignment of meaning has been done by Anglin (1970, 1977) and Clark and Clark (E.V. Clark, 1971, 1972, 1973a, 1973b, 1976; H.H. Clark, 1970a, 1970b, 1973; Clark & Clark, 1979).

Though Anglin (1970) purports "to provide a fairly detailed picture of how the internal lexicon evolves" (p. xi), it fails because the youngest children examined were in grades three and four. By this time, each child must have had a lexicon of several thousand words, and experience involving millions of utterances. In his later work, Anglin avoids this specific problem, his youngest populations being about 2.5, but his work is still not as useful as that of E.V. and H.H. Clark.

One of the thrusts of the research of the Clarks is that where polar items (in/out, up/down, even father/mother) are concerned, children generally first acquire one of the items and apply it to both situations. Subsequently, the other item is acquired, but the two are applied indiscriminately to both meanings. Finally, the two items are sorted appropriately. A vivid example of this phenomenon, which we have recorded, is that of a child wanting to watch a particular TV show, and protesting, "But I wanted to go to bed earlier!"

In an attempt at rationalizing the child's acquisition of spatial terms, H.H. Clark proposed that the child's perceptual (P) space is made up of "The perceptual features in the child's early cognitive development," where the language space is comprised of "the properties of the linguistic system" (1973:208). His contention is that "the properties of P-Space are strikingly close to the properties of the linguistic system the speaker of English actually uses in describing the locations of objects in space." Clark sees perceptually salient planes and directions as based on the physical properties of people in physical space, which allows positive or negative values to be assigned to locatives on an axial basis. Thus, for example, everything in front of a vertical plan is easily seen and so FORWARD may be considered as possessing a positive perceptual direction, BACKWARD a negative direction.

In scalar adjectives like *long/short*, length is the scale extending from the verticle plane, so LONG is the more general word: "Shortness is defined only with respect to the secondary point of reference—the zero point of no length" (1973:216), according to Clark. From our own research, and from the reports of others, it is clear that the order of acquisition of such pairs is the one predicted by Clark, and that *long* does precede *short, early* does precede *late*, and *up, down*. In fact, Clark's gneralization can be extended, as *mommy* and *daddy* frequently refer to either or both parents, and occasionally are generalized to any caretaker of either gender. Similarly, *coming* and *going* may be assigned to either direction of movement.

But while this helps us where the development of the child's lexicon is concerned, it does not account for the beginnings of the child's use of words.

It is our belief that taxonomic sorting of phenomena is basic to perception of those things which impinge upon our senses. And the way in which things are taxonomized cultures the system of phenomenological recognition. A seventeen-month-old, for example, may refer to everything in the water as a "fish," to every quadruped as a "doggie" or a "horsie," to everything on the water as a "duck," and to everything in the air as a "birdie." A crab or a lobster is thus a "fish"; a cat is a "doggie"; and a goose swimming is a "duck," but aloft is a "birdie")while a butterfly is a "birdie" as well. With the growth of vocabulary—and with parental and environmental correction—such a simplistic system is modified: "No, dear, that's a cat, not a dog"; "Look at the mouse"; and "See the butterfly!" are typical modificatory statements. And with each of these items, the child is constrained to restructure his or her universe to adapt to the limits the standard language puts upon the contents of his or her vocabulary.

Some of these adaptations are readily accessible to the investigator, especially at the early stages where the vocabulary is small and there is (quantitatively) but a small interval between the active and the passive vocabulary. But as time goes on just what the speaker's knowledge of the language is and the way in which that knowledge is organized and accessed becomes more difficult for the investigator to determine. We will return to this problem below, but first let us try to imagine a way in which we can account for both the child's perceptions and the growth of the vocabulary.

If, as we have claimed, comparison and classification are basic to perception, then in order to recognize something as "X" we must differentiate it from "not-X." At an early stage this may mean differentiating mommy from daddy or fish, birds, dogs, and people. The child's reference to crabs as fish, to giraffes as horses, to butterflies as birds, is the result of a taxonomy based on a smaller range of comparison than that applied by adults in observing these same creatures. In order to build up the conceptually exfoliating taxonomic universe each of us has internalized, we have had to build up a set of "features" to facilitate the decision-making process which is perception and cognition. Unfortunately, while this may describe the manner in which each of us has built up our cognitive and lexical store, and perhaps given us some sort of handle as to how we access some of the stored material, it does not answer the question "Why?"[2]

Polanyi pointed out more than a decade ago that "analytic descent from higher levels to their subsidiaries is usually feasible to some degree, while the integration of items of a lower level so as to predict their possible meaning in a higher context may be beyond the range of our integrative powers" (1968:1312). As human language would appear to be the highest achievement of the evolution of the central nervous system, we consider it foolish to attempt to trace perception and cognition from the euglena or the paramecium. However, in line with Polanyi's remark, it does not seem absurd to look back phylogenetically in an attempted explanation of just why a particular mode of organization has come about.

The mode of acquisition, and organization, which we favor is one based on opposition and polarity, on the recognition of "X" and "not-X."

If we consider the behaviors of protozoa, we note a very simple set of decision-making properties: if an object is small, engulf and eat it; if the object is large, rebound from it (or be eaten). As we move up the phylogenetic tree, while the behaviors become more complex, the decisions (for the most part) are still binary: eat or be eaten; attack or flee; mate or reject the suitor. From this phylogenetic point of view, oppositions are vital to survival; synonyms are of little importance. As will be seen below, we consider the organization of the internal lexicon to be the surface realization of the phylogenetic survival baggage that went into the decision-making processes of all of our ancestors.

In their most recent article, the Clarks concern themselves with coinages in adult language, and, in specific, with nouns used as verbs in adult speech (e.g. "She would not try to stiff-upper lip it through," *Time* magazine). They conclude that "the meanings are best accounted for by a theory of interpretation that specifies what the verbs mean on particular occasions of their use" (1979). Though their claims have been attacked by Aronoff (1980), we consider his comments to stem from devotion to orthodox transformational theory, rather than from an examination of real language phenomena.

In fact, we would carry the Clarks' claims a step further, again. It seems to us that children think of words in general as occurring in contexts and deriving their special meanings from those contexts. Though adults also derive meanings from contexts, one of the sources of the syntagmatic/paradigmatic shift in word association responses noted by a number of researchers investigating children's single-word associations to a variety of stimuli (Entwisle, 1966; Nelson, 1977) must be the change in the way the mental lexicon is dealt with by young children as opposed to older children and adults.

The reason that small children tend to give "next-word" responses to verbal stimuli is that the words only exist in contexts, they have no "solitary" existence of their own. It is only when the words have occurred in a vast variety of utterances that they are abstracted from the flow of speech and take on existence as entities in their own right. Stolz and Tiffany (1972) and M.W. Salus (1980) have shown that adults resort to "childlike" verbal behavior when confronted by unfamiliar verbal stimuli.

It has been traditional in linguistics for several decades to consider phonemes and morphemes as abstractions which are realized, in specific environments, by their allophones and allomorphs. What we are saying here is that the meanings of words, too, are abstractions, and that they are realized by specific uses in specific contexts. These contexts, incidentally, may be sentential or circumstantial. That is, the meanings of words are dependent on the phrases they occur in and on the social—the nonlinguistic—contexts within which they occur. The meaning of "out" or "go" to a young child may have much more to do with mommy's putting on her coat or sweater or picking up her purse than anything else.

We are used to saying that comprehension precedes production in language acquisition, but we have never really come to grips with just what this comprehension may be. It is quite clear that the child's comprehension of the noises made in its environs and of the noises it makes cannot be the same as the adult's comprehension of those noises. The child's lexical store is stocked with goods that are markedly different from the adult's store in terms of meanings, though the stock may be similar in terms of sounds. It was clear that the child we cited earlier knew that a fish was a fish; but she also called other objects in the water "fishes." Her comprehension of the item "fish" was different from the normal adult view of the meaning of the item.

We would suggest that the information in our mental lexicons has similar reasons for possessing organizational strategies: without organization, nothing is accessible. A garage, an attic or a storeroom are hoarding places, but knowing that your snowshoes or fishing rod or family photos are "somewhere" isn't much good—without organization, access is either impeded or rendered impossible.

Unfortunately, direct access to the mental lexicon is not afforded to the interested investigator. Two ways of gaining insight into the mental store are by means of pathological behavior and speech errors. But we can also examine "normal" behavior.

One of the remarkable things about normal speakers of a language is the rapidity with which they can recognize words of that language. Perhaps it is even more impressive that mature speakers can immediately recognize that an item is a possible, but not a real lexical item (Bower, 1970).

The earliest theories of lexical access were all "direct-access" models. The essential feature of these was the claim that familiar stimuli somehow contacted their appropriate memory traces directly. Given a stimulus—a written or spoken word—we would move sequentially down a decision tree and either find the item or not—if not, then we would conclude that the item was not a word. The direct access lexicon would thus look like Figure 1 and a partial, pruned, tree like Figure 2.

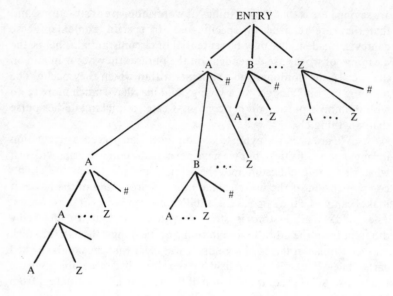

Figure 1. Direct access lexicon

By means of "lexical decision" experiments, the relative times required to decide whether a letter sequence is a word or not can be estimated (most of these experiments involved visually presented material). Typically, in such experiments, familiar words are classified in about 500 msec. and nonwords require about 650 msec. An exception to this general rule is that impossible nonwords (like *bfgklzxt*) are classified in about the same time as words. Impossibles thus do not require a search of the lexicon for a decision, though possible nonwords do require one. Furthermore, high frequency words are classified faster than low frequency ones, even when the low frequency items are words known to the participant (*mildew* or *perspire*). From this we are forced to the conclusion that we do not organize our lexicons on a letter base, nor do we gain access by means of letter-based decision trees.

Salus and Salus

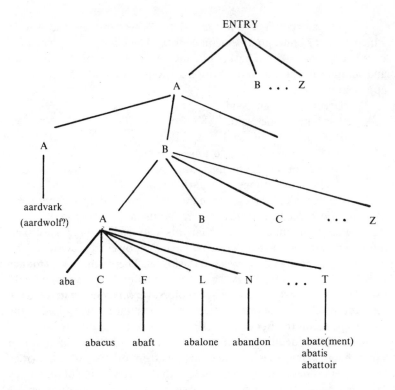

Figure 2. Direct access lexicon (pruned tree)

An alternative to this is the "threshold" model of Selfridge and Neisser (1960), which originally concerned machine pattern recognition. This model postulates a separate internal detector for each word which is extremely sensitive to "environmental stimuli." The main problem with this is that a series of experiments has shown that nonwords that are *like* words take longer to classify than other nonwords: *abount* takes longer than *obttle*, for example. Such results are destructive to the notion of a "detector" sensitive to each word, for if this were the case, all nonwords would be rejected with the same rapidity. The fact that there is a significant difference in response time where two types of nonwords are concerned, implies that the same mechanism is not operating in both cases.

Let us recount another anecdote to demonstrate the way in which a child's conceptual lexicon evolves. The child of a colleague of ours was playing with a basket of fruit. She was picking up each fruit and naming it and its color, bringing the items to her father for his approval in turn.

"Green pear," she said.

"Yes," her father said.

"Red orange," she said.

"No," said her father, "orange orange."

"Orange orange?" she queried.

"Yes, orange orange," her father repeated.

She deposited the orange in the basket, picked up another piece of fruit, and brought it to her father. "Apple apple," she said.

People are much smarter than rats. One trial learning is not at all infrequent. And even small children have the power to generalize. The child was exercizing her intellect to the fullest. There was no way for her to know that the orange was the anomaly among fruits (though we do use *plum*, and *cherry*, and *grape* for colors, we rarely do so in referring to plums or cherries or grapes), and so she instantly generalized to the next fruit, using the item name as a color name.

Children acquire the names of things in order to differentiate some things from others, some directions from others, some activities from others. These "names" exfoliate with the broadening of the child's experience and the concomitant need to make greater numbers of distinctions.

At the very beginning, children acquire these names by ostention: the actual object or activity is named while it is being displayed or demonstrated. But soon thereafter, the child begins to acquire words through the means of other words; and by the time the child enters school, nearly everything is being taught by means of words.

Storing and Accessing Words

As we have said before, each of us, child or adult, carries about a word hoard within our heads. We have chosen to call this store a mental lexicon. But while each of us can access our own lexicon—as we must do to speak and comprehend speech—just how the items in the lexicon are stored is far from clear. In fact, it is not at all clear just what the material making up the "lexical entry" is.

If one owns only one, two, or three books it is not hard to find them: you can readily locate the Bible, *The Joy of Cooking*, and *The Joy of Sex* on your shelf. If you own 50 or 100 volumes, you are forced to impose some sort of taxonomy upon them: books on invertebrate zoology over here, those on Velikovskian cosmology over there. This organization is necessary so that you do not waste time and effort attempting to locate *Worlds in Collision*. Economics and thermodynamics are relevant here: if there is only a given amount of energy within the system, then rationalization of the organizing factors is the only way to increase the number of accessible volumes. And once one graduates to a larger number of volumes—let's say a thousand—some sort of explicit organization becomes necessary, otherwise accessing any particular volume becomes either highly time-consuming or totally impossible. Finally, with a genuinely large library a more elaborate cataloging system becomes a necessity.

Yet another model is that of Forster. It assumes that mental lexical access differs from looking up a word in a printed dictionary only in its final stages. Forster notes that there are at least three different conditions under which each of us accesses the mental lexicon: reading, listening, and talking. He notes that writing may be yet another mode, but defers that issue. Where reading is concerned, Forster seems to feel that organization might proceed along orthographic lines; for listening, there might be greater sense in having things organized by phonological similarity; when we construct sentences, we need to find items with appropriate semantic and syntactic properties.

In order to organize the same set of entries in three ways, Forster is constrained to consider listing each item (each lexical entry) three times. However, in order to reduce the obviously cumbersome nature of having three lexicons, he assumes that there is but one master lexicon with three peripheral access files which refer to it: orthographic, phonological, and semantic and syntactic. He claims that an entry for a word in the master lexicon contains all the information we have about that word. The entries for that word in the peripheral access files contain descriptions of the appropriate stimulus features for that word (which he calls the access code) and pointers to the corresponding entry in the master lexicon. This schema is presented in Figure 3.

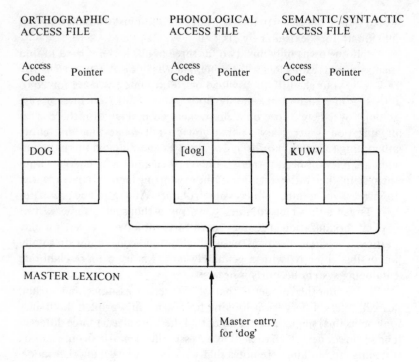

ORTHOGRAPHIC
ACCESS FILE

PHONOLOGICAL
ACCESS FILE

SEMANTIC/SYNTACTIC
ACCESS FILE

Access
Code   Pointer

Access
Code   Pointer

Access
Code   Pointer

DOG

[dog]

KUWV

MASTER LEXICON

Master entry
for 'dog'

Figure 3. Forster's mental lexicon

Forster's claim is thus that we access the master lexicon by first finding the word in question in the appropriate peripheral access file. This process involves preparing a coded description of the target item (the stimulus word) and then searching through the access file, comparing the coded description of the target item with the access code in each actual entry. A sufficiently accurate match of these terminates the search. The pointer specified in the entry provides access to the entry in the master lexicon. Forster uses the word *henchman* as an example. If we assume this to be a *read* item, then the visual stimulus would be concerted from a neural representation into a format compatible with the access codes. In this case, only the first few letters would have to be converted: only *hence* and *hench/man* begin with *henc-*. If we think of this as a phonological input, there is only one item in the file with *henc-*. In accessing orthographically, only four or five characters have to be encoded. In accessing phonologically, only one syllable. Forster seems to believe that items are grouped by similarity, and he refers to each of these groups as a *bin*.

Salus and Salus

At this point it may be relevant to enquire as to what direct (or indirect) evidence Forster has for all this. The answer is: not much. However, there is some evidence for rejecting other views of the lexicon. For example, Rubenstein, Lewis, and Rubenstein (1971) suggested that we might do away with the notion of orthographic representations by setting up a phonological file into which orthography was converted by rule—for after all, everyone who learns to read already has a phonological access file. But if this were true, then it would take no longer to decide that *trane* is pronounced as an English word than it takes to decide that *train* is an English word. In fact, the first takes nearly double the time (Taft, 1973; Bower, 1970). Furthermore, Forster's model suggests an exhaustive search for nonwords and a terminating search for words, which would explain just why the time differences occur. Another point is that if we ask whether a word like *year* is ambiguous, or whether it can be used as a verb, the search takes a very long time. Presumably this is because only a search beyond the orthographic or phonological files will reveal ambiguity, and only an exhaustive search will reveal the categorizability of a lexical item. Both of these findings have been confirmed experimentally. A further consequence is that if an exhaustive search is required, then word frequency should have no effect—no matter how rapidly the first entry is found, one still has to search—and this has also been demonstrated experimentally.

Forster's model of the lexicon is a highly structured one. But there is a model of human memory which is a totally unstructured one: that of Landauer (1975).[3]

Landauer's model is one which might be referred to as a "garbage can." Yet while things are just thrown into the memory, there is not total randomness in the garbage. While there may be no obvious organization in the layerings in the garbage can, it will be found that, for example, orange peels, egg shells, and coffee grounds frequently occur contiguously: all is not totally random. Landauer's view also breaks down the notions of different sorts of memory stores: there is but one memory which keeps all the information each of us has.

Landauer's view is that neither place of storage nor order of search during retrieval is influenced by the nature of the information stored or retrieved. Memory consists of a three-dimensional space in which a large number of homogeneously distributed loci are contained. Data of any nature may be stored at each of these loci. Data received near each other in time are stored at nearby loci. Searches of an undirected expanding sphere afford access. Landauer feels that every datum is stored. Thus, things that are encountered repeatedly and frequently occur more frequently in the memory than things which have been encountered but once or infrequently. As access is by means of a random search, the more points containing a given datum there are, the more rapidly it will be accessed.

This garbage can view is most congenial when one thinks of the fact that smells, sounds, tastes, and textures are as recollectable as are words, their orthographies, their pronunciations, and their meanings.

Landauer's model also fits in rather well with an observation made by Meyer and Schwanefeldt (1976). They showed that lexical decision time varies with contiguity of associatively related words. That is, it takes less time to process *nurse* if it follows *doctor* on a list, than if the list is of otherwise unrelated items. But let us imagine that for *doctor* to be found, the random search pointer had to stop in the proximity of a locus containing it. It will still be nearby just after *doctor* has been found. As associated words will tend to be stored near each other (due to history, not because of an organizational propensity), the next item will take less time to evaluate if it is an associate. This model also explains some of the material in Rubenstein, Lewis, and Rubenstein (1971) concerning judgments of items with ambiguities, like *yard.* Judgments concerning whether or not this is a word will be more rapid because of the number of different occurrences of the string as a length and as a space (as well as its less-frequent nautical meaning). Items with multiple meanings are thus stored in more disparate places because their experienced occurrences are themselves more widely distributed.

Landauer discusses at some length the relations of his model to the human brain, and comes to no useful conclusion. It is worth pointing out, however, that there is more recent work: for example, that of Pribram (to appear).

Pribram advocates our viewing the hologram as an analog of the way the brain stores information. We might think of cortical function as a distributed Fourier function, but this may be untenable. It is more likely that there are a number of nodes in neural networks of which Fourier transforms are only one type of projection. However, it is important to see in this most recent work that memory is viewed as a distributed function, with decisional operators involved in retrieval and coding which are more localized.

We will abandon this material here to recount some experimental evidence.

Some Experiments

Earlier in this paper, we mentioned the fact that most of what we do is inferential. Some of the methods used for accessing information concerning the mental lexicon and memory generally have been mentioned in the course of the previous section. One procedure we have not looked at is the word association task.

As the word association test is now over a century old, there is a vast literature surrounding it. We will not endeavor to review this literature. However, there are a few works over the past two decades which are relevant to our topic here.

In 1962, Carroll et al. concluded that a large proportion of the commonality scores obtained from word association tests were based on responses to opposite-evoking stimuli. They found that when these opposite-evoking stimuli were removed from consideration, the primary responses given to non-opposite-evoking stimuli accounted for but a small portion of the commonality score. They concluded:

> It would seem on the basis of this evidence that a large part of what is termed a commonality score is dependent on S's tendency to respond or not respond with an opposite to certain key stimulus words. If these key words were removed from the list, we would be left with a great heterogeneity of responses to the remaining stimuli. (1962:25)

Carroll's group decided among themselves just which items on the list were opposite-evoking and which were not. In a number of cases (table/chair, hand/foot, command/obey, sleep/wake) they excluded items we would include. They found that about two-thirds of the responses were opposites; if we take the larger number, about three-quarters of the responses are opposites. (For a fuller discussion of this, see Salus & Salus, 1978; P.H. Salus, to appear.)

Shortly after this, Deese published his work on adjective contrasts (1964) and his brilliant book on associations (1965). In the latter he complained that most psychological work on associations had concentrated on the serial nature of stimulus and response, and that "attention to this property has led to the neglect of structure" (1965:1). Inspired by this, and by two articles by H.H. Clark (1969, 1970b), we began collecting requests for opposites, as well as associations, and collecting responses to the same list from speakers of all ages (our current data comprises over 25,000 stimulus/response pairs from subjects ranging from 2½ to 55 years of age).

We have found that when opposites are requested, only three-quarters of the responses are opposites. The remainder of the responses are as diverse as the responses cited over twenty years ago by Carroll et al. However, like Clark (1970b), and counter to the statements made by Carroll et al., we have found that the response types are classifiable. Furthermore, as opposed to the remarks of Nelson (1977), but like Stolz and Tiffany (1972), we have found that adults do not shy from rhymes and syntagms. It is just that frequency and familiarity play a great role here. This is not at all disturbing and, in fact, lines up quite well with the sort of model proposed by Landauer. We will devote the next few paragraphs to illustrating just how the garbage can can be used to explain such real data.

The fact that oppositions occur so frequently in word-association responses is accounted for by the fact that such words occur contiguously quite often in normal language, no matter what their part of speech: "salt and pepper," "ups and downs," "king and queen," "fast and slow," "black and white," "come and go," and a thousand such pairs come to mind. This would mean that the two members of the pair are stored at loci either adjacent or near one another, and that the pointer would locate the second soon after locating the first. This would be merely another instance of the phenomenon noted by Meyer and Schwanefeldt (1976).

Rhyming responses would be explained on the basis of the randomly moving pointer having come across a phonological similarity prior to arriving at a semantic similarity.

Syntagmatic responses are, perhaps, the easiest to explicate: as items are stored as they arrive at adjacent loci, the items next to the target item must be those which occurred next when it was received. In fact, one might view the opposite responses here as special cases of syntagms.

The phenomenon of forgetting is an interesting one in the garbage can model. If the pointer moves randomly, it must randomly arrive at already-occupied loci when it has something to store. When it does so, it "overprints" the material already there with the new material. If the instance of the "old" material is a unique or an infrequent one, it has now been "forgotten" or made less accessible. If it was a salient datum, then there will still be sufficient instances of it for it to be recalled.

All of us have experienced the phenomenon of saying "I don't know X" and then coming up with X a few moments later. In some way, our pointer has not located X but continues searching. N.P. Moray (personal communication) has suggested that each of us has an internal timer, and that when that timer goes off, we respond, whether or not the appropriate answer has been found. In the sort of instance cited here, our pointer hasn't found X when the timer goes, so the response is that X is unknown. But, at the same time, the pointer keeps moving through the memory space, and when X is located, it "pops up."

Landauer's model consistently mentions "the pointer," and we have employed this usage. But there are implementations of computer modeling which do not require single-trace searches.

Another way of attempting a search through the memory would be by means of "partial-match retrieval" and the notion of superimposed codes (Roberts, 1979). Let us suppose that we had put the Suffolk County, New York, telephone directory into our digital computer. What we would like to obtain is a listing of the businesses beginning with BOBS on Main. In most computer systems, our machine would search its files for items beginning BOBS, put them into a "dummy" file, and serially search this file for Main. With more complex material, three or four or five searches might be required, each entailing the setting-up of a dummy file or files. This is time-consuming and takes up a good deal of space in the computer's memory. In view of the fact that the value of stored material (whether in computer memory or in human memory or in the library model used above) is a direct function of its accessibility, a system making the specification, location, and retrieval of material faster and simpler is of great importance. The notion of superimposed codes, developed in the computer language C (Kernighan & Ritchie, 1978) and the UNIX system (Ritchie & Thompson, 1974; UNIX is a trademark of Bell Laboratories), but following much earlier work (e.g., Luhn, 1958), enables a simultaneous search, rather than serial searches, to take place.

Conclusions

There are (basically) three current models for semantic memory: network models (Collins & Quillan, 1969), set-theoretic models (Meyer, 1970), and feature-comparison models (Smith, Shoben, & Rips, 1974). Each of these has been criticized and its shortcomings detailed. We would like to suggest a modification of Landauer (1975) as being both more realistic and answering more of the various points which have been brought up where the other models are concerned.

First of all, we advocate the garbage can, rather than the hierarchic or nested approaches to the human memory. Second, we adopt Moray's notion of the internal timer. Third, we advocate viewing Landauer's pointer as a multiple complex vector, though we see this vector moving in memory space randomly. Fourth, we envision this complex vector as capable of carrying material of several kinds, enabling it to perform partial matching of several superimposed codes. Fifth, we see this model as best fitting Pribram's concept of memory as a distributed (rather than a localized) function in the brain.

Afterword

We began this essay with the statement that the essence of reading was the transmodal process of gleaning information from visually presented verbal material. Since then, we have concerned ourselves with the nature of the mental lexicon and of human memory. At this point, we feel it is necessary for us to come full circle and return to the question of reading.

For reading to take place, the reader must find the visual representation in his or her memory and relate this visual representation to phonological and semantic material. The garbage can/partial match model would enforce the notion that exposure is crucial in becoming a skilled reader. The more practice, the greater the exposure, the larger the number of loci at which the image/verbal will be found. The larger the number of loci, the more quickly they will be found by the pointer, whatever its nature.

On the other hand, this model would only support a very limited use of the phonics method for teaching reading, for skilled readers do not make use of letter/sound relationships (such as they are) as much as larger contexts in interpreting visually presented verbal material.

In fact, any of the current models of memory would argue against the use of phonics as an adequate method for producing a skilled reader. Writers on reading development (e.g., Gibson & Levin, 1975) seem to think that there is a heuristic leap made by skilled readers from their previous method of utilizing phonics. But there is no evidence that phonics has anything to do with this development. We would suggest that the "conversion" made by children who become skilled readers is done on their own, and that the elaborate search, reconstruct, search-for-item process which must be done within the phonics approach works counter to the production of the skilled reader.

Notes

[1] Much of the research reported here was done from 1977-1979 while both authors were at Scarborough College of the University of Toronto, with the generous support of the University, which is gratefully acknowledged. It was continued during 1979-1980 at Boston University, and since then at the University of North Florida. While we have received many valuable comments from colleagues, we feel the following should be singled out: Robert I. Binnick, Dwight Bolinger, Paul Bouissac, James Deese, Ilse Lehiste, Lise Menn, Paula Menyuk, Neville Moray, Jacqueline Sachs, Ann Zwicky, and Arnold Zwicky. Our debt to several hundred school children, teachers, and parents is immeasurable.

[2] For these remarks we are indebted to Konrad Lorenz, whose gracious comments at a seminar in Salzburg in August 1977 have profoundly influenced our thinking.

[3] We would like to thank Charles Clifton for bringing Landauer's work to our attention.

Sticht notes that one of the traditional practices in teaching reading is the use of simultaneous auding (listening) and reading to improve reading speed and/or comprehension; further, he notes that most of this work is contradictory in its findings reflecting a lack of conceptualizing regarding the auding and reading processes and their relations. In this paper he examines simultaneous auding and reading tasks within the context of a developmental model of reading. The model leads to the hypothesis that maximal auding and reading rates are probably the same because reading uses the same language base (lexicon, syntax) and the same conceptual base (semantic memory) as auding. He argues that rates at which comprehension can be formed from language, and rates at which language can be formed, set upper limits to both auding and reading.

Rate of Comprehending by Listening or Reading

Thomas G. Sticht
American University

A time honored practice in reading instruction has the reading teacher read a passage aloud while students simultaneously listen and attempt to read along (Daly, Neville, & Pugh, 1975). With modern audio technology, the tape recorded speech has frequently replaced the teacher, and there has appeared extensive "read along" materials that aim, in large part, to improve the rate of fluent reading by having students read while listening to messages (Monteith, 1978).

An important aspect of audio technology are techniques that permit the controlled acceleration of speech rates of tape recorded messages without introducing the "chipmunk" sound that occurs whenever a phonograph or audio cassette is played at a rate faster than the original recording rate, for example, when a 33 1/3 revolution per minute (rpm) record is played at 78 rpm (Foulke & Sticht, 1969). This technology for controlled manipulation of the rate of recorded speech also permits the slowing down of speech rates without distortions of the pitch that occur when a recording is played at a rate slower than the original recording rate.

One of the aspects of rate controlled recordings which has intrigued many educators is their potential for improving reading speed and comprehension. Duker (1974) presents several reports which studied the effects of training via listening to various rates of speech or in simultaneously listening and reading at various rates of speech on reading speed and comprehension. Despite the general ambiguity of research findings—sometimes positive, sometimes negative, with no real understanding why—commercial publishers have produced complete sets of expensive instructional materials based upon listening to rate accelerated speech to improve reading comprehension and speed (Daly, Neville, & Pugh, 1975; Monteith, 1978).

Interestingly, one of the most useful applications of rate controlled speech has been to permit the blind to listen at rates comparable to typical silent reading rates of sighted high school seniors and college freshmen. Thus, the application is based upon getting listening rates equivalent to reading rates.

When using rate controlled recordings to improve reading rate, however, the interest is in getting reading rates equivalent to listening rates. That is, the rate of listening is used as a pacer or target rate to which it is hoped reading rate will increase. Sometimes, it is hoped that listening rate itself will increase, and that almost magically (since usually no mechanism or process is stated) reading rate will now rise to the new level set by the improved listening rate.

Examination of the various studies which have attempted to use rate controlled recordings to improve listening or reading skills reveals very little by way of analysis of listening and reading processes to suggest a strong basis for the research. For instance, few studies ask: In what respects are listening and reading similar, so that training in processing spoken messages at various rates could transfer to processing printed messages? What characteristics do listening and reading share? What characteristics differentiate the processes? How do these processes change developmentally? How does learning to read differ from learning to listen?

Without a conceptual base which will suggest answers to questions such as above, applications of rate controlled recordings will continue to be done on a completely hit and miss, empirical basis. This will result in a proliferation of theses and dissertations, but little knowledge, only an assortment of contradictory findings, unresolvable and incomprehensible in the aggregate.

A Developmental Model of Auding and Reading

As a beginning in providing a conceptual base for the rational study of listening and reading, we are conducting research to explore some of the basic perceptual, cognitive, and language factors involved in listening and reading. In pursuing this work, we have found it useful to consider relationships among listening and reading from a developmental perspective—that is, with attention to the chronological development of listening and reading skills, including the development of *rates* of listening and reading. A detailed presentation of much of the thinking we have done in this area is contained in Sticht, et al. (1974). Here we present only a brief summary of the developmental model; then we will discuss in greater detail implications of the model for understanding factors underlying rates of listening and reading. Finally, we will present some empirical research in which we attempt to measure one aspect of reading which may be the target for studies in which simultaneous listening and reading are used to improve reading—namely, the decoding of print to language.

The Developmental Model

Figure 1 presents the developmental model of literacy in schematic form. Briefly, the model formally recognizes what common sense tells us, and that is that when children are first born they are born with certain Basic Adaptive Processes for adapting to the world around them. These BAP include certain information processing capacities for acquiring, storing, retrieving, and manipulating information. This stored information processing capacity forms a cognitive content which, in its earlier forms, is prelinguistic (Figure 1, Stage 1). After some time though, the children develop skills for receiving information representing the cognitive content of others, and for representing their own cognitive content to others. This is accomplished through the specialization of the information processing activities of listening, looking, uttering, marking (Figure 1, Stage 2). The specialization is one use of these skills for the express purpose of externally representing one's own thoughts for others to interpret, and forming internal representations of the external representations of others' thoughts that they make. More specifically, though, the particular specialization of present concern is the representation of thoughts via the use of conventionalized signs (words) and rules for sequencing these signs (syntax) in speaking and auding—listening to speech in order to language (Figure 1, Stage 3).

Finally, if the children are in a literate society, they may acquire the specialized looking and marking skills of reading and writing. For present purposes, we presume we are talking about the "typical" case in our literate society, and assert that children typically learn to read and write (Figure 1, Stage 4).

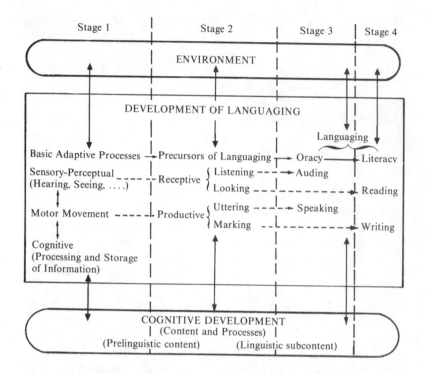

Figure 1. Overview of developmental model.

A further aspect of the developmental model is that it holds that the development of the oracy skills requires the development of the cognitive content through intellectual activity which we call conceptualizing ability. In other words, the development of the oracy skills of speaking and auding follows and is built upon a prelinguistic cognitive content and conceptualizing ability.

A final aspect of the model is that it asserts that the literacy skills utilize the same conceptual base (cognitive content, conceptualizing ability, knowledge) as is used in auding and speaking, *and* utilize the same signs and rules for sequencing those signs as is used in the oral language skills for receiving and expressing conceptualizations. Notice that this is an assertion based upon the developmental sequence, i.e., the literacy skills are built upon existing language and conceptualizing skills as the end of a developmental sequence. This does not mean that once literacy skills are acquired, they do not contribute anything new to knowledge or language capability; clearly they do. What is asserted is that when the literacy skills are initially acquired, they are essentially to be construed as a second way of utilizing the same language system the child uses in speaking and auding.

Rates of Auding and Reading

According to the developmental model outlined above, auding and reading utilize the same languaging and conceptualizing systems. Developmentally, one first develops auding skill, including the ability to process speech information into language and conceptualizations at some adaptive rate (or rates, depending upon the task at hand). We can speculate that this rate will have some upper limit, and that this limit will reflect the limits of languaging and conceptualizing rates. By languaging rate, we refer to the speed with which conceptualizations can be encoded as language forms (e.g., meaningful morphemes, or "words" for present purposes) for speaking to others, and the rate at which speech can be recoded from the acoustic form into an internal language form (e.g., "words") when auding the speech of others. By conceptualizing rate, we mean the rate at which concepts or thoughts can be formed in order to be expressed in language by speaking, and the rate at which language forms can be recoded into thoughts or conceptualizations during auding.

If, in fact, there are limits on how quickly we can recode speech into language, and language into conceptualizations during auding, and if, as stated in the developmental model, reading utilizes the same languaging and conceptualizing processes as used in auding, then we expect that maximal auding and reading rates will be comparable, following the acquisition of skill in recoding printed language into the internal representations of language as are formed during the auding of speech. This hypothesis follows from the fact that, in the present model, auding and reading utilize the same languaging and conceptualizing systems. Hence, the limiting factors underlying both auding and reading rate are skill in languaging and in conceptualizing.

Evidence for the Comparability of Maximal Auding and Reading Rates

While the concept of reading rate or "speed reading" is probably familiar, readers of this report may not be familiar with the concept of auding rate or "speed auding." Essentially, auding rates refers to how well one can comprehend spoken passages presented at different rates of speech. For instance, a paragraph might be read aloud to a listener at an average rate of 150 wpm, and a comprehension test administered immediately. This procedure is then repeated for comparable materials presented at rates of 200, 250, 300, and 350 wpm. Changes in immediate retention comprehension scores are used to indicate the influence of speech rate on auding. Thus, "speeding auding" means auding rapidly presented rates of speech.

In their 1969 review of research on rate of auding, Foulke and Sticht concluded that, when various studies are considered collectively, the relationship that emerges is one in which rate of auding comprehension declines slowly as word rate is increased, up to a rate of some 275 wpm; beyond this the decline in rate of auding comprehension is faster. Subsequently, Foulke (1971) reported data suggesting that rate of auding comprehension declined more rapidly when a wpm rate of 250 was exceeded. Carver (1973b) reported reanalyses of Foulke's data (1971) which indicated that, for very difficult test items, auding comprehension dropped off rapidly at 300 wpm., while for less difficult items, auding comprehension declined only a little over the range of speech rates from 125 to 400 wpm. In Figure 5 of the same article, Carver presented data of his own indicating that subjects' judgment of how well they understood spoken messages presented at various rates dropped off gradually for speech rates from 100 to 300 wpm, and then declined rather rapidly at rates beyond 300 wpm.

Carver also presented evidence (Figure 6 of his article) to suggest that a "threshold" for comprehending auding materials might be surpassed at speech rates as low as 150 wpm, depending upon how comprehension is measured (e.g., multiple-choice tests, judgments of understanding). However, in a subsequent unpublished paper, Carver (1973c) presented additional data to suggest that, for college students, auding comprehension drops precariously when rates exceeding 300 wpm are presented. Thus, although research exists to suggest that auding comprehension may or may not decline at rates of speech less than or equal to 250-300 wpm, evidence is strong for suggesting that rates above these levels will almost certainly lead to rapid losses of information by auding.

Regarding speed auding, then, current research indicates that, although most information that is presented for auding does not demand processing rates in excess of 150-200 wpm (newscaster, professional readers for the blind typically read aloud at around 175 wpm ± 25 wpm, Foulke & Sticht, 1969; Foulke, 1969), high school graduates and college students can aud at rates up to 250-300 wpm before their capacities for rapidly processing language information are overtaxed. If this represents some upper limit in rate of languaging, then the present model predicts that once reading skill is acquired, it will reflect this same limit in rate of languaging.

Data bearing on normative rates of silent reading are available from the 1972 National Assessment of Educational Progress (Report 02-R-09). This survey measured the rate at which respondents aged 9, 13, 17, and 26 to 35 (young adults) silently read materials with the knowledge that they would be tested for comprehension (memory for details) immediately afterward.

Table 1
Rate of Silent Reading for Four Age Groups[a]

				Reading Rate at Percentile[c]		
Age (years)	N	Passage	Grade Level of Materials[b]	25	50 Median	75
9	2195	1	4-8	86	117	158
		2	7-12	88	123	169
13	2196	1	5	133	173	217
		2	10-11	128	165	212
17	2220	1	10	160	195	247
		2	College	157	195	246
26-35	1239	1	10	145	188	231
		2	College	145	186	236

[a] Data are from the National Assessment of Educational Progress Report 02-R-09: *Reading Rate and Comprehension, 1970-71 Assessment*, December 1972.
[b] Grade levels are readability scores determined by 3 to 4 different readability formulas. Data presented are ranges.
[c] Reading rates are words per minute (wpm).

Data from the National Assessment report are summarized in Table 1. While a clear growth in reading rate is evident from 9 year olds to 17 year olds, there is no evidence for silent reading rates in excess of the 250-300 wpm reported previously for upper ranges of auding rates. For 17 year olds and young adults, only some 10 percent of the samples read in excess of 300 wpm. Only 17 people out of the 7,850 tested at all age levels read in excess of 750 wpm; and these readers could not consistently answer four out of five of the comprehension questions for two selections.

There is little evidence here, then, that people "typically" read at rates far in excess of rates they can contend with by auding. In fact, the median rates of silent reading for 17 year olds and young adults are not too much higher than the 175 wpm average oral reading rates of professional newscasters and readers for the blind (Foulke & Sticht, 1969). It is also relevant to note that trained oral readers can produce speech rates as fast as 220-344 wpm when asked to produce maximal, yet intelligible rates of speech (Carroll, 1968; Goldstein, 1940; Miron & Brown, 1971). The rates of reading aloud are fast enough to encompass the range of the sixteen hundred readers at the 75th percentile in Table 1. They are also within the range of silent reading rates for college students, which are typically found to be in the vicinity of 250-300 wpm (Carroll, 1968; Gray, 1956).

It appears that college students typically read silently at rates comparable to those at which auding can be performed, without serious decrease in comprehension. In turn, both auding and reading rates of college students seem to correspond to the upper rates at which oral reading can be processed. This suggests a common factor underlying all three processes, an idea we will return to later in this section.

The evidence reviewed regarding the comparability of auding and reading rates does not include direct comparisons of auding and reading. There are, so far as we can determine, only a handful of studies that make such a direct comparison. In an early study of the effects of rate of presentation in passages on auding and reading comprehension, Goldstein (1940) presented messages to adults at 100, 137, 174, 211, 248, 285, and 322 wpm. He found that comprehension scores, expressed in school grade equivalents, decreased from 11.1 to 10.8, to 10.6, to 10.5, to 9.4, to 9.3, and to 8.7, respectively. Thus, as the rate of presentation decreased, the amount of information available to be used in answering the comprehension questions also decreased. The largest drop occurred between 211 and 248 wpm, with a decrease from 10.5 to 9.4—a 1.1 grade equivalent drop.

In the same study, Goldstein also presented materials for reading at different rates using a moving picture projection technique to control rate of appearance of the printed text. For the same rates (100, 137, 174, 211, 248, 285, and 322 wpm) comprehension scores decreased as 10.6, 10.1, 10.1, 9.8, 9.4, 9.1, 8.7. It should be noted that the auding and reading comprehension scores are quite similar, and that both auding and reading scores decrease with increasing rates of presentation.

Jester and Travers (1966) presented passages for auding and reading rates of 150, 200, 250, 300, and 350 wpm. For auding, their college students had mean retention comprehension raw scores of 14.7, 14.2, 7.3, 4.9, and 2.1 respectively. Corresponding reading scores were 15.5, 10.8, 9.1, 10.1, 5.9. It is clear that at the fastest rate (350 wpm) auding and reading are comparable, while at 300 wpm, reading is clearly superior to auding. On the other hand, auding surpassed reading at 200 wpm. At best then, these data are inconclusive. It seems unlikely that reading would be more effective at 150 wpm—especially since both Mowbray (1935) and more recently Young (1973) found no differences in college students' auding and reading retention comprehension scores when materials were presented at 175 wpm.

Perhaps discrepancies between Goldstein's work and that of Jester and Travers relate in some way to the fact that the latter researchers used slide presentations to present nonmoving print displays. Whatever the case, it is clear that at the fastest rate—350 wpm—Jester and Travers found auding and reading performance to be comparable. Thus, there is no indication of differences in rate of languaging favoring reading.

Carver (1977-1978) and Sticht, et al. (1974) review extensive research using time compressed speech to accelerate spoken word rates to as fast as 500 words per minute with little signal distortion. Using this approach, it has been found that both auding and reading comprehension rates for college level readers are optimal at around 300 words per minute.

Fullmer (1980) indicates that maximal rates of reading, defined as the rate at which comprehension is no better than chance, may be somewhere in the neighborhood of 700 or so words per minute, while auding may fail to produce comprehension above chance level at some 500 or so words per minute. While these findings may reflect differences in the methods for controlling rate of presentation of information for auding and reading, it may also be indicative of separate language processing mechanisms for auding and reading. It may also indicate that auding and reading utilize the same internal mechanism, but that the auding display does not reach the limits of this mechanism in either ordinary speech or in time compressed speech, where it may lose intelligibility due to signal distortion produced by the compression process. If the latter is the case, we might expect to find that, in the early stages of learning to read, auding is more efficient than reading. With extensive practice in reading, however, we might expect to find reading more efficient than auding. That is indeed what the review of literature summarized by Sticht, et al. (1974) revealed.

Though the data on optimal and maximal auding and reading rates support the hypothesis that both reading and auding use the same, or a very similar, internal language process, as suggested by the developmental model, it does not rule out the possibility that it is the rate of thinking that limits information processing by eye and by ear, and not the rate of some internal language process (see Sticht, et al., 1974, pp. 92-107, for further analysis of this issue).

To summarize briefly, the research reviewed above indicates that:

1. Typical oral reading rates for professional oral readers (newsmen; readers for "talking books" for the blind) are around 175 wpm, with a standard deviation of 25 wpm, hence auding rates of 175 wpm are typical for persons auding such presentations.

2. A national sample of 17 year olds and young adults silently reading at rates of 185-195 wpm, suggesting that, typically, such persons do not read silently much faster than they aud newscasts or radio programs.

3. When requested to read aloud as rapidly as possible without loss of intelligibility, trained oral readers can produce speech rates as high as 250-340 wpm.

4. When adults are presented spoken materials for rapid auding, comprehension typically holds up well for speech rates up to 250-300 wpm, then declines more rapidly.

5. A national sample of 17 year olds and adults showed less than 10 percent of the population reading above 300 wpm, with the 75th percentile reading 231-247 wpm; additional studies indicate that high school students and college students—that is, the better readers in the country—typically read at rates of 250-300 wpm.

6. Studies which have directly compared the effectiveness of auding and reading, at different rates of presentation of the material up to 350 wpm, show comparable levels of comprehension for the two processes at the same rates.

From the foregoing we conclude that, to date, there is no clearly demonstrated superiority for the reading process in rate of processing to gauge information from print over what can be accomplished by the auding process in processing language information from speech. Rather, the available data suggest that both auding and reading processes may operate at the same rates of efficiency when the rate of presentation of language material is directly manipulated. This conclusion is consistent with the assessment in the developmental model that reading utilizes the same languaging abilities as auding. Hence, the rate at which languaging can be executed limits both the rate of auding and subsequently the rate of reading when that skill is acquired.

Speculation on the Rate of Languaging

It is of interest to note that the rates of 250-300 wpm, indicated by the foregoing as more-or-less "maximal" rates for auding and silent reading, correspond closely to the fastest rates at which trained readers can read aloud. This suggests that the same factors which limit rates of reading aloud may limit rates of auding and reading. One factor limiting oral reading is the rate at which articulatory movements can be made. Lenneberg (1967, pp. 88-124) discusses various aspects of speech production, including the rate at which articulatory movements (syllables) can be made. He reports that "...subjects between the ages of eight to about thirty could speed up production to eight and occasionally even nine syllables per second for the duration of a few seconds; the rate slowed down to about six per second if the alternating movements were to be sustained over more than three or four seconds" (p. 115).

Taking six syllables per second as an efficient level of production gives 360 syllables per minute. Then, assuming 1.42 syllables per word (the average for 33 of the 36 passages scaled for complexity by Miller & Coleman, 1967; Carroll, 1967 describes six passages with an average of 1.44 syllables per word), we obtain a rate of 254 wpm—a rate comparable to the average silent reading rate of high school students (Carroll, 1968). A rate of 300 wpm corresponds to a syllable per second rate of 7.1, midway between Lenneberg's rates of six syllables per second for sustained production, and nine syllables per second for brief durations of production.

There appears to be a close relationship between the rate of which syllables can be produced, and maximal auding and silent reading rates. It is as though, typically, auders and readers utilize the same mechanisms for decoding spoken or printed language *into* conceptualizations, as are used in signaling conceptualizations *to* others via speech.

This is, of course, an old idea. Huey (1908, reprinted in 1968) devotes two chapters to the role of "inner-speech" in reading. He states: "The simple fact is that the inner saying or hearing of what is read seems to be the core of ordinary reading, the 'thing in itself,' so far as there is such a part of such a complex process" (p. 122). While elsewhere Heuy states that the fact of inner speech forming a part of silent reading has not been disputed (p. 117), Kolers, in his introduction to the 1968 printing of Huey's book, expresses the kind of ideas that have obscured the relationship between languaging and auding and reading when he states that: "People who read faster than about three or four hundred words per minute, and certainly those who read at rates of a few thousand words per minute, simple have not enough time to form an auditory representation of all they read" (p. xxvii).

Of course, Kolers gives no data to indicate that people *can* read a "few thousand words per minute." In fact, Taylor (1962) presents eye movement records which clearly indicate qualitative differences between "normal" reading and "reading" at 3000 or more wpm. The latter recordings indicate that the "rapid reading" eyes move in a completely different manner than do the "normal reading" eyes. The latter move systematically to the right across a line of print making three or four stops (fixations), and then make a return sweep to the left margin and begin to move to the right again. The "rapid reading" eyes, on the other hand, may move down the left margin for 10 lines or so, then back to the left, and so on, quite clearly doing something other than "normal reading."

Thus, while "skimming" or "scanning" can most certainly be accomplished with printed displays, there is little evidence that readers can, or typically do, read at rates far above the rates at which they can aud or speak (see Edfeldt, 1960; Sikolov, 1972, pp. 202-211, for further discussion and research on inner speech and reading; Carver, 1971a, for discussion of speed reading).

The upshot of this analysis is that much of silent reading appears to involve the conversion of printed symbols into the same type of signing systems used in receiving and expressing oral symbols, which are then converted into, or directly give rise to, conceptualizations. Thus, the representation of meaning *directly* by written language does not appear to be a typical happening, as some have argued is the case with skilled readers (Goodman, 1973; Smith, 1971, pp. 44-45—again, we see here the claim that "...trained readers can cover [but not read one by one] many thousands of words in a minute" with no evidence given, and with a failure to carefully distinguish reading from skimming or scanning).

The fact that the maximal rates of syllable production closely match the optimal auding and reading rates should not be taken to necessarily imply the syllable as the "basic" unit of language. It may be, but there are many problems in adequately defining syllables (Shuy, 1969) both as units of speech and as units of print. For present purposes, it is sufficient to note the similarities among rate of syllable production (movement of articulators), rapid auding, and rapid reading, and to point out the relevance of this observation to the developmental model.

Speculation on the Rate of Conceptualizing

Lenneberg (1967, p. 90) points out that, while most adults are capable of producing common phrases or cliches at rates up to 500 syllables per minute, more frequently they speak at 210 or 220 syllables per minute (150 wpm). He then states: "Apparently, the most important factor limiting the rate of speech involves the cognitive aspects of language and not the physical ability to perform the articulatory movements. We may not be able to organize our thoughts fast enough to allow us to speak at the fastest possible rate."

It is likewise possible that in auding and reading we may not be able to merge the thoughts being presented with our own conceptual base fast enough to "track" the oral or printed message. Possibly, it is primarily lack of conceptualizing time which causes the gradual loss in comphrehension when auding and reading speeds are increased up to 250-300 wpm. Beyond 300 wpm, then, the loss in comprehension may reflect both lack of conceptualizing time and inability to mobilize inner language patterns rapidly enough to faithfully follow the message.

Evidence that ability to rapidly conceptualize is related to ability to comprehend rapid rates of speech is available in a study of Friedman and Johnson (1969). They administered a group of cognitive tests to college students who also auded materials presented at 175, 250, 325, or 450 wpm. One of the cognitive tests (the Best Trend Name Test) requires students to infer the semantic relationships among a set of words. For example, the words *horse, pushcart, bicycle, car* are presented and the student is asked to decide whether the relationship among the four terms is best described as one of speed, time, or size. The correct answer is *time* since the sequence describes an order of historical development; horses were the earliest means of transportation, cars the most recent.

Results of multiple regression analyses for predicting auding ability at each of the four rates listed indicated that while the Best Trend Name Test was a poor predictor of performance at the slowest rates, its correlation and beta weight increased significantly with the fastest rate of speech, identifying it as a major source of individual variance in the comprehension of highly accelerated speech. Thus, the ability to efficiently conceptualize semantic relations among vocabulary items facilitates comprehension of more rapid rates of speech.

The role of conceptualizing ability in comprehending auding materials is also demonstrated by the fact that, even at rates of speech of from 125 to 175 wpm, high aptitude men do not learn as much from materials written at grade level 14.5 or 8.5 as they do from materials of grade 5.5 difficulty (Sticht, 1972). Thus the effects of difficulty level of material appear to represent conceptualizing rather than languaging (encoding and decoding conceptualizations into and out of forms for communication) difficulties at normal rates of presentation, although research does not rule out the possibility that higher grade level materials may be more difficult to encode and decode for some individuals.

The role of conceptualization ability, or ability to "organize our thoughts," in comprehending auding messages presented at various rates is also evidenced by the differences in performance between "high" and "low" aptitude students. Sticht (1972) found that men of low verbal aptitude did not learn as much auding fifth grade materials as high verbal ability men did at 350 wpm. In another study (Sticht, 1968) it was found that low verbal ability men learned passages of sixth, seventh, and fourteenth grade level of difficulty as well by auding as they did by reading when materials were presented at 175 wpm, but in neither case did they do as well as higher verbal aptitude men. Thus, "low aptitude" or "low verbal" intelligence seems more likely to represent conceptualization problems than problems associated with rapid encoding or decoding of concepts into language to send or receive ideas.

The point we are making is that performance on immediate tests of retention of information typically used to evaluate auding and reading ability at various rates of presentation reflects a combination of the ability to encode and decode information from the conceptual base into or out of spoken or printed representations of our concepts, and the ability to formulate and reformulate concepts in keeping with the message being sent (speaking) or received (auding or reading). Other things being equal, the former ability will interfere with performance when rates of information display exceed 300 or so words per minute, while the latter ability will hinder or facilitate performance over all ranges of rates of presentation, and can be demonstrated by manipulating the difficulty levels of materials and the "mental aptitude" of the students. We are inclined at the moment to call the former a languaging problem, and the latter a conceptualizing problem.

Measuring Aspects of Languaging and Conceptualizing

We opened this discussion of auding and reading by indicating that there has been interest in improving reading skill by having students read passages while they simultaneously aud the passage. By increasing the rate of presentation of the auding passage—generally through the use of time compression devices—the attempt is made to increase the rate of reading.

As we have indicated above, the auding and reading processes contain both languaging and conceptualizing components. It is of interest to know which aspects of the reading process might be affected by practice in simultaneous auding and reading. For example, one aspect of languaging by reading is the decoding of printed words into the language forms used in the spoken language. This type of decoding training is found in phonics programs in which grapheme-phoneme correspondences are taught. This type of decoding skill apparently becomes overlearned in skilled readers, until it is completely unconscious, or automatic. Of course, the skill can be used consciously whenever a difficult word is encountered (e.g., sphygmomanometer) and we revert to "sounding it out."

One outcome of simultaneous auding and reading training, then, might be to help "automatize" the decoding component of reading. The use of faster and faster speech rates might provide practice in more rapid decoding and facilitate the automatization process.

We could also argue that a person who has great skill in decoding print to material language forms should be able to perform such a task at faster rates than a relatively unskilled person. Thus, if we presented simultaneous auding and reading passages at faster and faster speech rates, we might conclude that the person who can store the greater amount of information and use it later on to answer questions is the more skillful decoder of print to internal language. But of course this would be an improper conclusion, because the person might ignore the printed message and simply aud the spoken message. Because all of the information is in the auding message, a person might be quite unskilled at reading/decoding, but quite skilled at auding and do well on retention tests of comprehension.

In another case, the person low in reading/decoding skills who is also low in oral language and conceptualizing skills, would do poorly on a retention test even if he did ignore the print and attend only to the spoken message. But, if we have only the immediate retention test data, we cannot tell if poor performance reflects poor reading/decoding, poor oral language/conceptualizing skills, or both.

In order to better understand the effects of training in simultaneous auding and reading on the improvement of reading skill, we are exploring techniques for assessing the reading-decoding and language/conceptualizing components during simultaneous auding and reading. One technique we are exploring is described below.

Detection of Spoken and Printed Word Mismatches During a Simultaneous Auding and Reading Task

Our interest in this task is to obtain an indication of a person's skill in performing the reading-decoding process during simultaneous auding and reading. The procedure we are exploring has been tried out with children at the fifth grade level, and with adults of low and high reading skills. Here, I will describe procedures and data obtained with adults which demonstrates that the technique does seem to provide a measure of reading-decoding skill (or automaticity of decoding, as it will be referred to below).

The subjects of this research were four groups of adults; two groups having high reading ability (HRA) and two groups having low reading ability (LRA). The HRA adults were college students or out-of-school young men. Reading scores were 11th grade level or higher. The LRA adults were young men in a military literacy program with reading grade levels below the 6.0 grade level.

To assess the automaticity of decoding during simultaneous auding and reading, one group of HRA and LRA adults was presented a

2800-word selection from a fifth grade version of *Roland and Charlemagne* to be simultaneously auded and read. Then we arranged that at times during the presentation, there would occur a different, though semantically appropriate, word in the spoken message than that which appeared on the printed page. For instance, the printed story might state "With the air of a *lord* he walked. . .", while the spoken story would state "With the air of a *prince* he walked. . .". When subjects encountered a mismatch, they circled the printed word which did not match the spoken word. Following this procedure then, in order to perform the mismatch detection task, the subjects had to continually decode the print into a form comparable to the spoken word, and perform an internal comparison. To determine different levels of skill in tracking the message and performing this mismatch detection task, the audio tapes were time-compressed to produce speech rates of 228 and 328 words per minute, while the uncompressed rate was 128 wpm.

To gain additional evidence that the "tracking" task described above (detecting mismatches between aural and visual words) does indeed involve continuous decoding, a second set of HRA and LRA adult groups were presented a second version of the same material. But, in this case, the mismatch word was replaced on the printed page by three words (see example), one of which matched the word in the spoken message. In this case, the subjects' task was circling the matching words.

prince

Example: With the air of a king   he walked. . .

lord

With such an arrangement, the subject is able to skip a lot of the decoding required in the former task because he has a cue as to where his next decision must be made. We refer to this version of the tracking task as the "cued" version, while the first version is called the "uncued" tracking task. The "cued" version is also referred to as a low decoding demand task, while the "uncued" tracking task is a high decoding demand task.

In both the high and low decoding tasks, the first third of the story was presented at 128 wpm, the second third at 228, and the final third at 328 wpm. After each third of the selection, 15 four-alternative multiple choice questions were administered to the subjects. All questions called for retention of detail—no inference or reasoning items were included. These tests thus provided immediate retention indicators of comprehension.

Figure 2 presents the results of the studies. Part A presents the "tracking" task, in which one of the three alternatives (low decoding) or the printed/spoken word mismatch (high decoding) was circled during the presentation of the message for simultaneous auding and reading. Part B presents the immediate retention data.

Of major interest is the difference between the curves for the low and high decoding tasks in the tracking data (Part A). At the 128 wpm rate, in the low decoding task, both low and high reading ability people performed practically 100 percent correct. Under the high decoding conditions, however, the low reading ability people scored only 60 percent correct, while the high reading ability people maintained almost perfect performance. With the faster speech rates, under the low decoding condition, the high reading ability people maintained almost perfect "tracking" performance, while a systematic decrease is observed for the low reading ability people. Also, within each speech rate, there is a systematic difference between the low and high decoding conditions, with the latter always lower than the former. At the faster speech rates, even the high reading ability people show a drop in their tracking performance under the high decoding condition.

We interpret the tracking (Part A) data of Figure 2 as indicative of a person's skill in performing the reading-decoding process during simultaneous auding and reading. Skill is indexed in two ways: being able to maintain a high level of performance across low and high decoding tasks, and being able to maintain a high level of performance across all speech rates. The reading-decoding task is most difficult when each word in the printed page must be compared to each word in the spoken message (high decoding task) when the latter is rapidly presented at 328 words per minute. Under this condition, even highly skilled readers show a large (40 percent) decrement in performance.

The immediate retention data (Part B of Figure 2) indicate that the high reading ability people had no trouble in performing the tracking task and storing sufficient information from the message to be able to respond better than 80 percent correct across all three speech rates and under both decoding levels. Apparently this fifth grade material is well within the languaging and conceptualizing capabilities of these highly skilled readers.

For the poorer readers, however, increasing the speech rate produced a systematic decline in the amount of information which was stored in a retrievable manner during the simultaneous auding and

A. TRACKING

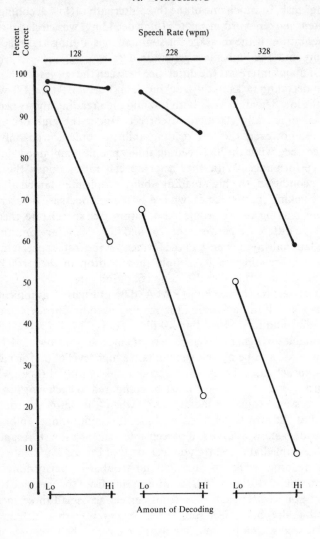

Figure 2. Part A. Tracking presents mean percent correct scores for the detection of mismatches between spoken and printed messages for cued (low decoding) and uncued (high decoding) conditions at three

B. RETENTION

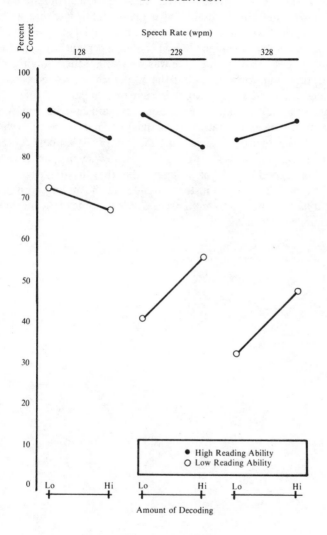

speech rates for high and low reading ability adults.   *Part B.* presents mean percent correct scores for immediate retention tests for the same conditions and subjects.

reading task, though the effects of decoding level were inconsistent for some unknown and uninterpretable (by us) reason. The fact that, at the 128 wpm rate, the low reading ability people performed at a fairly high level (almost as high as the high ability people: 70 percent compared to 80 percent) suggests that the message was well within their languaging and conceptualizing knowledge, but the 30 percent or so decrease in performance when the speech rate was increased to 228 and then 328 wpm suggests a lack of skill in processing the language information and/or forming conceptualizations from that information in such a way as to store much of it in a retrievable manner. This happened even though their tracking scores dropped to such low levels, particularly under the high decoding task, as to suggest that they may have ignored much of the reading task and instead attended to the auding message. This would have permitted them to process at least some of the message for subsequent retrieval.

PART THREE   Focus: The Structure of Prose

Calfee and Curley have designed a taxonomy of prose structures from a psychological perspective. In preparing their taxonomy, they attempt to determine the design facets that have significant influences on how a reader processes a text. Their taxonomy has been developed from an examination of prose in content area texts.

Structures of Prose in the Content Areas[1]

Robert C. Calfee
Robert Curley
Stanford University

> "I have taken all knowledge to be my province."
> Sir Francis Bacon (1561-1626)

When Bacon wrote these words early in the English Renaissance, it was conceivable that a single person might encompass the domain of "all knowledge." Though the printing press had been in England for a century, Bacon did not have to contend with today's torrents pouring from typewriters and linotypes, not to mention copiers, microfilms, and computers. Our store of knowledge is expanding at an enormous pace. The forms and instances for representing this knowledge are also increasing.

The purpose of schooling is to prepare youngsters to deal as adults with the flow of printed matter that they will encounter as adults. Most individuals, to succeed in modern society, must be able to handle information in many forms. The morning paper, the news magazine, and the documents telling you how to assemble a bicycle, fill out a tax form, improve your sex life, or chlorinate your hot tub (safely)—all of these and others provide knowledge to the person who can comprehend them. Nobel Laureate Joshua Lederberg (1981), asked to comment on the increasing use of computer-based word processers, had the following to say:

> I think text systems will put a premium on literacy...that has been vanishing with the preeminence of the telephone.... As people relate to language in a more deliberate and thoughtful way, as one looks at one's writing and has the

opportunity to see again what one had written some time ago, I think the more careful use of language is an inevitable and, to my view, generally desirable outcome.

In the primary school years, the young child is taught the preliminaries of reading, generally by means of one or another of the basal readers on the market. These texts are carefully constructed to confront the beginning reader with as few challenges as possible—the vocabulary is commonplace, and each word is repeated frequently; the sentences are short and simple; the text comprises short stories about presumably commonplace episodes from life, and is heavily illustrated by brightly colored pictures.

The gap between the primer level and the reading demands of "real life" is substantial. We have in mind both the academic and semiacademic reading that are demanded in colleges and trade schools, as well as the "functional" reading that all of us face in dealing with modern life. By the time students reach junior high school, they are expected to handle texts comparable to those encountered by adults—the vocabulary is determined by the topic rather than by word counts; the sentences are longer and more complex; the pictures are gone; both content and structures may be unfamiliar. We believe that many youngsters fail to make the step from the primer to the textbook. Our thesis is that this failure comes about partly because the school does not make clear to students what it is they have to learn, and that this shortcoming results because of a lack of conceptual clarity in the curriculum.

Two centuries after Bacon, Herbert Spencer observed that "science is organized knowledge." This epigram was not a truism so much as recognition of a significant shift in the way that human beings had come to understand what they know. Writing and its associated technologies have brought about many changes in the way that we represent information. Spencer lived at the turn of the century, by which time numerous styles of discourse had evolved as bases for communication—in science, in literature, and in a whole range of technical, governmental, and vocational domains. These areas are encountered by today's students in what is called "content reading." School children appear to read about "nothing in particular" in the early grades, and then are expected to shift automatically to literacy in science, social studies, home economics, and car repair.

Spencer was right—knowledge in the modern world is organized, and the forms of discourse in each domain of knowledge are often particular to that domain. Readers' tasks in learning to comprehend a text are: 1) to realize they should search for an organizational structure in the text, 2) to discover the various clues to that structure, and 3) to know how to modify the framework as they go along until they have constructed a representation of the text that suits their purposes. The teachers' tasks are: 1) to aid students to acquire an understanding of the importance of looking for structure, 2) to inform students about the most common structures and structural cues associated with various content areas, and 3) to encourage students to practice these tasks of comprehension.

It is probably best to think about a text structure as analogous to an outline—the bare-bones of the passage. What we are proposing is that student, teacher, and researcher all need to reach a mutual understanding of the different categories of outlines that are typically found in upper grade textbooks. We propose to tackle this question from the perspective of the experimental psychologist: What design facets are necessary to describe variations in prose structures? This perspective may seem somewhat esoteric, but to the extent that we are successful, the result should prove valuable in practice as well as in research. The curriculum developer, in selecting and creating the passages for a textbook, is best guided by a coherent design. The classroom teacher, in presenting and discussing the meaning of a text, performs best when he has a clear conception of the text structure. The researcher, in exploring the processes of comprehension, can generalize his findings most safely as he understands the structure of the domain under investigation.

Taxonomies from Rhetoric

We are by no means the first scholars to attempt a taxonomy of prose structures. The study of rhetoric, which is the basis for all such efforts, has a long tradition, and it is from this tradition that most contemporary work derives.

As a concrete example, we will review Levin's *Prose Models* (1978). In this fairly popular composition text for college students, the author illustrates the variety of organizational principles that are important in the construction of an essay. Levin organizes his presentation according to constituent levels—an essay can be examined as an entire structure, as a set of paragraphs within that structure, as a series of sentences within each paragraph, and finally as a choice of the most appropriate words within the sentence frame. The concept of levels is essential to any taxonomy of prose structures, and this topic is broached by most scholars. Levin's treatment is primarily physical-istic—for instance, a paragraph is defined as a collection of sentences set apart by space from the preceding and following sentences. We are convinced that a deeper understanding of the paragraph and relations between paragraphs would provide a more secure foundation for coherent design of text structures.

Levin also discusses a variety of rhetorical styles, each illustrated by a set of passages. He makes no attempt to classify these styles, nor to argue that they are associated with one level or another, though most are listed under the section on paragraphs. In Table 1 we have extracted Levin's list of styles, organized them in a way that seems reasonable to us, and added a few explanatory comments. Our purpose is to give you a concrete idea of the practical thinking of rhetoricians to compare with subsequent accounts by researchers and educational practitioners.

In addition to the discussion of levels and styles, Levin emphasizes the importance of a reasoned and orderly progression of the various parts of an essay. The beginning, the middle, and the end should be thoughtfully arranged. Transitions between elements should smooth the way for the reader. The author should have a single, clearly delineated thesis for the essay as a whole—"its central or controlling idea, the proposition or chief argument, the *point* of the essay" (p. 210). At another place he introduces the notion of *unity*:

> In a unified paragraph [or essay], each sentence [or paragraph] is related to a central, controlling idea. More than this, the relation of main to subordinate ideas is clarified for the reader, sometimes through transitional words and phrases, and sometimes...through parallel phrases, clauses, or sentences....The principles of order...are many: the writer may proceed from the least to the most interesting or important idea; or from the general to the specific...; or from the simple to the complex. (pp. 16, 17)

Here then is the domain of our investigation—the variety of prose styles employed, often unconsciously, by the skilled author. It is important for the competent reader to have some understanding of this domain, a knowledge sufficient to guide him in creating his own mental model of a passage. To be sure, not all compositions are well crafted. As Meyer notes, the teacher should help the student in attaining a knowledge of prose structures, but the teacher should also aid the student in learning to recognize poorly written material, and to reorganize the information into some reasonable structure. We will not pursue the point but, as you might suspect, we are inclined to think that learning to become a skilled writer will foster growth in comprehension, and learning to search out the structure of a text should lay a solid foundation for training a competent writer.

TABLE 1

Categories of Rhetorical Styles. After Levin (1978)

Description	
Definition	Definition elaborates on the meaning of a term. It may identify features, uses, or relationships with other known objects, events, or ideas.
Division and Classification	Division distinguishes the parts or members of an object or class. Classification relates groups of objects, events, or ideas according to a principle of similarity.
Comparison and Contrast	Comparison generally highlights similarities among two or more entities, while contrast emphasizes differences.
Illustration	
Analogy	"Illustrative analogy is...a comparison between two different things or activities for the purpose of explanation" (p. 72).
Example	Illustration through a sample of typical or outstanding instances.
Sequence	
Process	"Process is a series of connected instances, each developing from the preceding one, that result in something: a decision, a product, an effort of some kind" (p. 81).
Cause and Effect	A sequence of events which is related in a causal chain.
Argument and Persuasion	
Deductive Reasoning	An argument from generalities to particulars, where the conclusion necessarily follows from the premises.
Inductive Reasoning	An argument from particulars to generalities. A given outcome may be "characterized as more or less probable depending on the strength of the evidence in relation to the conclusion" (p. 354).
Persuasion	A line of argument laid out so as to present the ideas in the most *convincing* manner. The correctness of the argument is not necessarily a criterion.
Functional	
Introduction	An opening statement in which the author "will indicate a point of view and perhaps also [the] ways the subject is to be developed" (p. 246).
Transition	Establishes a framework for integrating prior information with forthcoming information. Emphasizes relationships among ideas or explains changes in theme.
Conclusion	Generally includes review of thematic material. Ties together any lines of thought left uncompleted.

Taxonomies from Research

A good deal of the current psycholinguistic work on prose structures has focused on the analysis of narrative passages. This research has been reviewed recently by Reder (1980), and we need only to recapitulate the major points from her paper.

Narration

A major breakthrough in the study of passage comprehension was the concept of a passage grammar. Rumelhart (1975) was one of the first to propose such a system; he worked out a scheme for generating simple narratives, shown here in much simplified form:

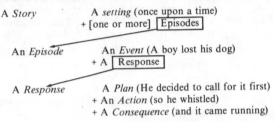

This example is incomplete in several respects, but it gives an idea of what a story grammar looks like, in case you have never encountered the approach. Several researchers have investigated memory for narrative prose, using the story grammar as a framework for constructing narratives with well defined internal structure, and for assessing the structural characteristics of the reader's retelling of a passage. There is now an extensive literature on this topic, the methodology has become quite sophisticated, and debates now center about fine points (Black & Wilensky, 1979; Mandler & Johnson, 1980; however, cf., Thorndyke & Yekovich, 1980). Experiments using this approach consistently find that a) the order of events specified by the story grammar is frequently an accurate description of "real" stories; b) readers seldom depart from this order if the story is well written (i.e., follows the grammar); and c) the ability to retell well written stories is acquired quite early, certainly by the age of 4 or 5 (Reder, 1980; Mandler & Johnson, 1977; Applebee, 1978).

All of us are submerged in narratives virtually from birth—fairy tales, "How was your day?", cartoons, situation comedies, and so on. It is not surprising that youngsters are familiar with the form, and are adept at using the model for remembering events. School experiences can deepen and enrich this knowledge, but the child has the basic skill when he first enters the classroom. It seems equally clear that most children are unfamiliar with the "nonnarrative" forms of prose that are referred to collectively as exposition. The dichotomy between narrative and expository prose, despite many shortcomings, has served until recently as the primary boundary for classifying types of prose structure. We turn next to research in the domain of expository text.

Exposition

Meyer's landmark research (1975a, b) on expository passages opened the way for a host of studies by Meyer and her colleagues as well as other investigators. Meyer proposed that expository structures could be described according to a set of hierarchically nested segments, which typically formed a tree diagram. She proposed further that the upper levels of the tree generally fell into one of five rhetorical relations, which share some similarity with Levin's categories.

1. *antecedent/consequent*—a causal relation between topics
2. *comparison* or *contrast*—pointing out the differences or similarities between two topics.
3. *collection* or *list*—showing how a set of topics is bound together on the basis of some commonality
4. *description*—giving more information about a topic by attributes, examples, or elaboration
5. *response*—including the remark-and-reply, question-answer, and problem-solution formats

Three levels of structure are distinguished—top-level structures bind the entire text together, macropropositions occur within the top level, and micropropositions fall at the lowest level. Meyer gives examples of rhetorical relations at the top and macrolevels; micropropositions are described by case grammar relations. The boundaries between levels are not always clear, but Meyer emphasizes that top level structures and macropropositions are the "main ideas" in a passage—they are explicitly stated, they occupy prominent positions in well written prose, and they are well remembered by competent readers (Meyer, Brandt, & Bluth, 1980; Meyer & Freedle, 1979).

Selinker and his colleagues (Selinker, Trimble, & Trimble, 1976; Selinker, Trimble, & Vroman, 1974; Lackstrom, Selinker, & Trimble, 1973) have proposed a structure for expository prose that, like Meyer's, is organized according to a hierarchy in which specific rhetorical functions are nested within a series of "fuzzy" levels." Their rhetorical functions do not always have the abstract character of Meyer's system—they include in their lists such entries as *detailing an experiment, making a recommendation, stating the problem, definition, description*, and *causality*. Neither do they attempt to support their hypothesized structure with experimental findings; their results are far more naturalistic and descriptive, and their subject sample is limited to students for whom English is a second language. Nonetheless, their observations warrant attention:

> The majority of the students appear to be able to read nontechnical material [in English] quite readily. . . . [However,] they often seem unable to comprehend the total meaning of [a technical] discourse even when they understand all the words in each sentence and all the sentences that make up the discourse. . . . [They] often lack an understanding of the relation between the individual clauses making up the supporting information in a paragraph. . .and the core generalizations of a paragraph. . . The non-native reader cannot recognize the existence of certain types of implicit presuppositional rhetorical information. (Selinker, Trimble, & Trimble, 1976, p. 282)

In short, Selinker et al. find that nonnative speakers/readers of English experience many of the problems in comprehending expository prose that appear in poor readers for whom English is the first language. One is tempted to conjecture that the underlying problem may be the same in both instances. Incidentally, Flick and Anderson (1980) have found that today's native born college students exhibit patterns of difficulty similar to those of foreign born students.

Next we want to call attention to studies by Bereiter and his colleagues at the Ontario Institute. In his first paper on the topic, Bereiter (1978) was puzzled that no one had previously tackled the problem of a taxonomy of prose structures:

> I truly believed, at the outset of the work leading up to this paper, that we would find already in existence a usable theory of discourse types and their processing demands. . . . We didn't find such a theory. We didn't even find the scraps of such a theory. Discourse researchers seemed to be concerned overwhelmingly with narrative, and it was obvious that children already have most of what it takes to understand narratives before they come to school. (p. 3)

As you can see, Bereiter's experience matches our own.

The taxonomy proposed by the Ontario group reflects a developmental orientation—comprehension strategies are assumed to progress from sequential narration to a peak in "abstract topical exposition":

1. Narrative—fictional and factual
2. Concrete process—descriptive and prescriptive
3. Description—fictional, factual particular, and factual general

4. Concrete topical exposition
5. Line of reasoning—rational narrative, physical and volitional cause-and-effect
6. Argument—dialogue, thesis and support, reflective essay
7. Abstract topical exposition

Bereiter sees these genres as forming an ordinal sequence, and he suggests that a "natural instructional plan...would be to introduce children gradually to literature that has fewer and fewer of the properties of narrative and that demands more and more of what the comprehension of abstract discourse demands" (p. 11). The basic proposition seems reasonable to us, although we do not think it necessary to propose a strictly developmental progression. Two additional points are worth noting.

First, it becomes increasingly apparent that although the various lists of rhetorical function overlap considerably, extensions of these lists might easily multiply beyond reason. How do we decide whether a genre has legitimate standing? Create a suitable name, and a new genre exists. This comment is not to criticize the Ontario group, but only to suggest that we lack a systematic approach for classifying prose models.

Second, these researchers' observations about students' level of processing deserve special attention. On the one hand, they report that many high school students seem to compose (and one suspects, to comprehend) at the sentence level. The compositions are generated one sentence at a time, generally without any guiding framework. On the other hand, the researchers have conducted several experiments demonstrating substantial growth in "top-level" structural awareness of prose organization when students are taught directly to look for such structure when composing a passage:

> We attempted to teach children a planning method that...was top down, in the sense that it required making choices first at a higher level than was customary...children can gain conscious access to implicit text grammar knowledge,...they are sensitive to the sequencing of text elements, and...they spontaneously recognize abstract text elements as potentially powerful concepts for thinking about writing. (Bereiter, Scardamalia, Anderson, & Smart, 1980, p. 1)

Finally, let us note the work of Spiro and Taylor (1980) at the Illinois Center for the Study of Reading. These investigators have attempted a "multidimensional psychological classification of texts," springing in part from the observation that school children seem to experience considerable difficulty in making the transition from narrative to expository prose. Research on this problem is hampered, as Spiro and Taylor note, by the fuzzy contrast between the narrative and expository genres. Structure, familiarity, ideational density, and complexity—all contrast these two prose types.

To lend some semblance of order to the situation, Spiro and Taylor (1980) propose a taxonomy, but first they issue several caveats:

> Our list of dimensions is not orthogonal, nor is it intended to be exhaustive. It is not even clearly delineated...our intention is to illustrate the complexity of the text classification problem though it is hoped that further developments...will permit...clarity.... (pp. 6, 7)

In the list of dimensions that follows the warnings, we find these entries (and their summary): *underlying structure* (order and hierarchy), *relevance of preexisting structural knowledge)* (perhaps overemphasized in the current literature), *form of linguistic expression* (readability, sentence complexity, metaphor, and so on), *content and semantic organization* (abstract, concrete, real, hypothetical, complex, single, explicit, implicit, and so on), *relevance and availability of preexisting content knowledge* (the impact of personal experience and knowledge), *discourse function* (the purpose of a passage), *subsequent use*, and *extratextual support*.

Spiro and Taylor argue, no doubt rightly, that the construction of a taxonomy for prose structures is a difficult and complex challenge. But one does not answer a challenge by giving in. Parsimony and clarity are still the chief goals of the scientific enterprise, and we believe that it is premature to accept complexity, confounding, and confabulation.

Taxonomies from Practice

Our focus in this chapter is on the prose structures found at the upper grades in the content areas. In earlier times, this topic did not exist as a specific concern of reading specialists (Smith, 1964a, cites about 1940 as the beginning of content area investigations). It was generally assumed that students beyond the sixth grade could read with fluency and comprehension; otherwise, they were not suitable candidates for further schooling, and they would be advised to leave school to seek a suitable vocation.

By the time "reading in the content area" became a recognized field, the objectives-based approach to instruction was in full flower. We will not attempt to trace this development (however, see Eisner, 1979); it must suffice to point to the scope-and-sequence charts that are commonplace today. A path reaching from Thorndike through Tyler and Bloom, emerging in Popham (1980) and others, has bequeathed us terms like *literal comprehension, main idea, inferential comprehension, judgment of fact versus opinion*, and so on. Taxonomies like the one ascribed by Clymer (1968) to Barrett (Smith & Barrett, 1974; Snow, 1980) had a major impact on the development of reading curricula, especially the questions and workbook exercises that direct much of the student's learning today. Although Barrett mentioned elements like comparison, cause-effect, sequence, and the like, he did not emphasize the character of the passages being read. If a "sequence" element can be found anywhere in a passage, that suffices as a basis for teaching and testing the sequence objective. (For a serious effort to apply an objective-based approach to different subject matters, cf. Bloom, Hastings, & Madaus, 1971.)

As more serious attention has been paid to the "content" of reading in the content areas, practitioners have been led to more serious consideration of the structures that undergird writing in the areas of science, social studies, and other fields. However, in the absence of a clear agreement on a taxonomy of prose structures, you might expect some degree of variation from one practitioner to another, and such is the case.

To give some idea of the present state of affairs, we examined five college textbooks on reading at the secondary level in the content areas. The results of our analysis appear in Table 2. The most frequently mentioned prose styles are Cause/effect, Compare/contrast, Time-order, and Listing. The last two are not in Levin's set of categories (1978). Time-order refers to any sequential structure, whether reflective of the passing of time or the progression of logic. This category thus encompasses all the subcategories in Sequence, as well as some of the entries under Argument. Listing applies to any passage structure in which enumeration is the chief principle. Argument is seldom dealt with as an organizational pattern in prose, though it is not unusual for students to be asked to distinguish between "fact and opinion." Robinson's treatment (1975) departs markedly from the other texts; it covers a broader range of structures and includes functional as well as substantive structures. Bader (1980) touches on a wide range of topics, but these are mentioned in passing as a series of lists, with little in the way of detailed discussion.

An interesting feature in most texts is the presentation of "signal words" for each of the major categories. The idea seems to have originated with Vacca (1973) who suggested the following lists:

> *Cause/effect:* because, since, therefore, consequently, as a result, this led to, so that, nevertheless, accordingly, if...then.
> *Comparison/contrast:* however, but, as well as, on the other hand, not only...but also, either...or, while although, unless, similarly, yet.
> *Time order;* on (date), not long after, now, as, before, after, when.
> *Simple listing:* to begin with...; first...second...; next; then; finally.

	Robinson	Friedman & Rawls	Herber	Bader	Olson & Ames
Description		2			
Definition		2		2	
Classification	1	2			
Comparison		1*	1*	2*	2
Illustration					
Analogy					2
Example				2	
Sequence		1§	1§	2§	2
Process		2			2
Cause/Effect		1*	1*	2*	2
Narration[a]	1	2		2	2
Argument					2
Deductive					
Inductive					
Persuasion	1				
Evidence					
Functional					
Introduction	1			2	
Transition	1			2	
Conclusion					
Summary	1			2	
(Other) Explanation	1	2		2	
Listing		1	1	2	
Instructions		2			

1 - explanation or example given
2 - mentioned
[a] - not in Levin's classification
* - lists appropriate signal words
§ - referred to as "time order"

The idea of giving the student explicit lexical clues to passage structure makes sense, if used properly—"students can use the signal words to establish mind sets as they read, enabling them to follow the author better through the development of the topic" (Herber, 1978, p. 79). This advice requires that the student also be taught the organizational frameworks. Unfortunately, we are convinced that the existing materials do an adequate job of accomplishing this objective. If our concern is justified, students are in the unhappy situation of having clues to differences that they do not understand. Meyer, Brandt, and

Calfee and Curley

Bluth (1980) investigated the effect of including or deleting signal words in expository passages. The students were ninth graders who were classified as good, average, poor, or underachieving comprehenders. All but the good readers recalled substantially more ideas just after reading a text which included signal words. Unfortunately, when they were asked to recall the passage a week later, the advantage of the signal words was lost, and students actually did slightly better if they had read passages without signal words. Apparently these clues provide a crutch for the short run, but lack staying power.

Another line of development worth mentioning is the attempt to characterize each content area according to the genre typical of the area. Smith (1964a, b) was one of the first to examine the writing patterns in the various content areas. She examined over 200 secondary textbooks and identified common patterns in literature, science, social studies, and mathematics. Within literature she classified patterns by genre: essay, drama, biography, and suggested that each "pattern" needs to be read with different purposes in mind. In science, classification, explanation of a technical process, instructions for an experiment, detailed statement-of-facts, and descriptive problem-solving were found to be the dominant patterns. Cause and effect, sequential events, comparison, statement of fact, and propaganda were cited in social studies. In mathematics, Smith distinguished word problems and explanation.

At a practical level, Robinson (1975) has done a particularly capable job of laying out the "patterns and strategies," as he calls them, for identifying and understanding the underlying structures in texts from science, social studies, mathematics, and English. He covers several other areas more briefly—business, bookkeeping, law, driver education, health, home economics, and industrial arts. His presentation illustrates good instructional design: general principles are introduced, reinforced by examples, and then summarized. To be sure, Robinson does not include all the patterns in his initial overview, and so the student teacher encounters new patterns almost incidentally within the various subject matters. Again, this discrepancy between the general and specific discussions of patterns is not so much a criticism of Robinson's exposition as a reflection on the lack of a well defined taxonomy for prose structures.

Our analysis of the conceptions of prose structures in practice today has not been particularly searching. Nonetheless, we think that researchers and curriculum designers can be informed by some aspects of practice—we have observed classroom teachers presenting expository networks with imagination and insight. Other experiences in the classroom have left us less satisfied. The training provided to teachers is often spotty and poorly organized. Techniques like signal words are presented as simple solutions to complex problems, and so lend themselves to misuse.

Many of the methods used for assessment in practical settings seem to us badly off the mark. The main idea is the typical label for text questions that purport to measure the student's structural knowledge. These questions generally encompass a single paragraph, which is to be summarized by a single sentence that incorporates the top-level structure of the paragraph. Normally the task would require the student to recognize the topic sentence. This approach is quite direct, and most students can do well if the paragraph is well written. As a result, such items have undesirable psychometric characteristics, and test writers are thus driven to less direct and less valid methods.

A Taxonomy of Prose Structures

In this section of the chapter, we will present our ideas about the creation of a taxonomy of prose structures. As mentioned earlier, we will pursue this problem from a psychological perspective; more specifically, our goal is to determine the design facets that might have significant influence on how a reader processes text. It seems likely to us that a skilled reader employs what are called *schemata*, mental frameworks acquired through experience and instruction, which provide a skeletal structure for organizing the information in a text (Anderson, 1977; Rumelhart, 1975). Mental schemata probably match closely the ways we "talk about things." For instance, if several people are asked to describe what it is like to have dinner in a restaurant, and if they all seem to touch on the same basic points, we might conclude that the set of points and the relations among them portray the "restaurant" schema in the minds of these people. Likewise, if we discover that most scholars in zoology use the same basic outline to describe various types of animals (appearance, habitat, food, behavior), we might reason that this outline reflects the expert's schema. We could go even further and suggest that the student's task in zoology is to acquire this schema, and learn how to use it to comprehend descriptions of animals. In any event, our quest is a system for organizing the set of textual outlines, and we think we are not far from the truth if we imagine that this system will help us understand how competent students organize textual information in their minds. Our proposal is not *de novo*, but relies extensively on the work of other scholars—rhetoricians, linguists, and psychologists.

Form and Level

Two facets are consistently found in earlier discussions of text structure—*structural form* and *level of discourse*. Structural form refers to lists like the one we generated from Levin's (1978) discussion of prose models. By level of discourse, we mean the distinctions between text, paragraph, and sentence; between top level macropropositional, and micropropositional (Meyer, 1975a); between conceptual and physical paragraphs (Selinker, Trimble, & Trimble, 1976).

Level has proven a fuzzy concept. None of the existing treatments make clear the boundaries between one level and the next. To be sure, one can make ordinal distinctions in a hierarchical network—Levels I, II, III, and so on can be defined with reasonable precision. But how do you tell when you move from a "top" or conceptual level to something lower?

Meyer (1975b) suggests that structural form is nested within level. She proposed one set of organizational relations at the upper levels of text (she called them rhetorical predicates, and they are similar to Levin's [1978] categories), and a different set of relations at the lower sentential levels (she called these role relations, and they are akin to Fillmore's [1968] case grammar).

Focus, Formality, and Elaboration

We want to introduce three new design facets that do not appear as such in the literature: *Topical focus, Structural formality*, and *Degree of elaboration*. We will characterize each of these briefly.

By *focus*, we mean the answer to the question, "What is it about?" It seems to us that most prose (written or spoken) can be placed in one of three topical categories: *object, sequence*, and *idea*. Under objects, we include discussions of things, persons, and even ideas, when these are objectified. Sequence has to do with any account in which progression is the key to the structure. Fairy tales, recipes, instructions for assembling a bicycle, an essay on the water cycle, all fit into this category. Our third category is fuzzier than the first two—it may become clearer through illustration, it may be inherently fuzzy, or it may be that we have not yet arrived at an adequate conceptualization. In any event, under this heading we place discussions intended to persuade, to convince, to anger, to enthuse—editorials, advertisements, essays, and so on.

Structural formality is akin to the distinction drawn by Olson and others between utterance and text (Olson, 1977; Calfee & Freedman, 1981). One of the most significant influences of the technologies of writing and the printing press has been the evolution of new structural forms. Writing allows us to represent our ideas visually, in nonsequential form (a listener can hear only one word at a time, and in the order determined by the speaker; not so with writing), and with physical support for memory. The very notion of an outline is difficult to conceive in the absence of the technology of print. We therefore propose that one can distinguish forms of prose that are commonplace in all societies and at all levels of human development, whether literate or not, from those forms that are less familiar, more typically used by educated people, and more formal in the sense that they fall with Bernstein's rubric of "restricted" language (1961). Thus, a simple story is commonplace, a recipe from a cookbook is more formal, and a technical discussion of how deoxyribonucleic acid (DNA) reproduces itself might be classified as very formal, not because of the complexity of the topic but because of the underlying structural constraints in the presentation.

Degree of elaboration is a concept which we think provides a better account of the notion of *level*. We begin with the writer and his decision to write about something—it is at this point that the focus is established. The writer also decides about the audience and the purpose for writing. These decisions influence the choice of style (more or less formal) and the degree of elaboration. The starting point, in any event, determines the overall theme and the uppermost level of structure for development of that theme. We assume a competent writer, so that this top level is *coherent* and *unified* to use Levin's terms (1978).

Once he has determined the topic and a general sense of the structural form, the writer then proceeds to elaborate the theme—literally, to "work it out." One approach to this task is to prepare an outline, which might be either quite detailed or a collection of sketchy notes. In either event, the writer works through a series of decisions, both hierarchical and sequential, that indicate how much and what to say about each element of the theme. These subsequent decisions, though guided by the topic and the style, are nonetheless relatively independent of one another. For each element, the author can choose a set of topics and styles within that element as a means of elaboration. Depending on the extent and character of the elaboration, a chapter, a section within a chapter, a paragraph, a sentence, or perhaps a single word may suffice. These segments, which bear a close resemblance to what others have referred to as levels, are described better according to their function within an exposition, rather than according to some inherent substantive existence.

Our account of the composition process is hardly news to many of our readers. Nor is it altogether novel to suggest that comprehension and composition bear a reciprocal relation to one another—we think the implications of this observation warrant serious investigation, and we would even suggest that the decline in writing instruction in the United States (Applebee, 1980) may be related to the decline in SAT scores. What is novel in our proposal is the suggestion that topical structures may appear at any level in a passage, and that for reader, curriculum designer, and scholar the important taxonomical undertaking is a scheme for reconstructing the network of interrelated elements. The author makes a series of decisions in creating a text; the reader's task is to retrace that path to the level of detail appropriate to his needs.

In Table 3 we have attempted to portray the main features of our analysis. The author first chooses a topical focus, and then selects a structural form appropriate to the topic and to the intended audience. For each element in the structure, the author then decides how extensive an elaboration to pursue. The choice may be a word or a sentence— lexical and grammatical constraints govern these choices. If the choice is to expand on the element to the extent of a paragraph, or perhaps even a subtext, then the process becomes iterative—depending on the element and the audience for this elaboration, the author chooses a topic and a structural form, and then proceeds to elaborate (i.e., work out) these choices until eventually an appropriate set of words and sentences is created.

One immediate outcome of this analysis is to modify the concept of the paragraph and perhaps of the chapter and the sentence. Rhetoricians (and psychologists as well) have tended to classify paragraphs according to their structural form (see Levin's 1978 classification scheme, which is designed for paragraphs). We are inclined to think that it makes more sense to examine the *function* of each element, including paragraphs, within the elaborated text structure.

TABLE 3
Decision Path for Creating a Text

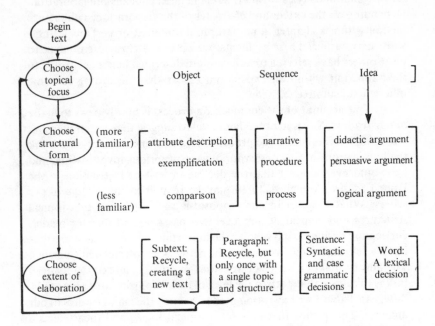

The paragraph is most clearly defined as a physical entity—one or more sentences set apart by indentations from the preceding and following parts of the text. The paragraph can also be defined formally—a single idea, usually comprised of a topic sentence and one or more supporting statements. The problem with the formal definition is to know when an idea has been captured. Moreover, some paragraphs seem to contain more than a single idea, and what are we to do with these instances?

We think that this problem and several others can be solved by examining the function of each paragraph within the content of the overall text or subtext of which it is a part. (A similar treatment of sentences is probably worth pursuing, though we should note that the case grammar analysis of words in a sentence may amount to just such a functional analysis.) A paragraph may serve various functions in a text. It may introduce the text or a subtext. It may provide a transition between major textual elements. It may summarize or conclude. It may comprise a textual element, or an entire text.

Calfee and Curley

The functional classification of the paragraph fits within a process-oriented taxonomy of prose structures. A well written text centers around a specific topical focus and a specific structural form. We suspect that the gist of the passage can be expressed in terms of this *topic-structure* combination. From this foundation, the passage then consists of a succession of elaborations. Depending on the degree of "working out" for each element, the reader may encounter a series of subtexts or paragraphs, each comprising a topic-structure combination in its own right. The reader's task is to reconstruct the process that created the text, to a level of detail sufficient to meet his particular needs for information.

The process of reconstruction poses an interesting challenge. The reader works most immediately from the products of the final stage of composition—sequences of words marked off into sentences, which in turn, are grouped into paragraphs, subsections, chapters, and so on. The eye can take in only a few words at a glance; it is impossible to "read" a passage as a whole. Rather, the reader is continually looking for the "joints" in a text that allow his mind to organize the information. The words, punctuation marks, section headings, and other sources of information are clues to the underlying structure. Much as the archeologist recreates the processes of an earlier life by combining sparse chunks of information with his own store of knowledge and imagination, so the competent reader must recreate the mental gyrations of the author. As de Beaugrande (1981) puts it:

> The initial processing unit is not the sentence (after all, many texts are not composed exclusively of sentences), but rather the stretch of text that can be comfortably held in working memory under current limitations of attention, familiarity, and interest. It would be important to learn whether that stretch is or is not usually a sentence, but we must not assume so in advance. Other candidates deserve consideration: a clause, a group of short sentences, a long noun phrase or verb phrase, a chunk of propositions, a discourse action, and so on. The goal of processing cannot be syntactic analysis, but rather *building a model of a textual world.* (p. 287)

We have proposed that most compositions are generated by a recursive series of decisions, each of which draws upon a relatively limited set of options. This proposal means that the set of all outlines is infinite in number, which agrees with our intuition. Nonetheless, it is possible to characterize this infinite set according to a relatively small number of decision rules. This situation parallels the classification of sentence frames according to the rules of a generative grammar. Finally, and as is true of generative grammars, the structure we have proposed is designed to account for the passages typically composed by a competent author. Unskilled writers are likely to produce structures which cannot be incorporated easily within this system—nor would we want to try to describe such compositions. Likewise, we cannot hope to account for the imaginative author who expresses himself uniquely by going outside the conventions. To explain the true artist is a challenge, but we will be content to attempt to describe the comprehension of well crafted prose.

Notes

[1] The preparation of this paper was funded in part by the following: Grant No. G007903258, U.S. Department of Education, Office of Special Education and Grant No. OE-G007803067, U.S. Department of Education, Teacher Corps.

In her paper, Hasan is concerned with placing the concepts of "coherence" and "cohesive harmony" in relation to each other. She argues that cohesion is the phenomenon on which the foundations of coherence is laid, but coherence requires a particular type of calibration of cohesive relations. She notes that the degree of coherence in a text does not vary either with the numerical or the categorial variation of cohesive ties. It does, however, display a correlation with the degree of interaction between cohesive chains.

Coherence and Cohesive Harmony

Ruqaiya Hasan
Macquarie University, Australia[1]

Introduction

What is cohesive harmony, and in what relation does it stand to coherence? One way of answering these questions would be to describe briefly how the concept of cohesive harmony evolved in my work.

In the late 1960s I was engaged in research on children's stories at the Sociological Research Unit at the University of London Institute of Education, under the general directorship of Basil Bernstein. One of the aims of my research project was to check if there existed any correlation between certain social factors and the degree of coherence perceived in the extemporae texts, produced by 6 to 7 year old children from different social backgrounds.

To set such an aim implies, on the one hand, some notion of the nature of coherence, and on the other, the possession of some means whereby a reliable measurement of coherence could be achieved. From the very start, my use of the term coherence has been fairly close to its every day meaning. I used the word to refer to the property of "unity," of "hanging together." By this definition, any object is coherent to the extent that its parts hang together.

Coherence, Language and Situation

It goes without saying that coherence in the text stands in some relation to some state of affairs in the extralinguistic universe, in roughly the same way that in normal, noncitational uses of language, the saying of sentences stands in some relation to a state of affairs in the world of our social or psychological experience. But, perhaps, in view of the prevailing climate of linguistics in the America of the 1960s, it needs to be added, that if for me all this went without saying even at that time, this was because the model I chose to work with is a functional one, in which a systematic relation between form and meaning is a fundamental assumption about the nature of human language, and therefore of the model for its description (de Saussure, 1916; Firth, 1935; Halliday, 1961; Hjelmslev, 1943, 1961; Lamb, 1964). It has been a cherished principle in this approach that "no study of meaning apart from a complete context can be taken seriously" (Firth, 1935). I, therefore, see no reason for making such a fuss over the fact that reference through pronominals, for example, normally implies that someone intends to refer through its use to some specific entity (Morgan, 1978). It is, in my view, wrong to give the impression that there are such specific problems as: how does pronominal reference succeed? or how does a whimperative get interpreted? The core of the problem lies not in accounting for any specific; it lies in a non ad hoc principled account of the relationship of language to the extralinguistic universe. The pronominal is simply a drop in this vast ocean.

Moreover, appeals to intention are notorious for their inability to solve any problems in this domain. More so, since it is obvious that to intend is not necessarily to achieve—witness ambiguities of pronominal reference, presumably unintended. Similarly, to make an assertion is not necessarily to commit oneself to the truthfulness of that which is asserted. The pervasiveness and the pliability of a sign-system is in inverse proportion to how closely this system is tied to individual intent and how far it is constrained to remain faithful in the representation of the exigencies of that which lies outside the system (Eco, 1976; Hasan, 1971a, 1971b; Morton, 1971). It would take me far from my present concerns to enter into a debate about the relative primacy of the individual vs. the community. Let me simply say that I reject as simplistic all those approaches to meaning which place the individual on a pedastal as the sole creator and architect of the meanings he means. I believe that the act of meaning is made possible only through the creation and existence of codes which provide the potential for meaning; and that in a very important sense, we are able to mean through language, by virtue of the fact that the signs of language have meanings quite irrespective of what any one individual might contrive to mean by them on an individual occasion. I raise these points at the start to explain why my explanations of the meanings of linguistic phenomena are not couched in the terminology popular here today (Van Dijk, 1977; Morgan, 1978). When I say that coherence in a text is the property of hanging together, I mean that the patterns of language manifest—or realize—the existence of semantic bonds, because it is in their nature to do so; not simply because someone is making them do so. The system of language is a resource for meaning (Halliday, 1977). The wordings make meanings accessible, just as meanings motivate wordings.

Coherence and Immediate Constituency

When we attempt to locate the lexico-grammatical means through which the semantic fact of hanging together is reflected, we are soon led into an examination of nonstructural relations. Since structure is a grossly overused term, let me clarify at once that it refers here to immediate constituency structures, through which a hierarchy of unit size is determined. For example, a clause is bigger than a phrase precisely because phrases function as immediate constituents of clauses.

Nonstructural relations are crucial to the creation of coherence not because structure is entirely irrelevant to it, but rather because structure is a uniformly integrative device; and as an integrative device, it does not go far enough in the explication of the notion. Let me elaborate these points further. It seems obvious that whatever is recognized as a structure must, by definition, hang together. This is irrespective of whether the content appears sensical or nonsensical. *The cow jumped over the moon* is a perfectly coherent sentence, even though one may doubt that it makes sense. In fact, barring word salads, the question of sense and nonsense arises only with regard to units perceived as a structure; and seen from this point of view, nonsense need not necessarily be incoherent.

However, if our notion of coherence took into account only such structural relations, then language pieces containing the same number of units would be equally coherent; the only correlate for variation in coherence would be the length of the piece measured in terms of some structural unit. For example, the more clauses a text contained the more coherent it would be. There is no difficulty in demonstrating that such views are empirically untenable. Consider the following examples:

1. I have a cat. It loves liver. It sleeps all day. It is black.
2. A cat is sitting on a fence. A fence is made of wood. Carpenters work with wood. Wood planks can be bought from a timberyard.
3. The captain has made a mistake. He will marry the female and bury her in an empty hole. He felt faint. So he sat against the drain which was under repair. The enemy were trapped. So the taxis had to hurry to the pleasant grassy slopes to save them.

Whatever method of analysis we adopt, 3 stands out: it is the longest piece and yet it is also the least coherent of the three, which is somewhat ironical since it is an actual example of language from a language teaching class! Note that each clause, and each clause complex, is coherent within itself, just as the clauses of 1 and 2 are. The latter two would also be seen as varying in coherence, with 1 being rated more coherent than 2. The semantic aspect of the coherence of 1 lies in the fact that it displays what we may refer to as "topical" unity. The lexico-grammatical reflection of this topical unity is provided partly by the construction of the identity chain through the pronominal reference *it*, and partly through the homogeneous selection of the (usitative) tense.

Hopefully this examination has revealed five things:

i. that normal speakers are sensitive to variation in coherence;
ii. that textual coherence is a relative, not an absolute property, so that it is possible to rank a group of texts on a cline (Halliday, 1961) from most coherent to least coherent; and as the membership of the group of texts changes, so might the position of individual texts on the cline;
iii. that coherence is an essential property of texts; consider that normal speakers of English would not regard 3 as a text;
iv. that wherever a textual fragment exceeds one simple sentence the variation in coherence does not correlate with structural facts. Such structure is only a necessary but insufficient condition.
v. that, therefore, an examination of coherence necessarily involves an examination of nonstructural relations of the type that we refer to as cohesion.

The Starting Point for the Analysis

Armed with these assumptions when I approached my data to determine the degrees of coherence in the texts, I assumed also, and perhaps with some justification, that the means for conducting such an enquiry were available to me. By this time the major part of my research into cohesive mechanisms had been completed and a preliminary draft of *Cohesion in English* (1976) was already in existence. This described in some detail the resources that a speaker of English has in the system for indicating the semantic bonds between parts of his utterance. A brief summary of these is presented in Table 1.

TABLE 1

I. REFERENCE	IV. CONJUNCTION
1. pronominal	1. *cohesive conjunctive*
2. definite article	a. additive
3. demonstrative	b. adversative
4. comparative	c. temporal
II. SUBSTITUTION & ELLIPSIS	d. causal
1. nominal	2. *continuative*
2. verbal	
3. clausal	
III. LEXICAL	
1. *reiteration*	
a. repetition	
b. synonymy	
c. super-ordinate	
d. general word	
2. *collocation*	

Each of the categories entered in Table 1 is a potential cohesive device; it represents a resource for the creation of cohesion. Cohesion is actually created when through the use of a member of any one of these categories, a semantic bond is created between this member and some other element in the textual environment. The two elements thus linked form a cohesive tie (Halliday & Hasan, 1976). Thus central to the notion of cohesion is the idea of "two-ness." In fact, where lexical cohesion is concerned, the very terms carry the implication of reciprocal elements since an element by itself can neither be its own repetition nor can it be synonymous with itself. So, when a language piece is analyzed for its cohesion, the focus is primarily on the ties, not solely on the occurrence of a member from some category listed in Table 1.

Cohesive Devices as the Realization of Semantic Bonds

It has been remarked (Dressler, 1978) that the above categories are surface phenomena. Neither the term "surface" nor "deep" appears to me to be well-defined or theoretically motivated. If by surface phenomena is meant "lexico-grammatical categories," then certainly the devices described above are surface phenomena. But in accepting this, I do not accept the implicit assumption that therefore they have little or nothing to do with "deep" phenomena, if by deep is meant semantic. It is not possible to view language as a sign system a la Saussure, and to maintain that there is an irreconcilable gulf between "surface" and "deep"—between "form" and "meaning."

To hold this position does not imply the simplistic idea of a one-to-one correspondence between formal and semantic categories. The postulate of any category in language—be it semantic or formal—involves an examination of its relation to other categories. As Halliday has argued, these relations are not limited to relations on the same level; in assigning a category a status, one needs also to look "above" to see what the category realizes, and to look "below" to see how it is itself realized (Halliday, 1977). One of the reasons for the indeterminacy of the semantic value of a formal category lies in the fact that it is seldom determined entirely by reference to formal or to semantic criteria (Hasan, 1971a). Thus although a one-to-one correlation between form and meaning, surface and deep phenomena does not exist, it is still possible to state the normal semantic value of a category (Hasan, 1971a; Belinger, 1977). As cohesion is a part of the system of language, these principles apply to it as well.

For example, when at least one term of a cohesive tie belongs to any category I:1-3 in Table 1, then typically the semantic bond between the members of the tie is that of co-referentiality (Hasan, 1979; Halliday & Hasan, 1980); this is the relation between *a cat* and *it* in the first two clauses of example 1 above. The word "typically" should be emphasized since the establishment of this relation is not an invariant condition. However it can be claimed that the pronominal functions, along with the definite article, as the most typical means of realizing the semantic bond of co-referentiality; the demonstrative has an overlapping but not identical function. The comparative is particularly interesting as it appears to be poised genuinely between I and II. When the categories of II:1-3 act as one member of a cohesive tie, the semantic bond is typically that of co-classification (Hasan, 1979; Halliday & Hasan, 1980). In a textual fragment such as:

4. My husband plays cello. My son does, too.

Although *does* is interpreted through its relation to *plays cello*, the playing of cello that my son does is not an event identical with the playing of cello that my husband does. The two events belong to the same class—are related through coclassification—they are two distinct members of that class. Comparative reference involves both coreferentiality and coclassification. For example in

5. Find me a riper mango!

The comparative *riper* can only be interpreted as *as ripe as some identified degree of ripeness plus a little more ripe.*

Note that all categories listed in the top left box of Table 1 involve co-interpretation (Halliday & Hasan, 1976). The potential for their cohesive function lies precisely in the fact that their interpretation is arrived at by relation to some other source, and it is the location of this interpretative source which determines the phoric status of the tie. If this source precedes the cohesive device, as in *a cat, it* in example 1, then the tie is anaphoric; if it follows as in 6, it is known as cataphoric.

6. *He who laughs last* laughs longest.

Alternatively, if the interpretative source is mediated through the extra-linguistic situation only, the direction of the source is said to be exophoric.

The devices of lexical cohesion do not involve co-interpretation. Although some of these devices are capable of indicating the semantic bond of co-referentiality under specifiable conditions (Hasan, forthcoming; Halliday & Hasan, 1976, 1980), their most typical semantic function is to indicate coextension, so that the lexical chain comes closest to the realization of some part of a semantic field.

The total set of cohesive devices I-III in Table 1 have something in common: they can all be regarded as "componential," in the sense that they realize only parts of individual messages. The integration between the messages is a product of the cohesion between specific parts of individual messages. In this respect the cohesive conjunctive differs from the devices in the left column, since these latter devices are the overt indication of a logical relation between two (or more) messages qua messages. The discussion has been brief by necessity, but hopefully it is clear that to talk about the lexico-grammatical devices of cohesion is not necessarily to remain divorced from semantic considerations.

Initial Hypotheses Regarding Coherence

In my analysis of the data, I started from two hypotheses:
  i. the larger the number of cohesive ties in a language piece, the greater the coherence;

ii. the greater the continuity of ties relating to each other, the greater the coherence.

Expressed informally my hypothesis was that degrees of coherence correlated with the density of the occurrence of cohesive ties; and if two texts containing the same number of cohesive ties displayed a difference in coherence, this would correlate with what proportion of the ties combined to form a chain. It is fairly easy to construct examples to show that these expectations were not unreasonable. Thus consider:

7. John was quite tired out (a) so he went to bed early (b). There was an old man (c) and he had two daughters (d).

8. John was quite tired out (a) so he went to bed early (b). However, not feeling sleepy (c) he decided to read (d).

Seen as a whole, 7 is obviously less coherent than 8. No doubt we can explain this fact by saying that, whereas 8 describes an integrated event, 7 does not. However, this is not a complete explanation; nor can it be used as the criterion for determining the perceived degree of coherence. Quite obviously, the integratedness of 8 is reconstituted for the reader through the normal operations of language as a meaning potential. In the last resort, the knowledge about the integratedness of the event in 8 is information processed; and since there is no other initial source of information here except the language piece itself, the form of the message must contain enough basis for the processing of this information. In the study of coherence in texts, it is these bases that must be made explicit. Thus note that although the number of cohesive ties in both 7 and 8 is the same, it is only in the latter that the ties form chains, as shown in Table 2.

TABLE 2

7	8
tie 1. John (a) ◄——— he (b)	tie 1. John (a) ◄——— he (b)
tie 2. message (a) ◄——SO———► (b)	tie 2. message (a) ◄——SO———► (b)
tie 3. an old man (c) ◄——— he (d)	tie 3. message (b) ◄———HOWEVER———► (c, d)
tie 4. message (c) ◄———AND———► (d)	tie 4. he (b) ◄——— he (d)
chain. NONE	chain 1. John (a) ◄——— he (b) ◄——— he (d)
	chain 2. (a) ◄——SO———► (b) ◄———HOWEVER———► (c, d)

Admittedly, the analysis overlooks some factors. In particular, instead of the comma between (c) and (d) in 8, I could have indicated another (covert) logical relation THEREFORE. But this would only have emphasized the fact that my initial hypotheses were not unreasonable, since there do exist some conditions under which they would appear to permit a correct characterization of the source of incoherence.

Hasan

Procedures for Initial Analysis

I tried to categorize the texts in my data on the basis of informal reader reaction. The analysis of the texts for cohesive patterns and its informal ranking for degrees of coherence were in random order to ensure that the knowledge of the rating of the text would not subconsciouly affect their informal analysis. This precaution was perhaps unnecessary, since most categories of cohesive devices are reasonably identifiable so that subjective interreferences were minimal and confined to specific areas (see A9).

To obtain the ranking for coherence, I would quite informally present a colleague with two (or more) of my texts to determine their relative coherence vis a vis each other. The texts produced below were judged by five such (unsuspecting) "informants," who all, unknowingly, agreed with my ranking of the three on the cline of coherence: A10 was judged most coherent of the three, A13 least, while A9 was considered less coherent than A10 but more than A13. Since then an unrecorded number of readers have agreed with these rankings.

A10   1. (there was) there was once a little girl and a little boy and a dog
         2. and the sailor was their daddy
         3. and the little doggy was white
         4. and they liked the little doggy
         5. and they stroke it
         6. and they fed it
         7. and he run away
         8. and then (um the little dog) daddy (um) had to go on a ship
         9. and the children missed 'em
       10. and they began to cry

A9   1. there was a girl and a boy
         2. there was a dog and a sailor
         3. the dog was a furry dog
         4. and the girl and the boy were sitting down
         5. and the sailor was standing up
         6. and the teddy-bear was lying down asleep
         7. and the sailor was looking at (the dog) the bear
         8. the little girl was laying down too
         9. she wasn't asleep
       10. and the boy was sitting up
       11. he was looking at the bear too

A13   1. once upon a time (there was two little) there was a little girl and a boy
         2. and they went aboard a ship

3. and the sailor said to them to go and find a carriage
4. don't go on the ship here because I'm trying to dive
5. but the dog came along
6. and threw himself into the sea
7. and then he came back
8. and (all) they all went home
9. and had a party
10. and they lived happily ever after

The conversations for the transcription and for the delimitation of the clause boundaries are discussed in Hasan (n.d., memo).

Grammatical Cohesion in Initial Analysis

I shall use the above three examples to show how my initial hypothesis was invalidated, so that it cannot be maintained that variation in coherence correlates with variation in either the number of cohesive ties or their proportion in chains. In demonstrating this, I shall focus primarily on those problems the search for whose solution finally made me move towards the notion of cohesive harmony. For various reasons which I need not enter into here, the analysis reported below ignores the cohesive conjunctives. Tables 3-5 present an account of all other grammatical cohesive devices which occurred in the three texts. The first column enumerates the cohesive devices, the second contains interpretative source, while the third column states the phoric status of the tie. The final column provides particulars of chain formation. The chain relation is stated in terms of the address of the preceding members in the same chain; thus in Table 3 the fourth entry 4-3-1 is read as: *it* clause 5 is in chain relation with *the (little doggy)* in clause 4, is in chain relation with *the (little doggy)* in clause 3, is in chain relation with *a dog* in clause 1. Note that when the tie is exophoric, a blank is entered in the second column; where the interpretation of a cohesive device is ambiguous, this is indicated by attaching a question mark to those items which could have functioned as the interpretative source (or part of); finally, for ease of reference, wherever the definitie article is involved, the noun of the relevant nominal group is shown within brackets.

An examination of these tables will show that the pattern of componential grammatical cohesion bears no significant relation to the variation in coherence. Neither the raw score of cohesive ties nor a tie-clause ratio appears to differ significantly from one text to another, as is clear from Table 6.

TABLE 3. Text A10

cohesive device	interpretative source	tie status	chain
2. the (tailor)	—	exophoric	
their	1. a girl, a boy	anaphoric	
3. the (..doggy)	1. a dog	"	
4. they	2. their, the sailor	"	2-1
the (..doggy)	3. the..doggy	"	3-1
5. they	4. they	"	4-2-1
it	4. the..doggy	"	4-3-1
6. they	5. they	"	5-4-2-1
it	5. it	"	5-4-3-1
he	6. it	"	6-5-4-3-1
9. the (children)	6. they	"	6-5-4-2-1
'em	7. it, the sailor	"	6-5-4-3-2
10. they	9. the children	"	9-6-5-4-2-1

TABLE 4. Text A9

cohesive device	interpretative source	tie status	chain
3. the (dog)	2. a dog	anaphoric	
4. the (girl)	1. a girl	"	
the (boy)	1. a boy	"	
5. the (sailor)	2. a sailor	"	
6. the (teddy bear)	—	exophoric	
7. the (sailor)	5. the sailor	anaphoric	5-2
the (bear)	6. the teddy bear	"	
8. the (..girl)	4. the girl	"	4-1
9. she	8. the..girl	"	8-4-1
10. the (boy)	4. the boy	"	4-1
11. he	10. the boy	"	10-4-1
the (bear)	7. the bear	"	7-6

TABLE 5. Text A13

cohesive device	interpretative source	tie status	chain
2. they	1. a girl, a boy	anaphoric	
3. them	2. they	"	2-1
the (sailor)	2. (aboard a) ship	"	
4. the (ship)	2. a ship	"	
here	3. (by) the sailor	"	
I	3. the sailor	"	
5. the (dog)	—	exophoric	
6. Subject-ellipsis	5. the dog	anaphoric	
7. he	6. Subject of	"	6-5
8. they	7. he		
	4. I ?	"	7-?
	3. them		
9. Subject-ellipsis	8. they	"	8-7-?
10. they	9. they	"	9-8-7, ?

TABLE 6

	clauses	cohesive ties	tie per clause
A 10	10	13	1.3
A 9	11	12	1.09
A 13	10	12	1.2

Halliday and Hasan (1976) had argued that the endophoric tie—where the interpretative source is provided by the co-text—is more germane to texture than the exophoric one. Since the interpretative source of the latter type of tie is text-external, the interpretation of the cohesive device is not accessible to those who lack information regarding the immediate context of situation—except in as much as some lexical selections in the text might guide the interpretation. But in this respect, the exophoric tie is somewhat like a tie whose ambiguity is never fully resolved. In neither case can we be certain of arriving at the correct interpretation; a cohesive device lacking endophoric source of explication is as opaque in the absence of the knowledge of the text's environment as is an ambiguous cohesive tie whose ambiguity cannot be resolved by reference to the co-text. For this reason, it seemed valid to separate out both these types of ties from the transparent endophoric ones. The result of this operation is displayed in Table 7.

TABLE 7

	clauses	transparent ties	transparent tie per clause
A 10	10	12	1.2
A 9	11	11	1.00
A 13	10	10	1.00

It is obvious that neither the facts reported in Table 6 nor those in Table 7 can be used to explain variation in the degree of coherence displayed by these texts. Before discussing the grammatical cohesive chains, let us ask if any conclusive evidence can be found from an examination of lexical cohesion.

Lexical Cohesion in Initial Analysis

Tables 8-10 display the facts regarding lexical cohesion, analyzed in terms of the categories in Halliday and Hasan (1976) and briefly summarized in the bottom left hand box of Table 1. In the following tables Roman numerals indicate chain number and the Arabic numerals state the clause number in which the lexical tokens have occurred.

TABLE 8.   Text A10

I. girl 1; boy 1; children 9	3 tokens 2 ties
II. daddy 2; daddy 9	2 " 1 "
III. sailor 2; ship 8	2 " 1 "
IV. dog 1; doggy 3; doggy 4	3 " 2 "
V. run-away 7; go (sail off) 8	2 " 1 "
VI. like 4; miss 9; cry 10	3 " 2 "
Total: 6 chains; 15 tokens; 9 ties	

TABLE 9.   Text A9

I. girl 1; girl 4; girl 8; boy 1; boy 4; boy 10	6 tokens 5 ties
II. sit 4; stand 5; lay 6; lay 8; sit 10	5 " 4 "
III. asleep 6; asleep 9	2 " 1 "
IV. bear 6; bear 7; bear 11	3 " 2 "
V. dog 2; dog 3; dog 3	3 " 2 "
VI. sailor 2; sailor 5; sailor 7	3 " 2 "
VII. look 7; look 11	2 " 1 "
Total: 7 chains; 24 tokens; 17 ties	

TABLE 10.   Text A13

I. ship 2; ship 4; sailor 3; sea 6	4 tokens 3 ties
II. girl 1; boy 1	2 " 1 "
III. * go 2; go 4; go 8; come 5; come 7	5 " 4 "
IV. dive 4; throw (self into sea) 6	2 " 1 "
Total: 4 chains; 13 tokens; 9 ties	
* Note that *go* in *go and find* clause 3 is not treated as a token of the lexical category GO	

The analysis of lexical cohesion in terms of the 1976 model (see Table 1; III) posed serious problems. However before I discuss these, one general point needs to be made.

The triumphs of modern linguistics are more noticeable in the realms of grammar and phonology; by comparison, lexis is a neglected area. Despite suggestive leads from different approaches (Firth, 1957; Halliday, 1966; Sinclair, 1966; Bendix, 1966; Fillmore, 1971), the categories for the description of lexis are no more than a shot in the dark. This has the consequence of creating problems of decision making at every step in the analysis. For example, can it be assumed that word and lexical token are coextensive? If so, how do *sit, sit down* and *sit up* relate to each other? Is *up* in *sit up* and *stand up* a realization of the same lexical category? Indeed, is it valid to use the term lexical category in relation to the traditionally "empty" words, *up, down, in, out, on* and *at*? And most basic of all, what are the ways in which a lexical category may be realized? Are *bachelor* and *unmarried human adult male* alternative realizations of the same lexical category?

These problems are troublesome and affect the analysis of lexical cohesion at every step; but it must be pointed out quite clearly that they are not problems arising from any particular view of cohesion. Rather, their roots lie in our conception of the form of language—and more particularly in our ideas about the relationship between grammar and lexis. In practice, each one of us, no matter what our views on cohesion and/or coherence, meets these problems in the course of attempting analysis; and in practice each one of us finds some working solution. For the analysis of my data, I prepared a flow chart as a heuristic device for the recognition of a lexical category. This operationalized my concept of "lexical category." It appears to me that although this does not ensure the viability of my solutions necessarily, it certainly overcomes the problems of the indeterminacy of what it is that is being analyzed. Thus the problems that I discuss below are solely problems of the analysis of coheshion in the Halliday and Hasan (1976) model.

Since in my approach to the study of coherence, the orientation was primarily quantitative, the question of the identity of a tie became doubly important. However, the counting of ties posed a problem in lexical cohesion. For example, repetition leads to the creation of a tie; so does collocation. Examine then chain III in Table 10. Do we have five ties in this chain or four? Either the state of affairs is as shown in Table 10 or there are three ties of repetition:

go 2 ⟷ go 4
                  go 4 ⟷ go 8
                                    come 5 ⟷ come 7

and also two of collocation between *come* and *go*

come 5 ⟷ go 4
come 7 ⟷ go 8

This problem arises in the first place because reiteration and collocation belong to two distinct dimensions. Tokens may enter into these relations at one and the same time; so that it is possible, if one wishes, to count them as constitution ties both through the relation of reiteration and that of collocation.

Altogether the notion of collocation proved problematic. While I firmly believe that behind the notion of collocation is an intuitive reality, I have come to accept the fact that unless we can unpack the details of the relations involved in collocation in the Firthian sense, it is best to avoid the category in research. The problems of inter-subjective reliability cannot be ignored. If someone felt that there is a collocational tie between *dive* 4 and *sea* 6 in A13, on what grounds could such a statement be either rejected or accepted?

In addition to this problem, the existing categories of lexical cohesion failed to take into account certain semantic bonds. An example would be the relation to equivalence between *sailor* and (*the children's*) *daddy* in A10. Such problems lead me naturally to a modification of the lexical categories of cohesion; but before I discuss these, let me take a brief look at the findings presented in Tables 8-10. Recall that chains had a significant status in the original hypothesis (see section 6); but as the table below shows, the findings were quite inconsistent with any possibility of correlation between lexical chains and variations in the degree of coherence:

TABLE 11

	chain per cl	token per cl	token per ch	tie per ch	tie per cl
A10	.6	1.5	2.5	1.5	.9
A9	.6	2.1	3.4	2.4	1.5
A13	.4	1.3	3.2	2.2	.9

Grammatical Cohesive Chains in Initial Analysis

An examination of the grammatical cohesive chains did not yield a more positive result. I reproduce the details of the grammatical chains to facilitate discussion.

TABLE 12.   Text A10

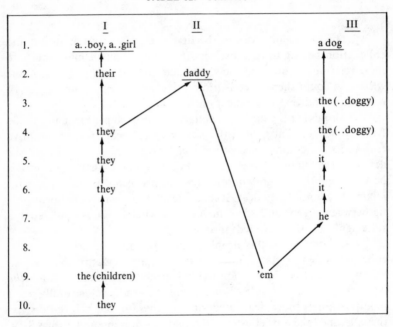

The ultimate referent of each chain is underlined; in addition, where this item is itself exophoric, it has been starred. The fact that one can talk about the "ultimate referent" indicates that the members of these chains refer to the self-same situational entity, whatever that may be. In other words, the semantic bond between the members of the tie is that of co-referentiality (see discussion in section 5 above). However, within limits, the referential value of such chains can vary from one point to another. There are two ways in which this can come about: either there is a conjunction of chains, or there is a disjunction; both possibilities are exemplified in A10.

TABLE 13. Text A9

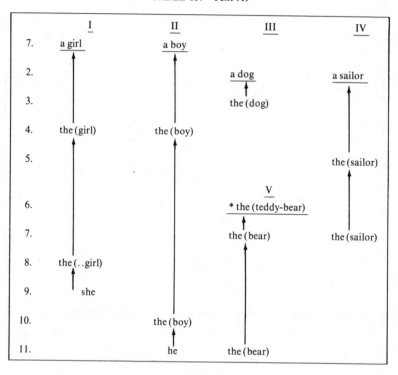

Chain Connection

Consider chain I (Table 12). The cohesive items *they, their* have to be interpreted as *girl* and *boy* mentioned in clause 1 of the text. In clause 4, however, the referent of *they* is not just *girl, boy* but also *daddy* (the justification for this interpretation is discussed below in section 13). This interpretation of chain I holds until clause 6. The chain is not picked up in clause 7, and in clause 8 there is lexical evidence for chain disjunction; *dad* is no longer a referent of chain I. In clause 9, chains II and III are combined through a joint reference to *daddy* and *dog*, both

TABLE 14. Text A13

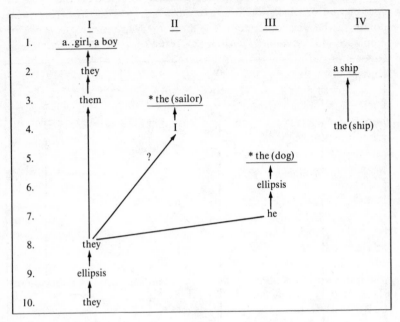

of whom were missed by the children. Thus schematically the chain pattern in A10 can be represented as follows:

TABLE 15

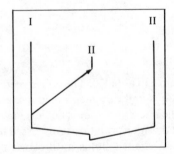

Hasan

Note that each chain connection, whether of the type of conjunction or of disjunction, is realizationally related to the crucial points in the development of the story. More recently, the work of Applebee (1978) would appear to support the hypothesis that chain connection patterns in texts are an expression of the development of the content of the text.

Chain disjunction is a possibility open to only complex chains. Such chains are created in two ways. Either a chain can start off with a composite referent as, for example, in A10 and A13, where the pronominal in the second clause of each text refers to more than one entity, or a complex chain may be created through the conjunction of two chains as exemplified in A10. A composite referent involves a negation of functional differentiation between two or more separate entities; note that both in A10 and A13 whatever is asserted of *girl* is also asserted of *boy*. When chain conjunction takes place, precisely the same principle applies in respect of the referent entities of the chains so connected. Nonetheless in both cases the option is open of introducing a differentiation of function between the separate entities. The point at which this option is taken is the point at which chain disjunction takes place.

It is interesting that the chain connection pattern in A13, the least coherent text, is something like a mismanaged echo of the chain connections in A10, the most coherent text. Here A9 is the odd one out: it contains five simple chains, none of which connects with another. Had our data not contained texts of the type A13, we might have been misled into believing that chain connection plays an important role in determining the degree of coherence in a text. I believe this is not the case. If the points in chain connection are related to the development of the content, the presence and absence—as well as probably the degree of chain connection itself—might correlate in interesting ways with text-genre variation. Note that A13 is a putative story in the same vein as A10, but A9 cannot be seen as a story, except by special dispensation.

Unresolved Ambiguity and Coherence

Table 14 presents a picture of chain connections in A13. Like A10 it has four chains, and but for the unresolved ambiguity of *they (all)* in clause 8, it might have displayed the same degree of chain connection. This ambiguity contaminates both the cohesive devices of 9 and 10. From the co-text only this much is clear, that whatever the interpretation of *they (all)* in clause 8 must also be the interpretation of the elliptical subject of clause 9 and the *they* of clause 10. We are, therefore, justified in putting 8, 9, and 10 in one chain, but quite unable to decide what the referents for these terms are. Do they cover *dog* as well as the *sailor*? The presence of *all* in 8 would normally imply that the referent of *they* should exceed two entities (at least); further, following the principles for the disambiguation of pronominals, *dog* would appear to qualify as one of the referents both because of its proximity to *they* and because of the thematic position of *he* and *they*. Both of these conditions can be overridden if there is good reason, but I believe no such reasons can be invoked in this case. The implication is that the entities referred to by *they* must include aforementioned *dog* and *boy* and *girl*. Whether ot not the *sailor* too is intended by the speaker cannot be determined. This explains the question mark attached to the line connecting *they* to *sailor*.

Questions Arising from Initial Analysis

My data consisted of 80 texts and a good proportion of it was analyzed following the above methods. This served the useful purpose of drawing attention to several questions. Two of these—relating to the analysis of lexical cohesion—have already been mentioned (see section 9 above); attention is drawn to others below.

It so happened that unresolved ambiguity co-occurred significantly frequently in the environment of textual incoherence. The question naturally arose: is there a logical relationship between the two phenomena? It is obvious from texts of type A9 that the lack of coherence went beyond unresolved ambiguity; texts could be judged incoherent even in the absence of unresolved ambiguity.

The examination of chain formation patterns revealed two facts. In the first place, the separation of lexical and grammatical cohesive chains quite clearly did violence to certain aspects of the text's semantic organization. For example, it is clear from a consideration of chains I and II in Table 12 that, if *daddy* (clause 8) cannot be included, the picture regarding chain disjunction is distorted. But between *daddy* (clause 8) and chain II, there is no grammatical cohesive relation; the token would be said to cohere through lexical repetition to *daddy* (clause 1). It became apparent that text being a semantic unity (Halliday & Hasan, 1976), the lexicogrammatical categories of cohesion occurring in a text should be so aligned as to reflect readily the fact of this semantic unity. This implied a search for some generally valid principle which would place both the lexical and grammatical cohesive facts in relation to each other. Secondly, the patterns of chain connection in the domain of lexical cohesion led me to wonder if analogous chain connections also took place where lexical chains were concerned.

The revision of lexical cohesive categories and the search for some answer to these three questions finally resulted in the definition of the concept of cohesive harmony.

The Revision of Lexical Cohesive Categories

The revision of lexical cohesive categories can be described under three heads:

    i. the introduction of new categories;
    ii. the elaboration of the existing ones;
    iii. the exclusion of collocation.

Lexical cohesion appears to belong to two primary types: that mediated through "general" lexical relations and that mediated through "instantial" ones. The 1976 model contained details of most of the former type; however, instantial lexical cohesion is a significant resource for textual unity.

The categories of general lexical cohesive devices are based upon semantic bonds which are supratextual, with a language-wide validity. Consider the cohesive device of the use of synonyms as an example: such synonyms as *write* and *scrawl* cohere with each other. The semantic bond between them is that of the identity of their experiential meaning. However, this identity of experiential meaning between these two is a fact of the system of English. That is why it is possible to provide a citation of the above type, where they are dissociated from a real context of utterance, and yet constitute a valid example of this meaning relation. Quite irrespective of particular texts, we know that each member of the pair is synonymous with the other; the relation exists in the system.

By contrast, instantial lexical relations are text-bound. Their validity is an artifact of the text itself, and does not extend to the system. There is, therefore, no shortcut to their exemplification, as the relation attains its validity only through the linguistic context of the utterance. For example, in A10 *(the) sailor* and *(their) daddy* are related to each other through an instantial cohesive relation of "equivalence"; the text equates *sailor* and *daddy*. But this relation of referential identity is a fact of *this* text; it cannot be maintained that in the system of English *sailor* and *daddy* are so related.

A glance at Table 1 (III: 1 a-d) will show that the main relations here are those of similarity and inclusion. In the 1976 model, similarity subsumed "same" and "different," while inclusion covered both "including" and "included." In the revision, these aspects were separated, and thus made, perhaps, more operational. The total set of these cohesive categories is listed in Table 16.

TABLE 16

Categories of lexical cohesion		
A. *General*		
	i. repetition	leave, leaving, left
	ii. synonymy	leave, depart
	iii. antonymy	leave, arrive
	iv. hyponymy	travel, leave (including co-hyponyms, leave, arrive)
	v. meronymy	hand, finger (including co-meronyms, finger, thumb)
B. *Instantial*		
	i. equivalence	the *sailor* was their *daddy*; *you* be the *patient*, *I'll* be the *doctor*
	ii. naming	the *dog* was called *Toto*; they named the *dog* *Fluffy*
	iii. semblance	the *deck* was like a *pool*; all my *pleasures* are like *yesterdays*

Note that Table 16 does not include collocation. It proved remarkably difficult to operationalize this category sufficiently to ensure consistent analysis. But the reason for its exclusion is not entirely negative. Many relations previously handled under this rubric are now subsumed in the revised version. This came about from a modified definition of lexical chain, which was now said to consist of that set of tokens where the members of any possible pair stand in any of the relations enumerated in A: i-v of Table 16, with the instantially related tokens being treated as one unity. The notion of chain connection applied to lexical chains further permits the inclusion of such chains as *pear, peel, core, pip* into another such as *sustenance, food, vegetable, fruit.* Note that such chain conjunction would be related to the topical development of the text in roughly the same way as that characteristic of grammatical cohesive chains. In practical terms, then, it is no longer necessary to think of *go* and *come* as related to each other through collocation; they fall within the same chain on the ground of being antonyms.

Although the above minimized the effects of the exclusion of collocation, it does not entirely cover the phenomena handled through collocation. Certain relations intuitively recognized as cohesive cannot be accounted for in the revised version. For example chain I in Table 10 reads *ship ship sailor sea*, where the relationship between *sailor* and *ship* and *sea* was said to be collocative. However, it was not possible to bring them together into the same chain under the revised version. Attaching greater priority to consistency of analysis, I accepted—with regret—this shortcoming of the analytical categories. My work in this area has since helped me to handle these relations as well; but since this latter development was not available when these texts were analyzed, its details are of no consequence here. I believe, however, that this shortcoming has not impaired my analysis since the examination of coherence will reveal that there are many ways in which a crucial relation can be picked up, so long as it is truly crucial.

Lexis and Unresolved Ambiguity

Given the definition of the lexical chain above, we could have a chain such as *sailor-daddy children girl boy*. In this chain *sailor-daddy* is seen as one unit; the semantic bond between the two tokens is that of co-referentiality, which is realized here through the cohesive device of instantial equivalence. But as pointed out in section 5, the typical realization of co-referentiality is through a tie, one member of which is either a pronominal or the definite article *the*.

In a very important sense, the grammatical cohesive ties are like the instantial lexical ones: both are text-bound—*they* cannot always be interpreted as *(the) children* or *it* as *(the) dog*. The justification for this interpretation is typically textually provided. This highlights the role of the lexical tokens in the text in determining the interpretation of what I have referred to as implicit cohesive devices (Hasan, 1975, 1979, 1980, forthcoming). If in A10 *the children* can be interpreted as the same *boy* and *girl* mentioned first in clause 1 of the text, this is because lexical and grammatical cohesion operates harmoniously and by doing so leads us to this interpretation.

It should follow from the above argument that unresolved ambiguity would occur in the environment of "lexical neutrality"

(Hasan, forthcoming), for where lexis is simply "incompatible," what we perceive is not ambiguity, but irrelevance. For example, the various occurrences of *he* in example 3 are not seen as ambiguous, but as irrelevant to (not cohering with) *the captain* in the first sentence. We are able to arrive at this conclusion because of the incompatibility of the lexical selections. An examination of unresolved ambiguity in my data is consistent with the hypothesis that it occurs in the environment of lexical neutrality. This is, for example, the case in A13. Consider what effect a rewrite such as the following for clauses 7-9 of A13 would have on the ambiguity:

A13.
      7'. and then he swam back
      8'. and they all went and found another carriage
      9'. and they played together

True, that clause 10 is still a rather hasty ritual closing of the narrative; but since lexical selections are no longer neutral, receiving support from selections in other parts of the text, most readers would interpret *they* in 8' as *the girl, the boy and the dog*.

Often in the data there were cases of potential ambiguity which went unnoticed, simply because of the harmonious functioning of lexical and grammatical cohesion. There is one such point, for example, in A10, where a sudden shift is made by the child from *it* to *he* to refer to *the dog*. Consider how unresolvable ambiguity can be created by a rewrite of clauses 5-10, as follows:

A10.
      5'. and it used to be in the garden
      6'. and it was nice and cuddly
      7'. and he run away
      8'. and then he had to go
      9'. and they were alone
      10'. and they were very very sad

In the original text we interpret *he* (clause 7) as *the little doggy* without any hesitation; in the rewrite this interpretation becomes subject to doubt. Those factors in the original text which permitted the treatment of *he* as unambiguous are not confined to any one location. On the one hand there is support from *stroke* and *feed*, and on the other hand from *daddy* and *children* and from *missing* and *crying*. These patterns cumulatively determine that *he=it* and that *it=dog*.

An interesting implication of the above discussion would be that a reader's tolerance for "ungrammaticality," incomplete structures, and unmotivated repetition is likely to remain in proportion to the harmonious operation of lexical and grammatical cohesion in a text. Such phenomena would affect the processing of a text adversely only to the extent that lexical and grammatical cohesion may not be seen as supportive of each other.

Revised Principles for Chain Formation

In section 5, I have argued that the categories of cohesive devices as shown in Table 1 are semantically motivated. This semantic motivation is general in nature. Thus the assertion that reference devices typically involve co-referentiality can be seen as a statement about the system of English. When we consider the importance of the mutual support that lexical and grammatical cohesion must provide for each other in specific texts, to enable correct processing, it becomes obvious that despite the systemic validity of their separation, the two should also be seen in relation to each other. And such a valid alignment of the two can be made by reference to their place in the economy of the text. The practical consequence of this approach is that we have to find principles for chain formation which face in two directions: they must be such as to permit the chain's valid relation to the system *and at the same time* they must be such as to permit the chain's relation to the text as a process.

From this point of view we can recognize two major categories of chain: the "identity chain" and the "similarity chain" (Hasan, 1979, 1980). The members of an identity chain are held together by the semantic bond of co-referentiality. This meaning relation may be realized either through pronominal cohesion as in *a. .girl* and *a. .boy←their* (clauses 1 and 2: text A10), or through simple equivalence as in *sailor←daddy* (clause 2: text A10), or through simple lexical repetition *if* entities in question are generic, or through a combined operation of grammatical and lexical cohesion as in *a. .girl* and *a. .boy←the children*, through the mediation of other intermediate pronominals (clause 1 and 9: text A10). The categories of English capable of realizing co-referentiality and the general conditions for the interpretation of these categories are facts of the system of language, but the specific content of the categories is determined by the text's status as language operative in a context of situation. This amounts to saying that the specifics of co-referentiality are situationally—and to that extent text-specifically—determined. In this sense the identity chain is always textbound. The identity chain (ic) is a requirement for the construction of the text because the entities, events, circumstances that one is talking about need to be made specific if there is to be repeated mention of the same.

Similarity chains (sc) are not textbound. The semantic bond between the members of such chains is either that of coclassification or of coextension (see section 5 above and Hasan, 1979, 1980). Coclassification may be realized either by substitutive or elliptical cohesion, or under certain conditions by simple lexical repetition, while coextension is realized only through lexical cohesive categories of the type listed under A: i-v in Table 16. Obviously the actual shape of a sc varies from one text to another; however, both the general conditions of its formation and the specific content of each of its terms are facts of the system of the language. And this is especially so in the case of coextension. Since the scs are a realization of particular portions of semantic fields, they have a dual function in the economy of the text: on the one hand they reflect the generic status of the text, and on the other they contribute to its individuality (Hasan, 1980).

In a normal nonminimal text, the presence of both types of chains is necessary. It is certainly possible to construct short texts in which only one IC may be found: the very first example in this paper is one such. But texts of this type tend to be "brittle": their unity can be broken very easily. So, if in example 1, the homogeneity of tense selection is disturbed, the unity of the text suffers greatly. By contrast, in A10, a couple of wrong tense selections are taken in stride; far from the text's unity being affected, the reader automatically reads *stroked* for *stroke* in clause 5 and *ran away* for *run away* in clause 7. It is also possible to construct short texts with only scs, but such texts tend to give an effect of oddness, perhaps because they often sound like an inventory of possible state of affairs, having no means for building specificity. Example 2 of this paper belongs to this type. In the last resort it is possible to construct minimal texts such that they display no cohesion whatever. But it would be shortsighted to argue from these texts that cohesion is not crucial to text construction, just as it would be shortsighted to argue about the properties of the grammar of English from a consideration of the language of telegrams. In my data consisting of 80 texts, there was not one single example with either just ICs or just scs; both occurred side by side.

The Analysis of Chains in Texts A10, A9 and A13

The ICs and the scs in these texts are presented in Tables 17-19. The top half of each table displays the ICs, the bottom half is concerned with the scs. The address of each token is provided. Where there is evidence of chain connection, the connected chains are boxed in. Tokens underlined with solid lines are those yielded from an interpretation of pronominals; those with broken underlining have been rendered coreferential partly through the functioning of the definite article *the*.

TABLE 17.   Text A10

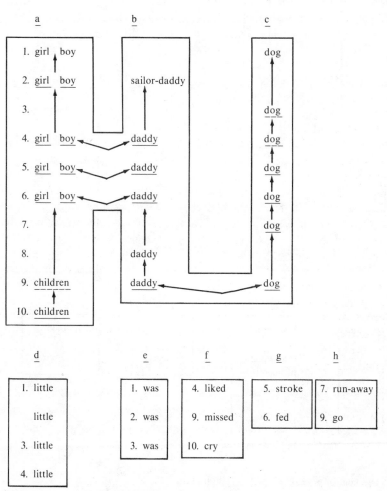

Total number of chains: 8   Total tokens in SCs: 14
Total tokens in ICs: 26   Total tokens in chains: 40

TABLE 18. Text A9

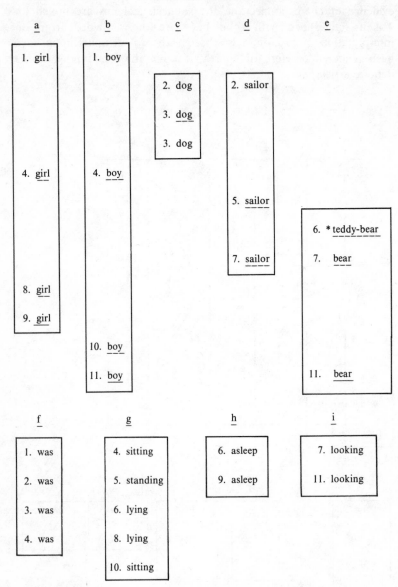

a	b	c	d	e
1. girl	1. boy			
		2. dog	2. sailor	
		3. dog		
		3. dog		
4. girl	4. boy			
			5. sailor	
				6. * teddy-bear
			7. sailor	7. bear
8. girl				
9. girl				
	10. boy			
	11. boy			11. bear

f	g	h	i
1. was	4. sitting	6. asleep	7. looking
2. was	5. standing	9. asleep	11. looking
3. was	6. lying		
4. was	8. lying		
	10. sitting		

Total number of chains: 9   Total tokens in SCs: 13
Total tokens in ICs: 17   Total tokens in chains: 30

208   Hasan

TABLE 19. Text A13

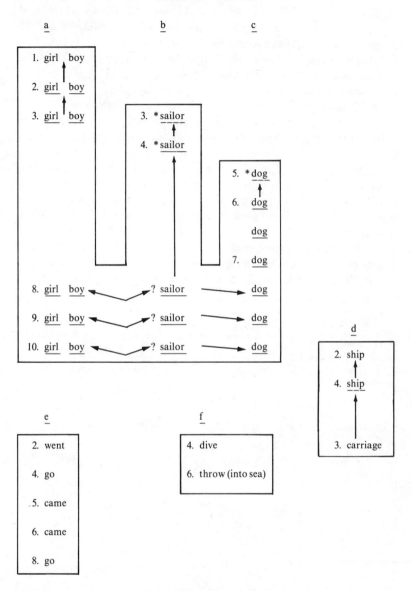

a	b	c

1. girl ↑ boy
2. girl boy
3. girl boy

3. *sailor ↑
4. *sailor

5. *dog ↑
6. dog

dog

7. dog

8. girl boy ← ? sailor → dog
9. girl boy ← ? sailor → dog
10. girl boy ← ? sailor → dog

d

2. ship ↑
4. ship ↑

3. carriage

e	f

2. went
4. go
5. came
6. came
8. go

4. dive
6. throw (into sea)

Total number of chains: 6   Total tokens in SC : 10
Total tokens in ICs: 24 (21)   Total tokens in chains: 34 (31)

Coherence and Cohesive Harmony   209

It would be useful to compare the top half of Tables 17-19 with Tables 12-14 and the bottom half with Tables 8-10. The facts presented in Tables 12-14 pertain to grammatical cohesive chains, those in 8-10 relate to lexical cohesive chains only. It is largely these same facts that are now realigned in Tables 17-19, by reference to their functioning in the economy of the text. But the foundation of these chains is still laid on cohesive categories. This is part of the justification for the claim that the basis for textual coherence lies in cohesion. A situationally chaotic scene of some accident, or a fight, for example, can be rendered coherently in a text. And to this extent, situational coherence is not a prior requirement for the existence of coherence in a text which describes these situations. Coherence is not a picture of reality; it is a representation—just like other semantic phenomena in language. The coherence arises from the imposition of a grid upon sensory precepts; the categories of cohesion are the lexicogrammatical indication of the details of such a grid.

Note that the total number of tokens occurring in each text is in excess of those subsumed in chains as shown in the above Tables. The details of tokens which fall outside chains in these texts are presented below:

TABLE 20

A10	A9	A13	
1. once		once-upon-a-time	little
2.			
3. white	furry	said	go-find
4.		trying	here (near sailor)
5.			
6.		sea	
7.			
8. ship	little	all	home
9.		had (pro-Verb)	party
10.		lived-happily-ever-after	

Those tokens in a text which are not subsumed in chains may be referred to as "peripheral tokens" (PT); this label reflects a hypothesis that such tokens are not crucial to the organization of the experiential and textual meanings. By contrast, tokens subsumed in chains may be referred to as "relevant tokens" (RT). The label is again mnemonic: such tokens were found to be relevant in two interrelated ways. In the first place, they are related to each other through cohesion, and secondly they are related to the topical development of the text. The sum of PT and RT in a text is the sum of its tokens. This for the three texts under review can be presented as in Table 21.

TABLE 21

	PT	RT	Total token (TT)
A10	3	40	43
A9	2	30	32
A13	12	34 (31)	46 (43)

Both in Table 19 and 21 the lines relating to A13 show two figures. The higher figure is calculated with *sailor* as one of the referents of the grammatical cohesive devices in clauses 8, 9, 10. Thus the ambiguity of the text is always being kept in focus, and further comments will be made about it in the section below.

Chain Interaction and Cohesive Harmony

The revised conception of chains has the effect of integrating the lexical and grammatical cohesive patterns of the text, so that they are seen neither as just lexical nor as just grammatical, but have a status by reference to their potential function in the text. Why is it then that Table 21 shows no significant correlation to the degree of coherence perceived by readers in these texts? This is because the final step which clinches the concept of cohesive harmony has not yet been taken. It remains still to enquire if, and how, these chains are related to each other. Table 17 has shown patterns of chain conjunction and chain disjunction; it was suggested that analogous patterns may also be found in similarity chains. But such chain connections are a matter of the internal organization of chains whereby a simple chain may be turned into a complex one or vice versa. What we need to ask now is whether individual chains—both simple and complex—interact with each other so that this interaction remains exocentric to the individual interacting chains but makes a significant difference to the unity of the text as a whole.

Such interaction does take place. It happens when two or more members of a chain stand in an identical functional relation to two or more members of another chain. Let me provide an example by a consideration of some of the chains in text A10; we can show that members of the complex chain *a-b* interact with members of chain *c* and *g*. This happens because the first-mentioned have the function of "actor" vis a vis the member of *g* while members of *c* have the function of "goal" vis a vis *g*. A schematic display is shown in Table 22.

TABLE 22

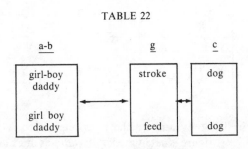

Note that each of these chains is itself constructed on a semantic principle which creates unity amongst its own members; now through the examination of the interaction of individual chains with each other a further source of unity is laid bare. This source resides in the fact that similar "things" are said about similar/same "entities," "events," etc. Why chain interaction is so important will be discussed in some detail below when I have demonstrated its relevance to the variation of coherence in texts. But first of all, I need to clarify the notion of chain interaction.

If we examine the example from A10 presented above, and recall the terms in which the relationship between the chains is described, it is at once obvious that interaction should be read as consistency of some grammatical relation. Chain interaction in the analysis of my data was studied only in terms of grammatical functions realizationally related to the experiential meanings (Halliday, 1977, 1978). There is no implication, however, that it would not be possible to study chain interaction in terms of functions realizationally related to, for example,

Hasan

interpersonal meanings; nor is there any implication that the former is more basic to the unity of the text than the latter. The decision to concentrate on experiential meanings was more or less made for me by the predilection of linguistics, which has for centuries concentrated on the description of experiential meanings as if these, and these alone, constitute the essence of language. Consider the very meaning relations by reference to which SCs are constructed—concepts such as synonymy, antonymy, etc. are all based on the consideration of relations in experiential meaning. The availability of the descriptive categories naturally pushes one into doing precisely what I did: analyze the texts in terms of categories which are more or less available readymade.

The units in which grammatical relations of the above kind were analyzed were the clause and the group. Thus not only is there interaction between *a-b*, *c* and *g* as shown in Table 22, but also there is interaction between *a*, *d* and *d*, *c*, as follows:

TABLE 23

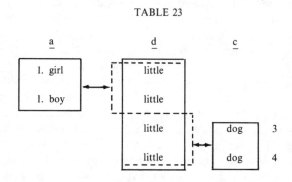

The interaction shown in Table 22 is intraclausal, that in Table 23 is intragroup.

A comparison of the two Tables also shows the fact that some given chain (*g* or *d*) can interact with two or more distinct chains; note, however, the difference between *g* and *d* in this respect. The former (*g*) is in simultaneous interaction with chains *a-b* and *c*, while the interaction of *d* with *a* and *c* is "staggered." Although staggering is a necessary attribute of multiple chain interaction when the grammatical function in question is group-internal, it is not confined solely to such interaction. In most texts of my data, staggered interaction was more common than simultaneous.

Note that in both cases, interaction is said to take place only if two or more members of a chain stand in the same functional relation vis a vis two or more members of some one specific chain. If in text A10 the attribute *little* had not been assigned to the *boy* in clause 1 and if it had not been recurrently assigned to *dog* in clause 4, we would have had two tokens of *little*, one functioning as epithet to *girl* and one to *dog* (in clauses 1 and 3 respectively). In such a case there would have been no chain interaction since *girl* and *dog* do not belong to the same chain and since the relation of *little* to a member of each chain remains unechoed. The principle of two-ness holds in chain interaction just as much as it does in the operation of componential cohesive devices. Later I shall discuss the significance of this requirement.

The grammatical functions in terms of which chain interaction was analyzed were largely borrowed from Halliday (1967, 1968, 1970). At various points, however, I had to work out the description for myself and there is no implication that the details of my analysis are necessarily in agreement with all details of Halliday's grammatical description.

Not all of the relevant tokens always participate in chain interaction. The picture here is somewhat analogous to componential cohesion: in the latter, although the actual cohering is done by the components of the message, the net result is the creation of unity between the messages as a whole. In the same way, a given chain *a* may be said to interact with a given chain *b*, not because all of its members interact with all of the members of *b*, but because some parts thereof do. This means in the first place that chains have the potential of entering into multiple interaction as for example in Table 23, where chain *d* would be said to interact both with *a* and *c*. Secondly, this means that not all relevant tokens need be in actual interaction. This gives us ground for a subdivision of the RTs in a text: that subset of relevant tokens which actively participate in interaction may be referred to as "central tokens" (CT).

The details of chain interaction are fairly involved and cannot be described in full here (see Hasan, forthcoming); however, the above remarks will permit the reader to follow the picture of chain interaction produced below for the three texts.

TABLE 24.   Text A10

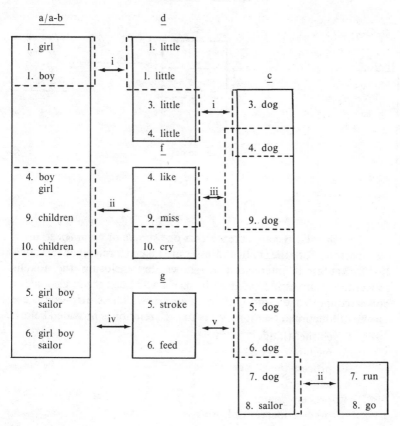

TABLE 25.   Text A9

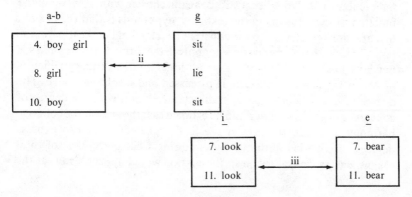

TABLE 26. Text A13

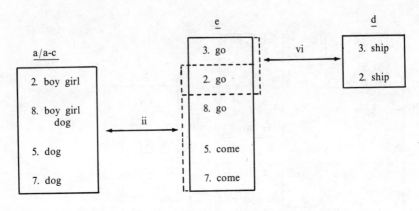

Each solid rectangle represents one simple or complex IC or SC (or a part thereof); the chain addresses are taken by reference to Tables 17-19. Staggered interaction is shown by enclosing the tokens concerned in boxes indicated by broken lines. Each rectangle and/or box is connected to some other by an arrow. These arrows are the arrows of functional relation. A key to each relation is provided below:

- i. epithet-thing
- ii. medium-process
- iii. process-phenomenon
- iv. actor-process
- v. process-goal
- vi. process-location of process

Tables 24-26 only display the CTs of each text. The CTs (central tokens) are that subset of the relevant tokens which are in actual interaction. The label "central" is again chosen with a view to the function of these tokens in the text. The hypothesis is that the CTs of a text are directly relevant to the coherent development of the topic in the text. Cohesive harmony consists not only in the formation of ICs and SCs but also in the creation of that additional source of unity which is provided by chain interaction as discussed and displayed above. The degree of chain interaction is in direct correlation with the degree of coherence in a text, so that it can be claimed that the greater the cohesive harmony in a text, the greater the text's coherence. We can express degrees of cohesive harmony by enquiring what percentage of total tokens acts as central token in the text. It would appear also that the

Hasan

ratio of peripheral to central token may be a significant factor, so that the higher the ratio of CT to PT, the more coherent the text would be. Table 27 supports these predictions with regard to the three texts under discussion.

TABLE 27

	TT	RT	PT	CT	CT as % of TT	CT per PT
A10	43	40	3	31	72.09%	10
A9	32	30	2	11	34.37%	5
A13	46 (43)	34 (31)	12	14	30.43% (32.55)	1

The figures in the last column of Table 27 represent only rough calculations; since the difference between the texts is so obvious, there seems no need for finer calculations. The penultimate column represents the degree of cohesive harmony in these texts: note that the order in which the three texts are ranked on this measure is precisely the same as that in which they are ranked by an informal judgment on their coherence. I would draw attention in particular to the double entries for A13. As pointed out before, they are there to focus attention on the ambiguity in that text. The figures in the bracket would be the correct ones if *sailor* could be definitely counted out. Note how close the cohesive harmony score of A9 and A13 would be in that case. These figures can be interpreted as demonstrating the part that unresolved ambiguity plays in the coherence ranking of the text A13. Had the *they all* in clause 7 read as *the boy, the girl and the dog*, there would have been no ambiguity; the TT for the text would have scaled down to 43 and the cohesive harmony would not be significantly different from that in A9. I suggest that if the readers were to reread the text with the suggested modifications, they would agree that the resultant is very close in coherence to A9, if not better.

At this point I would like to draw attention to another aspect of Tables 24-26. Note that both in 24 and 26, the chain interaction pattern presents a unity, so that the interacting chains are related to each other step by step: there are no gaps. In 25, pertaining to text A9, there is a gap in the interactive pattern. Like the low proportion of CT to PT, the gap in the interactive pattern is an associated feature of low coherence, so that if the measure of cohesive harmony is equal for two texts, then that text is likely to be seen as more coherent, in which the interactive pattern does not show gaps and/or in which the ratio of CT to PT is significantly higher. In my data, from which these three texts are taken, I found that any ranking by the measure of cohesive harmony, as determined by the percentage of the CT over the total, consistently correlated with readers' judgment on how the texts ranked vis a vis each other in coherence. Moreover, in the texts deemed unquestionably coherent, the central tokens consistently formed above 50 percent of the total token. Since then, this kind of analysis has been applied to data from other genres, and the hypotheses regarding the relationship between cohesive harmony and coherence have not been challenged. These can be summed up as follows:

  i. any text will be seen as coherent, in which the central tokens (CT) form at least 50 percent of the total tokens (TT). This percentage may be treated as a measure of their cohesive harmony;
  ii. ranking by cohesive harmony will match the ranking of the texts on the cline of coherence by reference to informal reader/listener reaction; cohesive harmony is the lexico-grammatical reflex of the semantic fact of coherence;
  iii. if two texts display no significant difference in their cohesive harmony, variation in their coherence will correlate with interactive gaps: all else being equal, the larger the number of such gaps, the less coherent the text would be;
  iv. whereas the percentage of PT over RT or TT is not significant for coherence (Hasan, 1980), the ratio of CT to PT is associated with coherence: the higher the ratio of CT to PT, the more coherent the text will be, all else being assumed equal.

The Significance of Cohesive Harmony

It remains now to comment on the place of cohesive harmony from the point of view of the system of language. If the Saussurean conception of paradigm and syntagm is brought to bear upon the phenomena capable of realizing coherence, it is obvious that the ICS and the SCS have the status of paradigms. Members of this paradigm are semantically tied to each other; to say that they cohere is to say precisely this. Each such chain then represents a relatively self-contained center of unity. When through chain interaction these centers of unity are brought together, this yields cohesive syntagms.

I discussed the integrative nature of structure in section 3. A clause structure yields one integrated unit, but such a unit by itself does not have a cohesive status. Central to cohesion is the notion of two-ness; and syntagms become cohesive when the principle of similarity or inclusion operate not only on the paradigmatic axis but also on the syntagmatic one. By itself *they stroke it* is not cohesive; it only becomes cohesive because of its similarity to *they fed it*. Thus it is neither the structure nor the content of any one particular clause that gives it the status of cohesiveness; what matters is the same principle of similarity following which the paradigms of cohesive chains are created. This is why a clause by clause, or a proposition by proposition analysis of a text will not reveal the nature of coherence in texts. When, however, a functional relation of the same type is mapped on lexical tokens which are already united by their internal similarities, and this relation is echoed, then the semantic bond between the components of the messages of the text is greatly augmented. The echoing of functional relations becomes a powerful device, but this happens only because the members of the chains echo one another in any event. Herein lies the rationale for insisting that the minimal condition for chain interaction is the "echo" of a functional relation, in other words, chain interaction can be recognized only if at least two members of a chain stand in the same grammatical relation to at least two members of some other specific chain.

Although the results of such analysis as has been carried out by myself and some of my colleagues are encouraging, this does not mean that there are no problems in this approach. For example, there yet remains the problem of integrating the cohesive analysis of the interpersonal meaning relations. In addition, and closely related to it, is the problem of the calibration of cohesive harmony with the analysis of logical relations between clauses. For instance, is it possible to perceive a message-to-message logical relation if a language piece lacks cohesive harmony? What are the relations between the clauses of example 3, for instance? Again, such componential devices as *this, from now on* which typically establish text-reference and are therefore meta-textual, raise serious problems. In my own data the genre was such and the speakers' prowess of such a level that this last question did not arise at all; but, if the schema is to be used generally, this problem will have to be solved. The discussion of any one of these will require another full length paper.

Note

[1] This paper is a revised version of a talk given at the IRA Annual Convention, 1980. The research reported herein was supported by Nuffield Foundation during 1968-1970.

In this paper, Kintsch and Miller present a perspective on readability in
which they note that readability is not a new field of inquiry but, rather, one
that continues to develop with new information from relevant fields of
scholarship. They note that readability is dependent upon the nature of the
text and the reader. They conclude that both variables have to be adequately
considered before readability can be finally determined. They suggest that
the answers to many of the questions on readability are yet to be known.

Readability: A View from Cognitive Psychology

Walter Kintsch
James R. Miller
University of Colorado

Readability

Identifying the qualities that make a text easy or hard to read is not only
a fascinating intellectual puzzle and a challenge to current theories of
reading, but is also a problem of great social importance. For our
society to function, people have to be able to understand what they
read; and documents, instructions, and explanations must be written in
such a way that people can understand them. Readability research is a
major part of this effort.

Far from being a new or unstudied problem, readability has
received a great deal of attention from educators and psychologists, and
has been one of the more prominent domains of applied experimental
research. Studies of readability have regularly appeared in the
psychological and educational literature since the 1920s, and publishing
houses frequently rely on the results of this research for evaluations of
their texts. But number of studies and amount of use guarantee neither
success nor progress. There are serious flaws in this research, many of
which are due to the atheoretical orientation that has dominated
readability research since its beginning.

It has been recognized for some time now that the ease with
which a text can be comprehended depends not only on the nature of the
text, but also on the person who reads it: an article in a scientific journal
may be perfectly readable to the scientist for whom it was intended but
unintelligible to the layman. Readability is not a fixed property of a

text, but rather the result of the interaction between a reader and a text. The goal of readability research must then be to identify ways to match a text to its reader as exactly as possible. This is easier said than done. Readability researchers have recognized the importance of the reader-text interaction for some time (Chall, 1958), but the absence of a theoretical understanding of this interaction has prevented researchers from incorporating it into their conception of readability.

Instead, the vast majority of this work has concentrated on deriving readability formulas that relate a collection of descriptive statistics about a text (such as mean sentence length or word frequency) to some objective measure of how easy the text is to read. Unfortunately, these purely descriptive variables tie the resulting formulas extremely closely to the surface structure of the text when, as the prose comprehension research of recent years has shown, the primary task facing readers is to develop a conceptual understanding of the text. It is certainly true that a difficult surface structure can impede the acquisition of that understanding, but the measurement of the conceptual complexity of a text inevitably requires conceptual tools and measures, which traditional readability formulas lack.

A second problem with readability formulas is that the measures used to establish the objective readability of the texts are themselves flawed. One of these measures has been the cloze test, in which perhaps every fourth word is removed from the text, and subjects try to identify the missing words. It has been presumed that the predictability revealed by this test reflects the global organization of the text, but recent results from our laboratory have cast some doubt on this assumption. A set of essays on various topics was collected; these texts were written so that their rhetorical organization was optimal. In fact, some of the texts were examples of good writing taken from rhetoric textbooks. These essays were then rewritten so that their content remained unchanged, but the rhetorical signals in the texts were removed, and the order of the paragraphs within each text was changed to obscure rather than reveal its internal structure. Only a few words per page had to be changed in producing the bad forms of the texts, and care was taken that the bad forms were in no way ambiguous. A cloze test showed that the rewritten texts and the originals were equally comprehensible: the success rate in guessing every fourth word was identical for the original and rewritten texts. Thus, local comprehension, as assessed by the cloze test, was unaffected. However, global comprehension was very different for the two versions of the text: subjects were able to identify a text's topic or main points more accurately when the rhetorical structure of the text was sound (see also Meyer & Freedle, 1979).

Readability   221

Other assessments of readability have relied upon question answering to evaluate the comprehensibility of the texts under analysis. Unfortunately, few of these systems have studied texts complex enough to require significant conceptual processing, resulting in a highly restricted range of question difficulty. In addition, this type of analysis makes little sense without a sound understanding of the relationship between a question, a text, and the structures and processes that lead to the understanding of that text. Questions can be focused on facts that are explicitly stated in a text, or on concepts that are the product of the detailed comprehension of the text. Only a well-developed theory of comprehension can identify which level of comprehension is tapped by a given question.

The traditional approach to this problem has been to try to predict a text's readability without bothering to understand that text, and we argue that this trick has failed. As a practical matter, the predictions from these formulas are often inaccurate. For example, readability formulas were used to argue that Adlai Stevenson's presidential campaign speeches were as easy to understand as Dwight Eisenhower's; Kurt Koffka's convoluted Germanic prose was ruled more readable than William James, and Gertrude Stein is given an edge over Henry James (see Kintsch & Vipond, 1979, for these and other examples). But these formulas continue to be used—and may even become enshrined by law—for lack of a plausible alternative.

The reason that readability formulas have worked at all is that the factors that make up these formulas are indeed correlated with the conceptual properties of texts: long sentences generally correspond to complex syntactic structures, infrequent words generally refer to complex concepts, and hard texts will generally lead to harder questions about their content. However, there are no causal—and thus truly predictive—relations between these formulas and a text's readability. Hence, their empirical accuracy is limited, and, perhaps more importantly, they are of virtually no use in guiding the composition of texts that are easy to read.

The goal of readability research should not simply be to identify easy or difficult texts, but rather to provide guidelines for the construction of easily comprehended texts. This research must then concentrate on the actual causes of comprehension difficulty. Although sentence length and word frequency may be correlated with readability, it is doubtful that these surface structure factors are its cause. This was clearly demonstrated by a recent Navy readability project that was searching for ways to produce usable texts for their recruits with poor

Kintsch and Miller

reading skills (Duffy, 1980). Difficult texts were rewritten with the explicit goal of increasing their readability, using the components of readability formulas, especially sentence length and word frequency, as guidelines for the rewriting. These new texts were then tried out on new groups of recruits who found them no easier to understand than the original texts, despite the striking improvement in readability scores. There is, of course, no reason why such a project should succeed: understanding cannot be guaranteed by the use of short sentences and common words. But the mere fact that such a project should be attempted shows how much a solution to this problem is needed.

We hope to have shown above that readability is best interpreted from the perspective of the more general process of prose comprehension, and that the ultimate answer to readability assessment lies in the detailed study of the prose comprehension system. This is an area that has received considerable study in recent years, with particular focus on three areas: the structural characteristics of texts, the cognitive processes that are responsible for prose comprehension, and the role in the comprehension process of a reader's prior knowledge about the topic of the text.

Text Structure

Many of the recent studies of prose comprehension have dealt with conditions that affect the amount recalled from a text or the time taken to read a text. One of the most prominent findings in this body of research concerns how the recall of a text is affected by the structural properties of that text. Thorndyke (1977) presented subjects with texts whose initial sentence, responsible for specifying the topic of the text, was displaced to the end of the text, or even removed altogether. Preventing or inhibiting the subjects from discovering the central point of the text greatly inhibited recall from the text. Kieras (1978) similarly found that disrupting paragraph structure by moving the topic-specifying sentence resulted in both poorer recall and longer reading times.

Such experiments presuppose a particular view of prose comprehension, one in which the content of the text can be expressed as a set of *propositions*, each of which represents a single relatively simple idea expressed by the text. The task of the reader is then to find a coherent way to organize these propositions into a structure that represents the concepts expressed in that text. Kintsch and van Dijk (1978) have argued that there are two general classes of processes involved in this organization: *macroprocesses*, which are concerned with the interpretation of the global organization and meaning of the text, such as those affected by the manipulations of Thorndyke and Kieras, and *microprocesses*, which are concerned with establishing coherence between individual text propositions, and which can also affect reading time and recall. For instance, Haviland and Clark (1974) found differences in reading times as a function of the form of these coherence relations. In the sentence pair,

John got the beer out of the trunk.

The beer was warm.

the explicit repetition of *the beer* makes the relation between the sentences coherent and easy to understand. However, in the sentence pair,

John got the picnic supplies out of the trunk.

The beer was warm.

there was no explicit coherence relations that can link the two sentences. Instead, the macrostructural inference that "*beer* is an instance of *picnic supplies*" is required, an additional step that is reflected in the longer reading times found for such sets of inferentially related sentences.

The local propositional structure of a text also affects the text's comprehension. Kintsch and Keenan (1973) constructed a set of texts that contained the same number of words, but that varied in the number of propositions expressed by these words. Reading time was found to be an increasing function of the number of propositions that could be recalled; each additional proposition that was recalled led to an additional 1.5 seconds of reading time. In addition, Kintsch, Kozminsky, Streby, McKoon, and Keenan (1975) found that a text's reading time was affected by the number of different concepts that were contained in a text: the more concepts that were discussed, the longer was the text's reading time.

It should be stressed that these aspects of text microstructure should not be considered properties of the text in the same way that sentence length and word frequency are. Rather, these propositional factors are relevant only with respect to their interaction with the reader's comprehension processes. Texts that contain many different propositions or concepts should cause problems with the reader's limited short term memory, requiring relatively more long term memory searches to retrieve propositions and concepts that have been lost from this short term store. Similar problems exist at the macrostructural level: texts with missing topic sentences should be difficult because these sentences contain information essential to the identification of relations among some of the text's propositions. If this information is missing from a text, it can be obtained only by means of inference generation, a process that is frequently complex and error prone. The interaction between the characteristics of a text and the reader's cognitive abilities and limitations means that a valid interpretation of a text's readability can be found only from the perspective of a general theory of text comprehension.

Comprehension Processes

Kintsch and Vipond (1979) investigated readability from such a position. Using the Kintsch and van Dijk (1978) prose comprehension theory as a foundation, several subprocesses of this proposed comprehension system were identified that might influence its efficiency. The Kintsch and van Dijk model assumes that the reader has a working memory of limited capacity, and that a text must therefore be processed in a number of cycles, each of which is concerned with some relatively small part of the text, perhaps a phrase or a sentence. A graph that represents the coherence relations between this segment's propositions is then constructed. In order for the reader to maintain coherence between successive text segments, a limited number of propositions is held in working memory from one cycle to the next. These allow the propositions of a new cycle to be interconnected with those of previous cycles. If the coherence among the propositions breaks down, the reader must search a long term memory representation of the text for a proposition that could be reinstated in working memory and successfully interconnect the old and new propositions. If no such proposition can be found, an inference must be generated that will serve as a connection between the parts of the text.

The characteristics of the text's representation discussed earlier—propositional density and the number of different concepts in the text—clearly affect reading time. In addition, several other aspects of the processing model should be related to the readability of the text. Contributing factors to a text's reading time should include the number of times long term memory must be searched for material that was read earlier but is no longer available, and the number of inferences that must be generated to maintain the coherence of the text. Readers with a relatively large working memory should be more efficient readers, since they would be able to retain more propositions across cycles and thus minimize the number of long term memory searches (Daneman &

Carpenter, 1980). Similarly, if a large number of propositions can be processed in each cycle, the likelihood that coherence can be maintained on purely propositional grounds should increase, and should reduce the number of long term memory searches.

Kintsch and Vipond found that these factors successfully predicted the relative difficulty of four texts that had not been properly assessed by traditional readability methods. Since these texts were relatively short, only limited macroprocessing was presumed to take place. A similar analysis also succeeded in discriminating the difficulties of the Eisenhower and Stevenson campaign speeches mentioned earlier. Kintsch and Vipond divided these speeches into macropropositions, derived from subjects' divisions of the texts into idea units, and applied the processing model to the resulting sets of macropropositions. As expected, the more easily comprehended speech by Eisenhower required far fewer inferences and long term memory searches, and benefited from a larger working memory to a much greater extent than did Stevenson's less comprehensible speech.

These ideas were examined in a more rigorous way by Miller and Kintsch (1980). A computer simulation model of the microprocessing component of the Kintsch and van Dijk theory was constructed and applied to twenty naturally occurring texts that varied greatly in their apparent readability. Experimental analyses, using reading time per proposition recalled as the index of the text's readability, confirmed these intuitions, and provided an empirical base for the application of the simulation model. An initial stage of the model divided the propositionalized text into "chunks"—relatively self-contained groups of propositions—for processing by the coherence system; this system used the original text and a specified input size to locate places in the text (typically sentence and phrase boundaries) where reasonable segmentations of the text might occur. The segmented proposition list was then analyzed by the coherence graph system, which was responsible for building the microstructure graph described by Kintsch and van Dijk, using argument repetition, long term memory reinstatements, and inference generation as tools for maintaining coherence.

The simulation model produced two kinds of predictions that could be compared to experimental data. Recall predictions were based on Kintsch and van Dijk's (1978) proposal that the probability of the recall of a proposition would be a function of the number of working memory processing cycles the proposition participated in. The model's reading time and readability predictions were evaluated by multiple regressions of variables associated with the surface text (such as word frequency and sentence length) and with the processing model (such as number of inferences, number of reinstatements, and working memory capacity) against the reading time and readability index (reading time per proposition recalled) for that text. Both sets of predictions were successful: the propositional recall of the texts was predicted well for all but four of the twenty texts, and the regressions of reading time and readability yielded multiple correlations of between .8 and .9. Most importantly, the variables that accounted for the largest amount of readability variance were, as predicted, the frequencies of reinstatement searches and inferences, with surface variables such as word frequency and sentence length accounting for comparatively little of the variance.

Knowledge-Based Processing

An important shortcoming of the Miller and Kintsch model was that it dealt only with the local microstructural coherence of the text. There has of course been no shortage of experiments demonstrating the importance of knowledge-based macroprocesses on comprehension. This absence indicates a serious flaw in the readability simulation above, and our recent theoretical work has been oriented toward incorporating such knowledge-based processes into the model.

It is clear that the ability to apply preexisting knowledge about the content of a text leads to marked increases in that text's readability. Bransford and Johnson (1972) studied a class of texts that were written so as to be virtually incomprehensible when presented without a title summarizing the text: texts read without these titles were rated much lower in comprehensibility and showed much lower recall. The title for such a text specified a body of semantic information that could be used to disambiguate the numerous vague references and terms in the text; without a title, the reader's search for the text's topic was disorganized, and was generally doomed to failure. From the present point of view, this experiment emphasizes the power of macrostructure and macroprocesses in discovering and maintaining the coherence of a text's propositional structure.

Not only is it easier to comprehend material that can be organized by prior knowledge structures, but this organization also provides a basis for retrieval. Chiesi, Spilich, and Voss (1979) found that subjects who were extremely knowledgeable about baseball were able to remember more about baseball game descriptions than were low-knowledge subjects; the differences were extremely pronounced in the retrieval of information critical to the game, and to event sequences from the game. Schustack and Anderson (1979) studied texts that described fictional persons; real historical persons were used as models for the fictional descriptions (e.g., a Japanese politician who had ended slavery and was assassinated near the end of a bloody civil conflict). When the subjects were told that these characters were similar to people they may already have known about (e.g., Abraham Lincoln), recall was significantly higher, providing that a correspondence between the real and fictional characters did, in fact, exist. This advantage was found only when the correspondence was stated to the subjects before both study and test sessions, suggesting that the memory representations of the fictional characters were closely tied to those of the corresponding real persons.

The Interaction of Knowledge and Structure

An additional kind of knowledge that is important in comprehending a text is knowledge about its structure. The interaction of this structural knowledge and more general semantic or world knowledge appears to be a critical part of comprehension, as has been shown in a set of experiments by Miller (1980; Miller & Kintsch, 1981). Subjects read texts one line at a time, and, after each line, stated how they believed the text would continue from that point. When these anticipation responses were scored against the actual continuation of the text, two trends were evident. First, the likelihood of a correct anticipation increased as the reader progressed through the text, suggesting that the information acquired increasingly constrained the possible ways that the text could develop. Second, the places where correct anticipations were generated were characterized by the presence of considerable world and text-structural knowledge. If the structure, but not the content, of the text was constrained, subjects could predict the general topic that would subsequently be discussed (e.g., that the result of an action would be discussed after the occurrence of the action is mentioned). If both text and world knowledge were present, however, highly specific and accurate anticipations, reflecting both the general topic and the detailed content of the text, could be generated. A second experiment collected reading times for the segmented texts and found shorter reading times for those segments that were accurately anticipated in the first experiment. These findings demonstrate that readers can and do use world and text knowledge to facilitate their comprehension, and that, correspondingly, a model of the comprehension processes that underlie readability must include knowledge about the world and about the structure of the texts.

Research Questions

We believe that the research described here has important implications for an appropriate conception of readability. It is, however, no more than a first step. Nothing could be more surely fatal to the budding relationship between cognitive psychology and education than to merely replace the old readability formulas with new formulas based on frequencies of reinstatement searches and inferences. That would be turning a promising research result into pernicious nonsense.

There are many reasons why such a step would be pernicious, and they have to do with the differences between research and practice. Educators need concrete answers, based on a reasonably complete and adequate understanding of the problems involved; we simply do not have such an understanding as yet. Our work has relied on the common research strategy of isolating and investigating some particular aspect of a problem, to the neglect of other doubtlessly important aspects. Our research has not dealt with the parsing of the text from natural language into propositions. There is good evidence that parsing requires a variety of strategies (Clark & Clark, 1977), which may interact with other strategies more directly concerned with, for instance, macrostructure formation. We cannot determine the ultimate effects of these interactions until a clear picture of the entire comprehension process is available. For instance, the earlier cited work of Haviland and Clark (1974) would suggest that comprehension can be facilitated by avoiding nonliteral references (and the accompanying coherence-maintaining inferences) between sentences whenever possible. Although their experiments clearly demonstrated this effect at the sentence level, constructing complete texts according to these principles may not be wise. Shuy and Larkin (1979) have shown that the over explicit language often used in legal documents and insurance policies can become a serious obstacle to understanding. Thus, while some of the inferences studied in Miller and Kintsch (1980) were potential trouble spots, blindly avoiding all inferences would not guarantee an easily readable text.

A further problem in applying our current research to readability is that our present theory is by no means static, and there will doubtlessly be many modifications and elaborations that cannot now be foreseen. For instance, the conditions that led to an inference in the Miller and Kintsch (1980) model can even now be seen to fall into several classes, each of which has quite different properties. Of particular importance is the relation between these "inferences" and the knowledge sources that are applied to a given text. Some inferences can simply be derived from already active knowledge structures, and so should have little or no effect on readability. Other inferences, however, require searching for and activating new knowledge structures: the resources expended in this search could significantly affect the text's readability. Also, new theoretical developments typically identify previously unknown problems that readers face. For instance, texts are occasionally written in such a way that certain pieces of information needed for understanding are neither provided by the text nor present in the reader's knowledge structures, and so are uninferrable. In this case, the model assumes that the needed information will eventually be provided by the text, but also creates an active expectation to watch for the appearance of this missing information. We do not yet know how subjects behave in these situations, but now that this potential problem has been identified by the theoretical work, we know what to look for, and an answer should not be hard to find. "Expectations" may then join the list of factors affecting readability, and there is no reason to suppose that this list will soon be completed.

As another illustration of the tentativeness of current research results, consider the fact that readability research has thus far been restricted to relatively short texts, where macrostructural considerations are relatively unimportant. However, one can safely predict that the overall structure of long texts will turn out to be crucial for their readability, as Kintsch and Vipond (1979) have argued with their Eisenhower-and-Stevenson example. Explicit models of the strategies responsible for macrostructure formation have only recently been proposed (Kintsch & Miller, 1980), and we suspect that a deeper understanding of these strategies will be of significance to our understanding of readability.

Prospects

Our point here is not that the research we have described is irrelevant to the question of readability, but only that the answers are not all in. The problems with the present approach to readability are clear, and we also know, in general, what needs to be done. Before educators can be advised on practical solutions to readability, we must simply learn more.

Practical applications of this work will eventually be possible, however, and some reasonable guesses about the nature of these applications can be made. It is now clear that comprehension, and therefore readability, is a complex, multilevel process, and that, correspondingly, no single indicator will be adequate. Instead, a battery of tests will be necessary to explore how well a text and a particular reader are matched. This battery of tests will have to be designed in such a way that separate diagnoses can be made for the various levels of understanding.

At the lowest level of comprehension, it will be necessary to detect problems at the parsing level—whether the text is written in such a way that the intended readers can readily decode its meaning, sentence by sentence and phrase by phrase. As noted earlier, sentence length and word frequency are at least correlated with the syntactic complexity of a text, and an index based on these and related variables might be feasible. Note that the measurement of a text's word frequency should of course reflect its intended audience: the jargon of a particular technical area might be of low frequency in the general linguistic corpus, but common in the literature of that area. Adjustments of this nature should be made as a matter of course.

Second, the local coherence of the text must be evaluated: whether the text is, in fact, coherent, or whether it requires potentially troublesome reinstatement searches, or inferences that are too difficult for the reader. A major part of this analysis would be an investigation of the knowledge sources that are presupposed by the text, that are needed to organize and integrate the text, and that are actually possessed by the intended readers. A model such as that of Kintsch & Miller (1980) could shed some light on the nature of the knowledge sources relevant to a particular text, although less cumbersome approximations may be preferable, based on the degree to which a text elaborates on a given topic, as well as the intended reader's knowledge of this topic.

Finally, a further set of diagnostic procedures will be required to assess the efficiency of macrostructure formation. It is probably fairly easy to find out whether the target population has problems in that respect, in view of the importance of macrostructure to recall. Once we know there is trouble, its sources need to be located through further testing before the text can be appropriately improved. It is clear that the assumed and existing levels of prior knowledge about the text will be critical to this process, as will the text's exploitation of good rhetorical structure.

Applying such a set of procedures would be far more difficult than computing a Flesch score, but it is by no means hopelessly complex. Once cognitive psychology has provided a sufficiently solid base of research, a test battery like the one outlined here should be possible. We can expect that a variety of related developments from educational and psychological researchers will converge in the next few years and help us to realize the possibilities that we can only now anticipate.

Kintsch and Miller

Chall suggests that researchers in two fields of inquiry, prose comprehension and readability, need to better understand the work of scholars in each of these fields to more ably attend to the fundamental issues involved in understanding texts.

Readability and Prose Comprehension: Continuities and Discontinuities

Jeanne S. Chall
Harvard University

This paper has a dual purpose. The first is to bring some of the enduring concepts of readability research to those currently engaged in the new research and theory on reading comprehension. The second is to alert readability researchers to some of the newer thinking and research on reading comprehension that may be of value to their work.

I have felt the need to write such a paper for some time, for I have had a growing concern that the researchers in each of these fields seem to pay little attention to the basic work of the other. A perusal of the published writings in each of these fields reveals a discontinuity between them. Since I believe that a discontinuity between two fields as closely related as these two can lead to a loss for both, I will attempt to indicate how the distance between them might be lessened.

The paper will present, first, some examples of how the new scholarship in prose comprehension tends to view readability research. This will be followed by an overview of "traditional" readability research and its applications. The final section presents some of the prose comprehension research that seems to hold promise for readability research.

Readability and the New Comprehension Research

For specific data on how readability research is viewed by the "new" prose comprehension researchers, I reviewed the papers in two

233

recently published volumes, *Theoretical Issues in Reading Comprehension: Perspectives from Cognition, Psycholinguistics, Artificial Intelligence, and Education* (Spiro, Bruce, & Brewer, Editors, 1980) and *Children's Prose Comprehension: Research and Practice* (Santa & Hayes, Editors, 1981).

A simple search of related categories in the indices was not possible, for neither volume contains a subject index. I had, therefore, to use the author index in each, searching for names prominent in readability. The search revealed only one readability researcher cited in each of the volumes—John Bormuth. Such well recognized contributors to readability theory and measurement as Irving Lorge, Rudolf Flesch, Edgar Dale, and George Klare were not cited for their works on readability, although several of them were cited for other research.

The sole reference to readability found in the Spiro, et al. volume follows:

> Attempts to apply surface structure concepts to practical problems, such as predicting text readability from a variety of statistical measures on the text, were relatively unsuccessful. Some of these measures, such as average sentence length and the number of subordinate clauses or prepositional phrases per sentence, attempted to account for syntactic factors. Others, such as the proportion of concrete as opposed to abstract words, were aimed at semantic factors. Although readability measures can be found that correlate fairly well with text difficulty (Bormuth, 1966), their main weakness is that the difficulty of a passage involved its comprehension, and surface structure descriptions capture only some of the syntactic variables necessary to comprehension. As an extreme example of the inadequacy of these formulas, most of them would yield the same readability index on a passage if the word order within each phrase, and the order of the phrases within each sentence, were scrambled. (Huggins and Adams, 1980, p. 91)

Although this is but one brief reference to readability in a 586 page volume, it may well represent some of the attitudes toward readability research held in much of the new comprehension research—a tendency to underestimate it, to confuse some of the facts, and to be ambivalent toward its research and practical uses (Harris, 1980; Warren, 1980; Davison et al., 1980).

Perhaps the discontinuity from readability that is revealed stems also from a difference in the styles and assumptions of educational research that each holds. The authors of the excerpt, as do most of the authors of the Spiro volume, seem to assume that through theory—mainly cognitive and/or linguistic theory—and perhaps *only through theory* can viable solutions to the reading problem be achieved. At the same time, there is a recognition that theory may not lead easily to workable solutions. But there also appears to be an assumption that solutions not grounded in theory cannot be expected to be ultimately useful for practice.

Readability research, on the other hand, tends to have a different set of assumptions. It is both theoretical and empirical, but its main objective is finding practical solutions. This difference can be seen in the last point of the above excerpt. The observation that one can obtain the same readability score even if the sentences and paragraphs are scrambled has been noted as a theoretical weakness of formulas by many readability researchers (Chall, 1958). But it was not considered a serious threat to practical use since it was expected that readability formulas would be used only for testing connected, natural text.

The history of readability research also contains poignant examples of the greater usefulness of empirical solutions in comparison with solutions based on more elegant theory. The painstaking, almost heroic attempts to use theories of transformational grammar to improve the measurement of syntactic complexity of the readability formulas is a recent example. After nearly a decade of trying to devise syntactic measures based on tranformational grammar, the more empirical and "theoretically weaker" average sentence length measure was used instead because empirical tests found it to be more predictive of comprehension difficulty (Bormuth, 1969; MacGinitie & Tretiak, 1971). Thus, while deep structure might be more satisfactory theoretically, surface structure measures seemed to work better for predicting the readability of prose.

The IRA volume, *Children's Prose Comprehension*, seems, also, to have just one reference to readability. As in the Spiro volume, Bormuth is the only readability researcher mentioned and for one of his studies on sentence understanding. His major works in readability are not referred to. Indeed, the term readability appears to be used only once in the entire collection. Trabasso uses the term to discuss the Kintsch and Vipond study (in press) which used traditional readability indices to rate passages which were then analyzed by their scheme of propositional analysis.

Although Trabasso does not discuss readability per se, he seems to conclude from his review of the three preceding chapters (Baker & Stein, "The Development of Prose Skills"; Levin & Pressley, "Improving Children's Prose Comprehension: Selected Strategies that Seem to Succeed"; and Johnson & Barrett, "Prose Comprehension: A Descriptive Analysis of Instructional Practices") that the text itself and its difficulty in relation to the ability of the readers probably makes the greater difference in comprehension of text, perhaps greater than metacognition, readers' strategies, questions asked, and the like. His concluding proposal for research is in fact one that has been asked traditionally in readability research: "We desperately need to know how we learn from what we read and what conditions promote this learning" (p. 111). One can find it running through the long history of readability research and practice. Indeed it is still being studied today (Chall et al., 1977; in press).

Readability—Research and Practice

Following is a brief introduction to the theories, research, and practice of readability. According to historian Geraldine Clifford (1978), it is a field that has had, more than most fields in reading and educational research, a cumulative and continuous development—with cooperation and sharing of knowledge among scholars. With vocabulary studies it has had an important impact on the practice of education through its influence on book selections and development in schools and in educational publishing.

The Concept of Readability

Since the early 1920s, readability researchers have had two major goals: 1) to understand what makes text easy or hard to read and comprehend, and 2) to use this knowledge for effecting an optimal match between readers and texts.

The most widely known outcomes of readability research are the readability formulas. More than 50 have been published to date but only a few are in wide use: Spache (1974), Dale-Chall (1948), Flesch (1948), and Fry (1968).

These formulas are best viewed as readability tests of text, similar to intelligence and standardized reading tests of students. Just as it is assumed that the true concept of intelligence or reading ability is broader than the tests used to measure them, so the concept of readability is broader than any readability formula.

Dale and Chall (1949) proposed a comprehensive definition of readability as "the sum total (including the interactions) of all those elements within a given piece of printed material that affects the success a group of readers have with it. The success is the extent to which they understand it, read it at an optimal speed, and find it interesting" (p. 23).

Such a definition is concerned not only with text comprehensibility, but with its being read at optimal speed and with interest. Although most of the readability formulas in current use do not measure interest directly, some of the early readability researchers were very much concerned with the interest factors that appealed to young children such as surprise, liveliness, animalness and moralness (Gates, 1930), and action and humor (Zeller, 1941). In fact, one of Gates' factors of interest for beginning readers was ease. Similar classifications were made recently of the characteristics of the TV show, *The Electric Company*, with regard to factors of interest and to learning gains (Chall & Popp et al., 1977).

Comprehension, speed, and interest have generally been found to be positively related; speed of reading is usually a good measure of comprehension, and ratings of ease and interest have also usually been associated positively.

Physical features, such as size of print, number of words in a paragraph and on a page, and the number and relationship of pictures to text have also been found important for a comprehensive estimate of readability. These are still not included in the widely used readability formulas, and hence are judged separately.

The concept of readability which has been used most widely in research and practice has dealt with text comprehensibility or learnability, and less often with readership and acceptability. Most readability measures have been validated against reader comprehension as determined by some kind of comprehension test.

The Domain of Readability Research

Readability research has been concerned with the relationship between three interacting variables. First, the textbook or passage— which is comprehensible depending upon its internal characteristics, broadly seen as features of content, style, linguistic, and cognitive characteristics. The second, the reader—who brings to the book his reading ability, language, cognition, previous knowledge, interests, purposes, and the degree of comprehension required. And third, the present context, the instructional help from a teacher or the text, the strategies used by the reader, and the degree and kind of comprehension expected.

What Makes Text Easy or Hard to Read and Comprehend?

The research in readability has uncovered over one hundred factors related to difficulty—such factors as vocabulary, sentences, ideas, concepts, text organization, content, abstractness, appeal, format, and illustrations. Of these factors, the two found consistently to be most strongly associated with comprehensibility are vocabulary difficulty and sentence length. Various forms of these two factors are included in most of the currently used readability formulas. The stronger factor of the two is vocabulary difficulty—measured either by a count of unfamiliar words, hard words, words of low frequency, words of three or more syllables, or words of 7 letters or more. All word measures are highly interrelated. Once a vocabulary factor is used in a formula, another adds little to the prediction. Average sentence length is the second strongest and second most widely used measure of difficulty in readability formulas. It is very highly related to other measures of syntactic difficulty, and therefore only one sentence factor is usually used in a formula. It is also substantially associated with vocabulary difficulty.

A vocabulary and a sentence factor together predict the comprehension difficulty of written text to a high degree of accuracy. The multiple correlations run about .7 to .9 with reading comprehension on multiple-choice or cloze tests.

This long, empirically established high predictive power of a semantic and a syntactic factor for reading comprehension has considerable theoretical confirmation from psychological theories of language and cognitive development. It is confirmed by the long history of reading comprehension studies designed to test whether comprehension is composed of separate skills or of a general factor (Thorndike, 1973-1974). Whether the authors conclude for a general factor or for specific factors, they all conclude that vocabulary or verbal reasoning is the most potent factor in reading comprehension. Also, the history of intelligence testing finds that a test of vocabulary (word meanings) is consistently the best predictor of intellectual development (Wechsler, 1978; Stanford-Binet, 1937).

Indeed much of the current research on schema theory, particularly that of the importance of previous knowledge and attitudes on reading comprehension, is a kind of confirmation for readability in its concern for a match vocabulary (and concepts) as well as with the syntax of the reader's schema (Anderson, 1979).

In spite of these high predictions—as high, generally, as the association between two standardized reading comprehension tests—most readability researchers have, from the beginning, acknowledged that there are other factors of readability not measured by the readability formulas that need to be considered and estimated. These include conceptual difficulties which may not be fully accounted for by the difficult word count (particularly when difficult ideas are presented in familiar short words, as in metaphor), organization of paragraphs and entire texts, and difficulty and density of ideas (Chall, 1958). It is important to note that the new prose comprehension research has also moved away from a more direct study of linguistic factors toward a study of the more subtle, qualitative aspects of the relation between sentences and "propositions," and larger units of text (Kintsch & Vipond, in press; Halliday & Hasan, 1976).

Cloze as a Measure of Comprehension and Readability

Completion tests have a long history in the assessment of reading comprehension. For nearly thirty years they have also been used as a measure of readability (Taylor, 1953), known as cloze. In its most common form, a cloze test deletes every fifth word in a passage's readability. Unlike the readability formulas that predict difficulty by analyzing the text characteristics, the cloze procedure requires a group of readers. The literature reports that a 40 percent cloze accuracy score is equivalent to a 75 percent accuracy score on a multiple choice test (Almeida, 1978).

Recently, researchers including Coleman (1965), Bormuth (1966), and Sticht (1973) have used cloze rather than multiple choice tests for constructing criterion passages used in the development of readability formulas. Cloze has advantages, including high scoring reliability and ease of construction.

Formulas as a Measure of Readability

Readability formulas are the most widely used method for predicting difficulty. Since the formulas (multiple regression equations) have been correlated to reader comprehension, this method requires no reader participation, but is based on analysis of the text.

Most of the formulas in current use are based on only two factors—vocabulary, measured by word familiarity, frequency, or length, and syntax, most usually measured by average sentence length. The Dale-Chall formula (1948)[1] uses the Dale List of 3,000 Familiar Words (words known to fourth graders) as does the Bormuth (1969); Spache (1974) uses the Stone Revision of the Dale List of 769 Words (1931); Harris and Jacobson use their own word lists (1975); and Fry uses a syllable count (1968). The 1950 Flesch formula also counts syllables in addition to a percentage count of definite words (1950).

Besides identifying potent measures of difficulty, readability research is concerned with determining the relationship of these factors to an independent criterion of difficulty. The most widely used criterion for the construction of readability formulas has been the McCall-Crabbs Standard Test Lessons in Reading first used by Lorge in 1939. These are graded passages with multiple choice questions. The grade level assigned to each is based on the number of correct responses by pupils of known reading achievement. The recently devised formulas tend to use criteria based on cloze tests (Bormuth, 1966). The Harris-Jacobson (1975) used criteria determined by other readability formulas, as did the Fry (1968). The Spache used the grade levels assigned by publishers to reading and content textbooks (1974).

Most readability formulas predict difficulty in terms of reading grade levels needed to read and understand the material. Grade level refers to a reading grade equivalent, not to a grade placement. There is some variation in formulas with regard to the standard of success. For most formulas a grade level of 5.0 for example, means that those who read on a 5th grade level on a standardized reading test can be expected to read and understand the material at about a 75 percent accuracy on a multiple choice test, or a 40 percent accuracy on a cloze test, other things being equal. The Flesch formula uses only broad descriptors such as *easy, very easy,* or *hard* to indicate levels of difficulty.

Like other tests, readability tests (formulas) have limitations. They are suitable only for estimating difficulty of material falling within the range of difficulty of the criterion passages on which the formulas were standardized. For example, the Spache formula is suitable only for reading levels 1 to 3. The Dale-Chall formula covers reading levels 4 to 16+ (college graduate level). The Harris-Jacobson formula is actually two different formulas, one for the primary grades and the other for the higher grades.

Readability formulas do not yet make adequate provision for such aspects of difficulty as conceptual load, idea density, organization, and the like. To a certain extent, however, conceptual difficulty and idea density are measured in the word and sentence factors and in a prepositional phrase count since, in natural writing, abstract conceptions are usually expressed in uncommon words.

In spite of these limitations, studies have shown that most readability indices can predict quite well teacher and pupil judgment of difficulty, and tested comprehension. There is also evidence of high correlations among the formulas themselves, particularly those with similar factors such as the Dale-Chall, Bormuth, and Fry. There is less agreement, however, on the grade level scores from the different formulas.

Readability Scales

Recently, researchers have been testing the validity of using scaled passages to guide judgments for measuring readability. Actually, this method is a revival of probably one of the oldest measures of difficulty—subjective judgment, with an added dimension of objectivity. Such a scale of graded passages in health education was developed by Chall (1947) and was proposed as a method for measuring the readability of health materials of use particularly to writers.

Scales of graded passages recently developed and validated as benchmarks for matching samples of materials to "exemplars" of difficulty include those by Carver, Singer, and Chall et al. Carver's Rauding Scale (1975-1976) uses a set of anchor rating passages at grade levels 2, 5, 8, 11, 14 adn 17. Singer's Seer Technique (1976) includes eight paragraphs from grades 1.5 to 6.8. The Readability Assessment Scales of Chall, Bissex, Conard, Harris (in press) include passages at 10 levels from primary to college, in three subject areas—literature, social studies and science. This type of readability measurement requires less time than for a formula analysis and seems to rely more on the rater's knowledge of language, experience, and insight. Validation studies to date seem to indicate predictions as good as or better than readability formulas at a fraction of the time. These scales will probably be of most use to teachers, editors, and writers. It is doubtful whether they would replace readability formulas used by publishers and textbook adoption committees who need more "objective" measurements, i.e. ones relying less on the analyst's experience and "schema."

Uses of Readability Measurement

Readability research has had a long history of application in education, in the selection and development of textbooks, and other instructional materials; in the construction of achievement tests; in the development of curricula, etc. (Chall, 1958, 1979; Clifford, 1978; Klare, 1963, 1974-1975). It has also been used in the improvement of the readability of newspapers and magazines, legal documents, advertising copy, and the like.

In education, the primary users of readability measurement are publishers, editors, and writers. Few teachers seem to do their own readability analyses, although they use the grade level estimates made available to them by publishers.

The readability scores and the formulas from which they were derived are increasingly listed in brochures and catalogs of educational publishing companies. Most of the multilevel reading kits and high-interest, low-vocabulary programs and books use formulas to estimate reading levels. Each of the selections in a basal reading series is usually tested for readability with more than one readability formula.

Outside of educational publishing, the overwhelming volume of printed materials and the increasing demand for clear communication have led to the need, in many groups and organizations, for accurate measures of difficulty. Governmental agencies, health and welfare organizations, and branches of the Armed Forces are using readability measurement to evaluate the suitability of their publications for intended audiences. In business and industry, an awareness of readability has grown and the difficulty levels of application forms, bulletins, and corporation annual reports are appraised. Legal documents, insurance policies, and tax forms have also been evaluated using readability measures. Journalists have made use of the concept, applying it to newspapers, magazines, comics, and even to appraising the difficulty of spoken commentaries and newscasts (Chall, 1979).

Computer technology for readability measurement has also contributed to its current wide use. Publishers of educational materials can not obtain computerized readability scores on texts using several readability formulas for their own use and for textbook adoption committees. Some publishers conduct their own computer analysis of readability. Usually, it appears, schools rely on others for such information.

Old and New Misconceptions

Misconceptions about readability are not uncommon—about the nature of readability, readability formulas, and the ways in which the formulas may be used. One tends to find that as each new group discovers readability measurement, it may be too optimistic about the comprehensiveness of the measures. With overconfidence may come overuse. Then dissatisfaction sets in.

There have been complaints that the readability scores for the same textbooks are not always the same when reported by different sources. That could well be, even when the same formula is used, since each formula tests only samples of text. When the sample taken is below that recommended or if the recommended sample is very small, it is not unreasonable to find unreliable scores. Generally, most of the widely used formulas give readability indices that are positively correlated, although the grade scores may differ (Chall, 1958).

The instructions should be followed as for standardized reading tests. A formula is not valid when used on a book too difficult or too easy as compared to the range of difficulty used to standardize it. Rules cannot be changed if the score is to have standard meaning. Adjustments made without explanation would be similar to changing the key or scoring system on standardized reading tests without a proper explanation.

The growing requests for readability scores of textbooks by schools and state textbook adoption committees may have contributed to what some call the "readability numbers game." Publishers seem to compete for the best scores, although it is not always clear what the best score is. Though no hard data exist as to what readability level is optimal, it would appear that some textbook committees and educational publishers seem to assume that, generally, the lower the readability score for textbooks to be used in a given grade the better. And yet, recent research in our laboratory would question this assumption (Chall et al., 1977). A comparison of the readability levels of the most widely used textbooks over a thirty year period with SAT verbal scores revealed that, generally, the textbooks decreased in difficulty and that the SAT verbal score decline was associated with the decrease in difficulty. Thus, readability of textbooks may have long term effects. Knowledge about optimal difficulty is important both for comprehension of the text and for the development of reading ability.

Readability does not tell how easy or hard the material should be for a reader or a class. Readability measures—whether based on formulas, cloze, or scales—give only estimates of how hard the materials probably are. Whether the difficulty is appropriate for a group of readers is a judgment that depends on the reading ability of those who will read it, their previous knowledge, their motivation, the amount of instruction they will receive before, while, or after they read it. Determining optimal difficulty with regard to learning of content is not a simple matter. Even more difficult is determining standards of optimal difficulty for the development of general reading and related verbal abilities. How easy or hard textbooks should be at each higher grade to assure the learning of content and the continuous development of reading and language skills, for students of varying abilities, are questions still in need of serious study (Chall, 1979a).

Readability grade scores can help in this quest by providing an estimate of how hard the material probably is. A readability formula can predict the reading level generally needed for comprehension of the text—at about 50 to 75 percent accuracy on multiple choice questions—

in unaided reading. When teachers preteach concepts, teach the needed background knowledge, help students to work through any difficulties with syntax and organization, and direct the students' attention with proper questioning, the readability levels can probably be higher in relation to tested reading levels of students. Indeed, if one always selects texts that are on the students' tested reading levels (or below, as some people seem to be recommending) it is doubtful whether the students would grow in their reading ability. It would seem, then, that for growth in reading ability, students must be exposed to materials that are above their current level of development. Indeed, this has long been part of the theory of cognitive, developmental psychologists concerned with the means by which children and students can be helped to move from lower to higher cognitive structures. The recent works of Bruner, McV. Hunt and the earlier works of Vygotsky tend to stress the importance of experience (education) keeping ahead of development (Conard, 1981).

Some people are claiming that because of the readability formulas, students are kept from reading more mature texts which would be more suitable to their language development, because publishers avoid using certain words that are not found on graded word lists. It is unfortunate that the formulas are blamed for their misuse. No word list, as no formula, tells writers or publishers the words that can or cannot be used for certain grades. The lists have been compiled to help writers, publishers, and teachers make judgments by informing them how well known or widely used certain words are. Certainly they were not devised to "dictate" the words to be used for the different grades.

Another dilemma—an old one, but one that is becoming ever more vocal—is that readability formulas do not measure all of the important aspects of readability. They fail to take account of such factors as concept difficulty and density, organization, previous knowledge, interest, illustrations, and the like. As noted earlier, this limitation has been acknowledged almost from the start of readability research. Indeed, there have been several attempts to measure these more qualitative, elusive aspects of text, including an "Idea Analysis Technique" by Morriss and Halverson (1938). Attempts have also been made to measure abstraction and organization. These were found to be significant predictors of comprehension difficulty, but were not sufficiently practical because of lower inter-rater reliability or they were too cumbersome (Chall, 1958; Klare, 1963, 1974-1975). Researchers have therefore advised users of formulas to be cautious in their use, suggesting further that the use of formulas can be tempered with wisdom and judgment, and that users judge the factors not included in the formulas.

Another persistent misconception is that any formula can be used on any text. Actually each formula can be used only for testing the kinds of materials on which it was standardized. As far as I know there are no readability formulas appropriate for arithmetic examples and mathematical formulas, and for poetry and highly poetic prose.

An old conception and also one that is being rediscovered is that readability formulas cannot serve as guides for writing, except in general ways. This has been noted from the very beginnings of readability and vocabulary studies. Ernest Horn (1937) was one of the first to research the use of word lists for simplifying text and concluded that to mechanically substitute easier for harder words does not necessarily make the text more readable. However, large changes or a restructuring of the text through reorganization and improvement of tone of the text do seem to make a difference (Chall, 1958). Thus, cutting sentences and substituting easier for harder words which results in lower readability scores does not necessarily mean that the text becomes easier to read. Indeed, such editing suggests that the text might have become harder to understand through loss of organization and cohesion and loss of clarity of concepts. There is more to readable texts than words and sentences. Although readability measurement can help in obtaining a first estimate of difficulty, the root of difficulty and how it might be lessened usually depend on more than changing words and sentence length. Many readability researchers have therefore developed guides for text selection and development (Bormuth, 1975; Chall et al., 1977; Dale & Chall, 1949, 1956). The concern for simplification that may distort the true readability has been the subject of recent research at the Center for the Study of Reading (Davison et al., 1980).

Current Trends and Future Developments

In recent years there has been a new upsurge of interest in readability measurement stemming perhaps from greater concerns for adult literacy, declining SAT scores and lowered reading achievement of high school and college students, minimal competency testing, the stress on individualization, as well as on basic skills.

Researchers have been looking for more comprehensive measures of the syntactic complexities of written text (Botel, Dawkins, & Granowsky, 1973). The cloze procedure has been adopted as another measure for matching the reader to a specific text (Almeida, 1978; Bormuth, 1968). But it has been used more generally as a measure of reading comprehension. Many word lists have recently been developed

(Carroll et al., 1971; Dale & O'Rourke, 1976) which are relevant to the vocabulary knowledge of contemporary children.

The new research in prose comprehension has, potentially, much to offer to readability measurement. Its major contribution will be, I believe, to the measurement of the more qualitative, elusive factors that have been tried by readability researchers, but which were not fully satisfactory. Generally, although the basis for some of the ideas may stem from a different theoretical tradition—cognitive psychology, linguistics—than that of traditional readability studies, they are contiguous with it. Thus, the propositional analysis of text by Kintsch and Vipond (in press) which has a positive relation with rate and recall is a promising way to get at the difficulty and density of ideas proposed by Morriss and Halverson (1938). The work of McConkie (1977) suggests improved ways for measuring the difficulty of the overall structure of the whole text. The work of Halliday and Hasan (1976) suggests still further ways for measuring cohesion and organization. Another area of research that needs to be incorporated is that of adjunct questioning, which also appears to affect comprehension positively (Slobody, 1981). And still another area from which to benefit is the growing research on writing and its development.

To Conclude

I have attempted in this paper to effect a better understanding and appreciation between two areas of scholarship and research. It would indeed be a loss if the newer prose comprehension scholars were to accept the traditional field of readability in terms only of its superficial products and misguided applications, and were therefore to inadvertently reinvest the enduring readability concepts—because they were useful and needed. It would be equally sad if readability scholars would not be challenged by the new prose comprehension and writing research to produce a fuller understanding of what makes text easy and hard to understand.

Note

[1] A revision including an update of the 3000 list is in press (McGraw-Hill).

References

Alessi, S.M., Anderson, T.H., & Goetz, E.T. An investigation of lookbacks during studying. *Discourse Processes*, 1979, *2*, 197.

Allen, J. *A plan based approach to speech-act recognition.* Toronto: Department of Computer Sciences, University of Toronto, Technical Report 131/79, 1979.

Almeida, P.M. The cloze test as a measure of reading comprehension. Qualifying paper, Harvard Graduate School of Education, 1978.

Anderson, I.H. Eye-movements of good and poor readers. *Psychological Monographs*, 1937, *48*, 1-35.

Anderson, R.C. The notion of schemata and the educational enterprise. In R.C. Anderson, R.J. Spiro, & W.E. Montague (Eds.), *Schooling and the acquisition of knowledge.* Hillsdale, New Jersey: Erlbaum, 1977.

Anderson, R.C., & Freebody, P. *Vocabulary knowledge.* Urbana, Illinois: Center for the Study of Reading, University of Illinois, Technical Report No. 136, August 1979.

Anderson, T.H. Study skills and learning strategies. In H.F. O'Neil & C.D. Spielberger (Eds.), *Cognitive and affective learning strategies.* New York: Academic Press, 1979.

Anderson, T.H. Study strategies and adjunct aids. In R.J. Spiro, B.C. Bruce, & W.F. Brewer (Eds.), *Theoretical issues in reading comprehension.* Hillsdale, New Jersey: Erlbaum, 1980.

Andre, M.D.A., & Anderson, T.H. The development and evaluation of a self-questioning study technique. *Reading Research Quarterly*, 1978-1979, *14*, 605-623.

Anglin, J.M. *The growth of word meaning.* Cambridge, Massachusetts: MIT Press, 1970.

Anglin, J.M. *Word, object, and conceptual development.* New York: W.W. Norton, 1977.

Applebee, A.N. *The child's concept of story.* Chicago: University of Chicago Press, 1978.

Applebee, A.N. A study of writing in the secondary school. Final Report NIE-G-79-0174. Urbana, Illinois: National Council of Teachers of English, 1980.

Aronoff, M. Contextuals. *Language*, 1980, *56*, 744-758.

Bader, L.A. *Reading diagnosis and remediation in classroom and clinic.* New York: Macmillan, 1980.

Baker, L. *Comprehension monitoring: Identifying and coping with text confusions.* Champaign: University of Illinois, Center for the Study of Reading, Technical Report No. 145, September 1979.

Baker, L. *Do I understand or do I not understand? That is the question.* Champaign: University of Illinois, Center for the Study of Reading, Reading Education Report #10, July 1979.

Baker, L., & Anderson, R.I. *Effects of inconsistent information on text processing: Evidence for comprehension monitoring.* Unpublished manuscript, University of Maryland, 1980.

Baker, L., & Brown, A.L. Metacognitive skills and reading. In P.D. Pearson (Ed.), *Handbook of reading research.* New York: Longman, in press.

Baker, L., & Stein, N. The development of prose comprehension skills. In C. Santa & B. Hayes (Eds.), *Children's prose comprehension: Research and practice.* Newark, Delaware: International Reading Association, 1981.

Barclay, J.R., & Reid, M. Semantic integration in children's recall of discourse. *Developmental Psychology*, 1974, *10*, 277-281.

Bartlett, F.C. *Remembering.* Cambridge, England: Cambridge University Press, 1932.

Bearison, D.J., & Levey, L.M. Children's comprehension of referential communication: Decoding ambiguous messages. *Child Development*, 1977, *48*, 716-720.

Becker, A.L. A tagmemic approach to paragraph analysis. *College Composition and Communication*, 1966, *17*, 237-242.

Beebe, M.J. The effect of different types of substitution miscues on reading. *Reading Research Quarterly*, 1980, *15*, 324-336.

Bendix, E.M. *Componential analysis of general vocabulary.* The Hague: Mouton, 1966.

Bereiter, C. *Discourse type, schema, and strategy: A view from the standpoint of instructional design.* Paper presented at AERA, Toronto, March 1978.

Bereiter, C., Scardamalia, M., Anderson, V., & Smart, D. *An experiment in teaching abstract planning in writing.* Paper presented at AERA, Boston, April 1980.

Bernstein, B. Social class and linguistic development: A theory of social learning. In A.H. Halsey, J. Flood, & C.A. Anderson (Eds.), *Education, economy and society.* New York: Free Press, 1961.

Bever, T. The integrated study of language behavior. In J. Morton (Ed.), *Biological and social factors in psycholinguistics.* Urbana: University of Illinois Press, 1970, 158-209.

Bever, T.G. The influence of speech performance on linguistic structures. In G. Flores d'Arcais & W. Levelt (Eds.), *Advances in psycholinguistics.* Amsterdam: North Holland, 1970.

Black, J.B., & Wilensky, R. An evaluation of story grammars. *Cognitive Science,* 1979, *3,* 213-230.

Black, J.B., Wilkes-Gibbs, D., & Gibbs, R.W. *What writers need to know that they don't know they need to know.* New Haven, Connecticut: Yale University, Cognitive Science Program, Technical Report N8, 1981.

Bloom, B.S., Hastings, J.T., & Madaus, G.F. *Handbook on formative and summative evaluation of student learning.* New York: McGraw-Hill, 1971.

Blumenthal, A.L. *Language and psychology.* New York: Wiley, 1970.

Bobrow, R. The RUS system. In B. Webber & R. Bobrow, *Research in natural language understanding.* Cambridge: Bolt, Beranek, and Newman Technical Report #3878, 1978.

Bolinger, D. *Aspects of language.* New York: Harcourt Brace Jovanovich, 1975.

Bolinger, D. *Meaning and form.* London: Longman, 1977.

Bond, G.L., & Tinker, M.A. *Reading difficulties: Their diagnosis and correction* (3rd ed.). New York: Appleton-Century-Crofts, 1973.

Bormuth, J. Readability: A new approach. *Reading Research Quarterly,* 1966, *1,* 79-132.

Bormuth, J. The cloze readability procedure. *Elementary English,* 1968, *45,* 429-436.

Bormuth, J. Reading literacy: Its definition and assessment. In J.B. Carroll & J.S. Chall (Eds.), *Toward a literate society.* New York: McGraw-Hill, 1975.

Bormuth, J. *Development of readability analysis.* University of Chicago, Office of Education (DHEW), Bureau of Research, No. BR-7-0052, March 1969. (ED 029 166)

Botel, M., Dawkins, J., & Granowsky, A. A syntactic complexity formula. In W. MacGinitie (Ed.), *Assessment problems in reading.* Newark, Delaware: International Reading Association, 1973.

Bougere, M. Selected factors in oral language related to first grade reading achievement. *Reading Research Quarterly,* 1969, *5,* 31-58.

Bower, G.H. *Emotional mood and memory.* Paper presented at Annual Meeting of the American Psychological Association, Montreal, September 1980.

Bower, T.G.R. Reading by eye. In H. Levin & J.P. Williams (Eds.), *Basic studies on reading.* New York: Basic Books, 1970.

Bowey, J. *Aspects of language processing in the oral reading of third, fourth and fifth grade children.* Unpublished doctoral dissertation, University of Adelaide, Australia, 1980.

Brachman, R. *A structural paradigm for representing knowledge.* Cambridge: Bolt, Beranek, and Newman Technical Report #3605, 1978.

Bransford, J.D. *Human cognition: Learning, understanding and remembering.* Belmont, California: Wadsworth, 1979.

Bransford, J., & Johnson, M. Considerations of some problems of comprehension. In W. Chase (Ed.), *Visual information processing.* New York: Academic, 1973, 383-438.

Bransford, J.D., & Johnson, M.K. Contextual prerequisites for understanding: Some investigations of comprehension and recall. *Journal of Verbal Learning and Verbal Behavior*, 1972, *11*, 717-726.

Bransford, J.D., & McCarrell, N.S. A sketch of a cognitive approach to comprehension. In W.B. Weimer & D.S. Palermo (Eds.), *Cognition and the symbolic processes*. Hillsdale, New Jersey: Erlbaum, 1974.

Brazil, D. *Discourse intonation*. Birmingham: English Language Research, 1975.

Brown, A.L. Knowing when, where, and how to remember: A problem of metacognition. In R. Glaser (Ed.), *Advances in instructional psychology*. Hillsdale, New Jersey: Erlbaum, 1978.

Brown, A.L. Metacognitive development and reading. In R.J. Spiro, B.C. Bruce, & W.F. Brewer (Eds.), *Theoretical issues in reading comprehension*. Hillsdale, New Jersey: Erlbaum, 1980.

Brown, A.L., Campione, J.C., & Barclay, C.R. Training self-checking routines for estimating test readiness. Generalizations from list learning to prose recall. *Child Development*, 1979, *50*, 501-512.

Brown, A.L., Campione, J.C., & Day, J. Learning to learn: On training students to learn from texts. *Educational Researcher*, 1981, *10*, 14-21.

Brown, A.L., & Smiley, S.S. The development of strategies for studying texts. *Child Development*, 1978, *49*, 1076-1088.

Brown, A.L., & Smiley, S.S. Rating the importance of structural units of prose passages: A problem of metacognitive development. *Child Development*, 1977, *48*, 1-8.

Brown, A.L., Smiley, S.S., & Lawton, S.C. The effects of experience on the selection of suitable retrieval cues for studying texts. *Child Development*, 1978, *49*, 829-835.

Brown, A.L., Smiley, S.S., Day, J., Townsend, M., & Lawton, S.C. Intrusion of a thematic idea in children's recall of prose. *Child Development*, 1977, *48*, 1454-1466.

Burns, George. *Living it up, or they still love me in Altoona!* New York: Putnam, 1976.

Calfee, R.C., & Freedman, S. *Understanding and comprehending*, Unpublished manuscript, Stanford University, 1981.

Canney, G., & Winograd, P. *Schemata for reading and reading comprehension performance*. Champaign: University of Illinois, Center for the Study of Reading, Technical Report #120, April 1979.

Carbonell, J.G. *Subjective understanding: Computer models of belief systems*. Doctoral dissertation, Department of Computer Science, Yale University, Research Report #150, 1979.

Carbonell, J.G. Politics. In R. Schank & C. Riesbeck (Eds.), *Inside computer understanding*. Hillsdale, New Jersey: Erlbaum, 1981.

Carpenter, P.A., & Just, M.A. Reading comprehension as eyes see it. In M.A. Just & P.A. Carpenter (Eds.), *Cognitive processes in comprehension*. Hillsdale, New Jersey: Erlbaum, 1977.

Carroll, J.B. Problems of measuring speech rate. In E. Foulke (Ed.), *Proceedings of the Louisville conference on time compressed speech*. Louisville, Kentucky: University of Louisville, 1967.

Carroll, J.B. *Development of native language skills beyond the early years*. Research Bulletin. Princeton, New Jersey: Educational Testing Service, 1968.

Carroll, J., Davies, P., & Richman, B. *Word frequency book*. New York: American Heritage, 1971.

Carroll, J.B., Kjeldergaard, P.M., & Carton, A.S. Number of opposites vs. number of primaries as a response measure in free association tests. *JVLVB*, 1962, *1*, 22-30.

Carver, R. Measuring prose difficulty using the rauding scale. *Reading Research Quarterly*, 1975-1976, *11*, 660-685.

Carver, R.P. Understanding, information processing, and learning from prose materials. *Journal of Educational Psychology*, 1973, *64*, 76-84.

Carver, R.P. Effect of increasing the rate of speech presentation upon comprehension. *Journal of Educational Psychology*, 1973, *65*, 118-126.

Carver, R.P. Toward a theory of reading comprehension and reading. *Reading Research Quarterly*, 1977-1978, *13*, 8-63.

Chall, J.S. *Graded reading paragraphs in health education.* Unpublished master's thesis. Columbus: Ohio State University, 1947.

Chall, J.S. *Readability: An appraisal of research and application.* Columbus: Ohio State University Press, 1958. Reprinted in 1974 by Bowker. Essex, England: Epping.

Chall, J.S. *Textbook difficulty, reading achievement, and knowledge acquisition.* Proposal submitted to the Spencer Foundation, Harvard Graduate School of Education, May 1979.

Chall, J.S. Readability: In search of improvement. *Publishers' Weekly*, 1979, *216*.

Chall, J.S. Middle and secondary school textbooks. In T.G. Sticht & J.Y. Cole (Eds.), *American education*, in press.

Chall, J.S., Bissex, G., Conard, S., & Harris-Sharples, S. *Readability assessment scales for literature, science, and social studies.* New York: McGraw-Hill, in press.

Chall, J.S., Conard, S., & Harris, S. *An analysis of textbooks in relation to declining SAT scores.* Princeton, New Jersey: College Entrance Examination Board, 1977.

Chall, J.S., Conard, S., & Harris, S. *Readability from a research viewpoint.* Unpublished paper presented at Houghton-Mifflin Readability Conference, 1979.

Chall, J.S., et al. *Characteristics of the Electric Company related to learning to decode by poor readers*, a final report. The Electric Company Lowest Decile Study, Children's Television Workshop, December 1977.

Charniak, E. Ms. Malaprop, a language comprehension program. *Proceedings of the fifth international joint conference on artificial intelligence*, 1977.

Chiesi, H.L., Spilich, G.L., & Voss, J.F. Acquisition of domain related information in relation to high and low domain knowledge. *Journal of Verbal Learning and Verbal Behavior*, 1979, *18*, 257-274.

Chomsky, N. *Syntactic structures.* The Hague: Mouton, 1957.

Chomsky, N. *Aspects of the theory of syntax.* Cambridge: MIT Press, 1965.

Chomsky, N. Conditions on rules of grammar. *Linguistic Analysis*, 1976, *2*, 303-351.

Christensen, F. A generative rhetoric of the paragraph. *College Composition and Communication*, 1965, *16*, 144-156.

Chu-Chang, M. *The dependency relation between oral language and reading in bilingual children.* Unpublished doctoral dissertation, Boston University, 1979.

Clark, E.V. On the acquisition of the meaning of before and after. *JVLVB*, 1971, *10*, 266-275.

Clark, E.V. On the child's acquisition of antonyms in two semantic fields. *JVLVB*, 1972, *11*, 750-758.

Clark, E.V. What's in a word? On the child's acquisition of semantics in his first language. In T.E. Moore (Ed.), *Cognitive development and the acquisition of language.* New York: Academic Press, 1973.

Clark, E.V. Nonlinguistic strategies and the acquisition of word meanings. *Cognition*, 1973, *2*, 161-182.

Clark, E.V. Universal categories: On the semantics of classifiers and children's early word meanings. In A. Juilland (Ed.), *Linguistic studies offered to Joseph Greenberg on the occasion of his sixtieth birthday.* Vol. 1. Saratoga, California: Anma Libri, 1976.

Clark, E.V., & Clark, H.H. When nouns surface as verbs. *Language*, 1979, *55*, 767-311.

Clark, H., & Clark, E. *Language and psychology.* New York: Harcourt Brace Jovanovich, 1977.

Clark, H.H. Linguistic processes in deductive reasoning. *Psychology Review*, 1969, *76*, 387-404.

Clark, H.H. The primitive nature of children's relational concepts. In J.R. Hayes (Ed.), *Cognition and the development of language.* New York: John Wiley & Sons, 1970.

Clark, H.H. Word associations and linguistic theory. In J. Lyons (Ed.), *New horizons in linguistics*. Baltimore, Maryland: Penguin Books, 1970.

Clark, H.H. Space, time, semantics, and the child. In T.E. Moore (Ed.), *Cognitive development and the acquisition of language*. New York: Academic Press, 1973.

Clay, M.M. *Reading: The patterning of complex behavior*. Auckland, New Zealand: Heinemann Educational Books, 1973.

Clifford, G.J. Words for schools: The application in education of the vocabulary researches of Edward L. Thorndike. In P. Suppes (Ed.), *Impact of research on education*. Washington, D.C.: National Academy of Education, 1978.

Clymer, T. What is reading? Some current concepts. In H.M. Robinson (Ed.), *Innovation and change in reading instruction*. The sixty-seventh yearbook of the National Society for the Study of Education, Part II. Chicago: The University of Chicago.

Coleman, E.B. *On understanding prose: Some determiners of its complexity*. Final Report. NSF-GB-2604, National Science Foundation, 1965.

Collins, A., Brown, J.S., & Larkin, K.M. Inference in text understanding. In R. Spiro, B. Bruce, & W. Brewer (Eds.), *Theoretical issues in reading comprehension*. Hillsdale, New Jersey: Erlbaum, 1980.

Collins, A., & Loftus, E. A spreading-activation theory of semantic processing. *Psychological Review*, 1975, *82*, 407-428.

Collins, A.M., & Quillian, M.R. Retrieval time from semantic memory. *JVLVB*, 1969, *8*, 240-248.

Conard, S. *The difficulty of textbooks for the elementary grades: A survey of educators' and publishers' preferences*. Thesis, Harvard Graduate School of Education, May 1981.

Conrad, R. The developmental role of vocalizing in short term memory. *Journal of Verbal Learning and Verbal Behavior*, 1972, *11*, 521-533.

Cosgrove, J.M., & Patterson, C.J. Plans and the development of listener skills. *Developmental Psychology*, 1977, *13*, 557-564.

Cullingford, R. *Script application: Computer understanding of newspaper stories*. Department of Computer Science, Yale University, Research Report #104, 1978.

Cullingford, R. *Script application: Computer understanding of newspaper stories*. Doctoral dissertation, Department of Computer Science, Yale University, Research Report #116, 1978.

Cullingford, R. SAM. In R. Schank, & C. Riesbeck (Eds.), *Inside computer understanding*. Hillsdale, New Jersey: Erlbaum, 1981.

Dale, E. A comparison of two word lists. *Educational Research Bulletin*, 1931, 484-489.

Dale, E., & Chall, J.S. *A formula for predicting readability*. Columbus: Bureau of Educational Research, Ohio State University, 1948.

Dale, E., & Chall, J.S. The concept of readability. *Elementary English*, 1949, *26*, 19-26.

Dale, E., & Chall, J.S. Techniques for selecting and writing readable materials. *Elementary English*, 1949, *26*, 250-258.

Dale, E., & Chall, J.S. Developing readable materials. *Adult reading*, fifty-fifth yearbook of the National Society for the Study of Education, Part II. Chicago: 1956, 218-250.

Dale, E., & O'Rourke, J. *The living word vocabulary: The words we know*. Field Enterprises, 1976.

Daly, B., Neville, M., & Pugh, A. *Reading while listening: Annotated bibliography of materials and research*, Paper No. 13. The University of Leeds Institute of Education, 1975.

Daneman, M., & Carpenter, P.A. Individual differences in working memory and reading. *Journal of Verbal Learning and Verbal Behavior*, 1980, *19*, 450-466.

D'Angelo, F.A. A generative rhetoric of the essay. *College Composition and Communication*, 1974, *25*, 388-396.

Danner, F.W. Children's understanding of intersentence organization in the recall of short descriptive passages. *Journal of Educational Psychology*, 1976, *68*, 174-183.

Davison, A., et al. *Limitations of readability formulas in guiding adaptations of texts.* Chicago: University of Illinois, Center for the Study of Reading, Technical Report #162, 1980.

de Beaugrande, R. *Text, discourse, and process.* Norwood, New Jersey: Ablex, 1980.

de Beaugrande, R. Design criteria for process models of reading. *Reading Research Quarterly*, 1981, *16*.

de Beaugrande, R. *The science of composition.* In preparation.

de Beaugrande, R., & Colby, B.N. Narrative models of action and interaction. *Cognitive Science*, 1979, *3*, 43-66.

de Beaugrande, R., & Dressler, W. *Introduction to text linguistics.* London: Longman, 1981.

de Beaugrande, R., & Miller, G. Processing models of children's story comprehension. *Poetics*, 1980, *9*, 181-201.

Deese, J. The associative structure of some common English adjectives. *JVLVB*, 1964, *3*, 347-357.

Deese, J. *The structure of associations in language and thought.* Baltimore: Johns Hopkins, 1965.

Dejong, J. *Skimming stories in real time: An experiment in integrated understanding.* Doctoral dissertation, Department of Computer Science, Yale University, Research Report #158, 1979.

de Saussure, F. *A course in general linguistics*, 1916.

deVilliers, J.G., & deVilliers, P.A. Competence and performance in child language: Are children really competent to judge? *Journal of Child Language*, 1974, *1*, 11-22.

Dewey, J. *How we think.* Boston: Heath, 1910.

Dewey, J. *Psychology.* Carbondale: Southern Illinois University Press, 1967 (1887).

DiVesta, F.J., Hayward, K.G., & Orlando, V.P. Developmental trends in monitoring text for comprehension. *Child Development*, 1979, *50*, 97-105.

Dressler, W.U. Review of Halliday & Hasan: Cohesion in English. *Language*, 1978, *54*.

Duffy, T.M. *The use of readability formulae and readable writing techniques to control text comprehension.* Unpublished manuscript, Navy Personnel Research and Development Center, 1980.

Duker, S. *Time-compressed speech: An anthology and bibliography in three volumes.* Metuchen, New Jersey: Scarecrow Press, 1974.

Dyer, M., & Lehnert, W. *Memory organization and search processes for narratives.* Department of Computer Science, Yale University, Research Report #175, 1980.

Eco, Umberto. *A Theory of semiotics.* Bloomington: Indiana University Press, 1976.

Edfeldt, A.W. *Silent speech and silent reading.* Chicago: University of Chicago Press, 1960.

Eisner, E.W. *The educational imagination: On the design and evaluation of school programs.* New York: Macmillan, 1979.

Entwisle, D. *Word associations of young children.* Baltimore: Johns Hopkins, 1966.

Ervin-Tripp, S. Social backgrounds and verbal skills. In R. Huxley & E. Ingram (Eds.), *Language acquisition: Models and methods.* London: Academic Press, 1971, 29-36.

Fahlman, S. NETL: *A system for representing and using real world knowledge.* Cambridge: MIT Press, 1979.

Fairbanks, G. The relation between eye-movements and voice in oral reading of good and poor readers. *Psychological Monographs*, 1937, *48*, 78-107.

Fareed, A.A. Interpretive responses in reading history or biology: An exploratory study. *Reading Research Quarterly*, 1971, *6*, 498-532.

Fillmore, C. An alternative to checklist theories of meaning. *Proceedings of the first annual meeting of the Berkeley linguistics society*, 1975, *1*, 123-131.

Fillmore, C. The case for case reopened. In P. Cole & J. Sadock (Eds.), *Syntax and semantics, VIII: Grammatical relations.* New York: Academic, 1977, 59-81.

Fillmore, C. Types of lexical information. In D.D. Steinberg & L.A. Jakobovits (Eds.), *Semantics*. London: CUP, 1971.

Firbas, J. Nonthematic subjects in contemporary English. *Travaux linguistiques de Prague*, 1966, *2*, 239-256.

Firth, J.R. The technique of semantics. TPS, 1935.

Firth, J.R. *Papers in linguistics*. London: OUP, 1957.

Flavell, J.H. Cognitive monitoring. In W.P. Dickson (Ed.), *Children's oral communication skills*. New York: Academic Press, in press.

Flavell, J.H. Metacognitive development. In J.W. Scandura & C.J. Brainerd (Eds.), *Structural process theories of complex human behavior*. The Netherlands: Sijthoff and Noordhoff, 1978.

Flavell, J.H., Speer, J.R., Green, F.L., & August, D.L. The development of comprehension monitoring and knowledge about communication. *Monographs of the society for research in child development*, in press.

Flavell, J.H., & Wellman, H.M. Metamemory. In R.V. Kail, Jr. & W. Hagen (Eds.), *Perspectives on the development of memory and cognition*. Hillsdale, New Jersey: Erlbaum, 1977.

Flesch, Rudolf. A new readability yardstick. *Journal of Applied Psychology*, 1948, *32*, 221.

Flesch, Rudolf. How to test readability: Measuring the levels of abstraction. *Journal of Applied Psychology*, 1950, *34*, 384-390.

Flick, W.C., & Anderson, J.I. Rhetorical difficulty in scientific English: A study in reading comprehension. TESOL *Quarterly*, 1980, *3*, 345-351.

Flood, J.E. The influence of first sentences on reader expectations within prose passages. *Reading World*, 1978, *17*, 306-315.

Flood, J., & Menyuk, P. *Detection of ambiguity and production of paraphrase in written language*. Final Report to National Institute of Education, November 1979.

Forrest, D.L., & Waller, T.G. *Cognitive and metacognitive aspects of reading*. Paper presented at the meeting of the Society for Research in Child Development. San Francisco, March 1979.

Forster, K.I. Accessing the mental lexicon. In R.J. Wales & E.Walker (Eds.), *New approaches to language mechanisms*. Amsterdam: North-Holland, 1976.

Forester, K.I. Accessing the mental lexicon. In E. Walker (Ed.), *Explorations in the biology of language*. Montgomery, Vermont: Bradford, 1978.

Foulke, E. *The comprehension of rapid speech by the blind: Part 3*. Final progress report on cooperative research project 24-30. Louisville, Kentucky: University of Louisville, 1969.

Foulke, E. The perception of time compressed speech. In D. Horton & J. Jenkins (Eds.), *The perception of language*. Columbus, Ohio: Charles E. Merrill, 1971.

Foulke, E., & Sticht, T.G. A review of research on the intelligibility and comprehension of accelerated speech. *Psychological Bulletin*, 1969, *72*, 50-62.

Fredericksen, C. Discourse comprehension and early reading. In L. Resnick & P. Weaver (Eds.), *Theory and practice of early reading*. Hillsdale, New Jersey: Erlbaum, 1976.

Friedman, H.L., & Johnson, R.I. *Time-compressed speech as an educational medium: Studies of stimulus characteristics and individual differences*, Report No. R69-14. Silver Spring, Maryland: American Institutes for Research, 1969.

Fry, Edward. A readability formulas that saves time. *Journal of Reading*, 1968, *11*, 513-516.

Fullmer, R. *Maximal reading and auding rates*. Doctoral dissertation, Harvard University, 1980.

Garner, R. Monitoring of understanding: An investigation of good and poor readers' awareness of induced miscomprehension of text. *Journal of Reading Behavior*, 1980, *12*, 55-64.

253

Garner, R. Monitoring of passage inconsistency among poor comprehenders: A preliminary test of the "Piecemeal Processing" explanation. *Journal of Educational Research*, in press.

Garner, R., & Kraus, C. *Monitoring of understanding among seventh graders: An investigation of good comprehender-poor comprehender differences in knowing and regulating reading behaviors.* Unpublished manuscript, University of Maryland, College Park, 1980.

Garner, R., & Taylor, N. *Monitoring of understanding: An investigation of the effects of attentional assistance.* Unpublished manuscript, University of Maryland, College Park, 1980.

Garrett, M.F. Does ambiguity complicate the perception of sentences? In G. Flores d'Arcais & W. Levelt (Eds.), *Advances in psycholinguistics*. Amsterdam: North Holland, 1970, 48-60.

Garrod, S., & Sanford, A. Interpreting anaphoric relations: The integration of semantic information while reading. *Journal of Verbal Learning and Verbal Behavior*, 1977, *16*, 77-90.

Gates, Arthur I. *Interest and ability in reading*. New York: Macmillan, 1930.

Gibson, E. Perceptual learning and theory of word perception. *Cognitive Psychology*, 1971, *2*, 351-368.

Gibson, E., & Levin, H. *The Psychology of Reading*. Cambridge, Massachusetts: MIT Press, 1975.

Gleitman, H., & Gleitman, L. Language use and language judgment. *Individual differences in language ability and language behavior*. New York: Academic Press, 1979, 103-125.

Goldsmith, S. *Reading disability: Some support for a psycholinguistic base.* Paper presented at Boston University Conference on Language Development, 1977.

Goldstein, H. *Reading and listening comprehension at various controlled rates.* Doctoral dissertation, Teachers College, Columbia University, 1940.

Goodman, K.S. Reading: A psycholinguistic guessing game. In H. Singer & R. Ruddell (Eds.), *Theoretical models and processes of reading*. Newark, Delaware: International Reading Association, 1976.

Goodman, K.S. The 13th easy way to make learning to read difficult: A reaction to Gleitman and Razin. *Reading Research Quarterly*, 1973, *8*, 484-493.

Gough, P. One second of reading. In J. Kavanagh & I. Mattingly (Eds.), *Language by ear and by eye*. Cambridge: MIT Press, 1972.

Gough, P., & Cosky, M. One second of reading again. In J. Castellan, D. Pisoni, & G. Potts (Eds.), *Cognitive theory, Vol. II*. Hillsdale, New Jersey: Erlbaum, 1975, 271-288.

Grady, M. A conceptual rhetoric of the composition. *College Composition and Communication*, 1971, *22*, 348-354.

Granger, R.H. Foul-up: A program that figures out meanings of words from context. *Proceedings of the fifth International Joint Conference on Artificial Intelligence*, 1977.

Granger, R.H. Foul-up: A program that figures out meanings of words from context. *Proceedings of the Fifth International Joint Conference on Artificial Intelligence*, 1977.

Gray, C.T. Types of reading ability as exhibited through tests and laboratory experiments. *Supplementary Educational Monographs, 5.* Chicago: University of Chicago, 1917.

Gray, W.S. *The teaching of reading and writing*. Glenview, Illinois: Scott, Foresman, 1956.

Graybeal, C. *Memory for stories in language impaired children*. Unpublished doctoral dissertation, Boston University, 1981.

Greeno, J.G., & Noreen, D.L. Time to read semantically related sentences. *Memory and Cognition*, 1974, *2*, 117-120.

Greimas, A.J. *Semantique structurale*. Paris: Larousse, 1966.

Guthrie, J.T. Reading comprehension and syntactic responses in good and poor readers. *Journal of Educational Psychology*, 1973, *65*, 294-299.

Halliday, M.A.K. Categories of the theory of grammar. *Word*, 1961, *17*.

Halliday, M.A.K. Lexis as a linguistic level. In C.E. Bazell, J.C. Catford, M.A.K. Halliday, & R.H. Robins (Eds.), *In memory of J.R. Firth*. London: Longman, 1966.

Halliday, M.A.K. Notes on transitivity and theme in English. *Journal of Linguistics*, 1967, *3*, Nos. 1, 2; 1968, *4*, No. 2.

Halliday, M.A.K. Language structure and language function. In J. Lyons (Ed.), *New horizons in linguistics*. Harmondsworth: Penguin, 1970.

Halliday, M.A.K. *Systems and function in language: Selected papers*, G. Kress (Ed.). London: OUP, 1976.

Halliday, M.A.K. Text as semantic choice in social contexts. In Teun A. van Dijk & J.S. Petofi (Eds.), *Grammars and descriptions*. Berling: W. de Gruyter, 1977.

Halliday, M.A.K., & Hasan, R. *Cohesion in English*. London: Longman, 1976.

Halliday, M.A.K. *Text and context: Language in a social-semiotic perspective*. Sophia Linguistica VI. Tokoyo: Graduate School of Languages and Linguistics, Sophia University, 1980.

Harris, A.J., & Jacobson, M. The Harris-Jacobson readability formulas. In A.J. Harris & E. Sipay (Eds.), *How to increase reading ability*. New York: David McKay, 1975.

Harris, S. *Analyzing written text: A look at discourse analysis from a readability research perspective*. Qualifying paper, Harvard Graduate School of Education, 1980.

Harris, Z.S. *Methods in structural linguistics*. Chicago: University of Chicago, 1951.

Hasan, R. Syntax and semantics. In J. Morton (Ed.), *Biological and social factors in psycholinguistics*. London: Logos, 1971.

Hasan, R. Rime and reason in literature. *Literary style: A symposium*. New York: OUP, 1971.

Hasan, R. *Ways of saying: Ways of meaning*. Talk given at Wenner-Gren Conference on Semiotics of Language and Culture. Bourg Wartenstein, Austria, memo, 1975.

Hasan, R. *On measuring the length of a text*. memo, n.d.

Hasan, R. On the notion of text. In J.S. Petofi (Ed.), *Text vs sentence: Basic questions of text linguistics*, second part. Hamburg: Helmut Buske, 1979.

Hasan, R. *Cohesive harmony: A measure for textual coherence*, forthcoming.

Haviland, S.E., & Clark, H.H. What's new? Acquiring new information as a process in comprehension. *Journal of Verbal Learning and Verbal Behavior*, 1974, *13*, 515-521.

Herber, H.L. *Teaching reading in content areas*. Englewood Cliffs, New Jersey: Prentice-Hall, 1978.

Hjelmslev, L. *Prologomena to a theory of language*. F.J. Whitfield (Tr.). Madison: University of Wisconsin Press, 1961.

Holmes, J., & Singer, H. *The substrata factor theory*. Berkeley: University of California, 1961.

Horn, E. *Methods of instruction in the social studies*. New York: Charles Scribner's & Sons, 1937. (Report of the Commission on Social Studies, American Historical Association).

Huey, E.B. *The psychology and pedagogy of reading*. Cambridge, Massachusetts: MIT Press, 1968 (first published in 1908 by Macmillan).

Huggins, A.W.F., & Adams, M.J. Syntactic aspects of reading comprehension. In R.J. Spiro et al. (Eds.), *Theoretical issues in reading comprehension*. Hillsdale, New Jersey: Erlbaum, 1980.

Ironsmith, M., & Whitehurst, G.J. The development of listener abilities in communication: How children deal with ambiguous information. *Child Development*, 1978, *49*, 348-352.

Isakson, R.L., & Miller, J.W. Sensitivity to syntactic and semantic cues in good and poor comprehenders. *Journal of Educational Psychology*, 1976, *68*, 787-792.

James, W. *The principles of psychology*. New York: Holt, 1890.

Jester, R.E., & Travers, R.M.W. Comprehension of connected meaningful discourse as a function of rate and mode of presentation. *Journal of Educational Research*, 1966, *59*, 297-302.

Johns, J., & Ellis, D. Reading: Children tell it like it is. *Reading World*, 1976, *16*, 115-128.

Judd, C.H., & Buswell, G.T. Silent reading: A study of the various types. *Supplementary Educational Monographs, 23*. Chicago: University of Chicago, 1922.

Just, M.A., & Carpenter, P.A. A theory of reading: From eye fixations to comprehension. *Psychological Review*, 1980, *87*, 329-354.

Just, M.A., & Carpenter, P.A. *Toward a theory of reading comprehension: Models based on eye fixations*. Pittsburgh: Carnegie-Mellon Psychology Department Technical Report.

Karabenick, J.D., & Miller, S.A. The effects of age, sex, and listener feedback on grade school children's referential communication. *Child Development*, 1977, *48*, 678-683.

Katz, J., & Fodor, J. The structure of semantic theory. *Language*, 1963, *39*, 170-210.

Kavale, K., & Schreiner, R. The reading process of above average and average readers: A comparison of the use of reasoning strategies in responding to standardized comprehension measures. *Reading Research Quarterly*, 1979, *15*, 102-128.

Kay, H. Learning and retaining verbal material. *British Journal of Psychology*, 1955, *46*, 81-100.

Keele, S. *Attention and human performance*. Pacific Palisades: Goodyear, 1973.

Kernighan, B.W., & Ritchie, D.M. *The C programing language*. Englewood Cliffs, New Jersey: Prentice-Hall, 1978.

Kieras, D.E. Good and bad structure in simple paragraphs: Effects on apparent theme, reading time, and recall. *Journal of Verbal Learning and Verbal Behavior*, 1978, *17*, 13-28.

Kimball, J.P. Seven principles of surface structure parsing in natural language. *Cognition*, 1973, *2*, 15-47.

Kintsch, W. *Memory and Cognition*. New York: Wiley, 1977.

Kintsch, W., & Keenan, J.M. Reading rate and retention as a function of the number of propositions in the base structure of sentences. *Cognitive Psychology*, 1973, *5*, 257-274.

Kintsch, W., Kozminsky, E., Streby, W.J., McKoon, G., & Keenan, J.M. Comprehension and recall of texts as a function of content variables. *Journal of Verbal Learning and Verbal Behavior*, 1975, *14*, 196-214.

Kintsch, W., & Miller, J.R. *Knowledge-based processes in prose comprehension*. Paper presented at the 21st annual meeting of the Psychonomics Society, St. Louis, 1980.

Kintsch, W., & van Dijk, T.A. Toward a model of text comprehension and production. *Psychological Review*, 1978, *85*, 363-394.

Kintsch, W., & Vipond, D. Reading comprehension and readability in educational practice and psychological theory. In L.G. Nillson (Ed.), *Memory process*. Hillsdale, New Jersey: Erlbaum, 1979.

Klare, G.R. *The measurement of readability*. Ames, Iowa: Iowa State University Press, 1963.

Klare, G.R. Assessing readability. *Reading Research Quarterly*, 1974-1975, *10*, 61-102.

Kobasigawa, A., Ransom, C.C., & Holland, C.J. *Children's knowledge about skimming*. Unpublished manuscript, University of Windsor, Ontario, 1979.

Koch, W.A. *Taxologie des Englischen*. Munich: Fink, 1971.

Koen, F., Becker, A., & Young, R. The psychological reality of the paragraph. *Journal of Verbal Learning and Verbal Behavior*, 1969, *8*, 49-53.

Kolodner, J.L. *Retrieval and organizational strategies in conceptual memory: A computer model*. Doctoral dissertation, Department of Computer Science, Yale University, Research Report #186, 1980.

Kosslyn, S., & Bower, G. The role of imagery in sentence memory. *Child Development*, 1974, *45*, 30-38.

Kotsonis, M.E., & Patterson, C.J. Comprehension monitoring skills in learning disabled children. *Developmental Psychology*, 1980, *16*, 541-542.

LaBerge, D., & Samuels, S.J. (Eds.), *Basic processes in reading: Perception and comprehension.* Hillsdale, New Jersey: Erlbaum, 1977.

LaBerge, D., & Samuels, S.J. Toward a theory of automatic information processing in reading. *Cognitive Psychology*, 1974, *6*, 293-323.

Lackstrom, J., Selinker, L., & Trimble, L. Technical rhetorical principles and grammatical choice. *TESOL Quarterly*, 1973, *7*, 127-136.

Lamb, S.M. *An outline of stratificational grammar.* Georgetown: Georgetown University Press, 1964.

Landauer, T.K. Memory without organization: Properties of a model with random storage and undirected retrieval. *Cognitive Psychology*, 1975, *7*, 495-531.

Lashley, K.S. The problem of serial order in behavior. In L.A. Jeffress (Ed.), *Cerebral mechanisms in behavior.* New York: Wiley, 1951, 112-146.

Lebowitz, M. *Generalization and memory in an integrated understanding system.* Doctoral dissertation, Department of Computer Science, Yale University, Research Report #186, 1980.

Lederberg, J. *Computer based text systems: Four user reports.* Videotape produced by Center for Information Technology, Stanford University, 1981.

Lehnert, W., et al. *BORIS: An experiment in the in-depth understanding of narratives.* Department of Computer Science, Yale University, Research Report #188, 1980.

Lehnert, W.G. *The process of question answering.* Hillsdale, New Jersey: Erlbaum, 1978.

Lenneberg, E.H. *Biological foundations of language.* New York: John Wiley & Sons, 1967.

Le Ny, J.F. *Le semantique psychologique.* Paris: Presses Universitaires de France, 1979.

Levelt, W. A survey of studies in sentence perception: 1970-1976. In W. Levelt & G. Flores d'Arcais (Eds.), *Studies in the perception of language.* New York: Wiley, 1978.

Levin, G. *Prose models* (4th ed.). New York: Harcourt Brace Jovanovich, 1978.

Liberman, I.Y., Liberman, A.M., Mattingly, I.G., & Shankweiler, D. Paper presented at Cross-Language Conference on Orthography, Reading and Dyslexia, sponsored by NICHD and Fogarty International Center of NIH., Bethesda, Maryland, September 18, 1978.

Loritz, D. *Children's knowledge of advanced phonics rules.* Unpublished doctoral dissertation, Boston University, 1981.

Luhn, H.P. Superimposed coding with the aid of randomizing squares for use in mechanical information searching systems. In R.S. Casey, J.W. Perry, M.M. Berry, & A. Kent (Eds.), *Punched cards.* New York: Reinhold, 1958.

Lloyd, P., & Pavlidis, G.T. *Child language and eye movements: The relative effects of sentence and situation on comprehension.* Unpublished manuscript, University of Manchester, 1978.

MacGinitie, W.H., & Tretiak, R. Sentence depth measures as predictors of reading difficulty, *Reading Research Quarterly*, 1971, *6*, 364-377.

MacKay, D.G. To end ambiguous sentences. *Perception and Psychophysics*, 1966, *1*, 426-436.

Mandler, G. *Mind and emotion.* New York: Wiley, 1975.

Mandler, J.M., & Johnson, N.S. Remembrance of things parsed: Story structure and recall. *Cognitive Psychology*, 1977, *9*, 111-151.

Markham, E.M. Comprehension monitoring. In W.P. Dickson (Ed.), *Children's oral communication skills.* New York: Academic Press, in press.

Markham, E.M. Realizing that you don't understand: A preliminary investigation. *Child Development*, 1977, *46*, 986-992.

Markham, E.M. Realizing that you don't understand: Elementary school children's awareness of inconsistencies. *Child Development*, 1979, *50*, 643-655.

Marslen-Wilson, W. Sentence perception as an interactive parallel process. *Science*, 1975, *189*, 226-228.

Masson, M.E. *Cognitive processes in skimming stories.* Boulder: University of Colorado Institute for the Study of Intellectual Behavior Technical Report 84-ONR, 1979.

McConkie, G. *Learning from text: A review of research in education,* L. Shulman (Ed.). Itasca, Illinois: Peacock, 1977.

McConkie, G.W. The use of eye-movement data in determining the perceptual span in reading. In R.A. Monty & J.W. Senders (Eds.), *Eye movements and psychological processes.* Hillsdale, New Jersey: Erlbaum, 1976.

McNeill, D. The development of language. In P.H. Mussen, *Carmichaels Manual of Child Psychology.* New York: John Wiley & Sons, 1970, 1061-1162.

Meehan, J.R. *The metanovel: Writing stories by computer.* Doctoral dissertation, Department of Computer Science, Yale University, Research Report #74, 1976.

Menyuk, P. Relations between acquisition of phonology and reading. In J. Guthrie (Ed.), Aspects of reading. Baltimore: Johns Hopkins University Press, 1976, 89-111.

Menyuk, P. *Language and maturation.* Cambridge: MIT Press, 1977.

Menyuk, P. Nonlinguistic and linguistic processing in normally developing and language disordered children. In N. Lass (Ed.), *Speech and language: Advances in basic research and practice.* New York: Academic Press, 1980, 1-97.

Menyuk, P. Syntactic competence and reading. In J. Stark & S. Wurzel (Eds.), *Language, learning, and reading disabilities: A new decade.* Cambridge: MIT Press, in press.

Menyuk, P., & Flood, J. *Metalinguistic processes in oral and written language.* In preparation.

Meyer, B.J.F. *The organization of prose and its effects on memory.* Amsterdam: North-Holland Publishing, 1975.

Meyer, B.J.F. Identification of the structure of prose and its implications for the study of reading and memory. *Journal of Reading Behavior,* 1975, *7,* 7-47.

Meyer, B.J.F., Brandt, D.M., & Bluth, G.J. Use of top-level structure in text: Key for reading comprehension of ninth grade students. *Reading Research Quarterly,* 1980, *1,* 72-103.

Meyer, B.J.F., & Freedle, R.O. *Effects of discourse type on recall.* Prose Learning Series Research Report No. 6, Arizona State University, Summer 1979.

Meyer, D.E. On the representation and retrieval of stored semantic information. *Cognitive Psychology,* 1970, *21,* 242-300.

Meyer, D.E., & Schwanefeldt, R.W. Meaning, memory, structures, and mental processes. *Science,* 1976, *192,* 27-33.

Miller, G.R., & Coleman, E.B. A set of thirty-six passages calibrated for complexity. *Journal of Verbal Learning and Verbal Behavior,* 1967, *6,* 851-854.

Miller, J.R. *The role of knowledge and text structure in prose comprehension.* Unpublished manuscript, University of Colorado, 1980.

Miller, J.R., & Kintsch, W. Knowledge-based aspects of prose comprehension and readability. *Text,* in press.

Miller, J.R., & Kintsch, W. Readability and recall of short prose passages: A theoretical analysis. *Journal of Experimental Psychology: Human Learning and Memory,* 1980, *6,* 335-354.

Miller, J.W., & Isakson, R.L. Disruptive effect: A new technique for reading research. *Educational Research Quarterly,* 1978, *3,* 45-51.

Miller, J.W., & Isakson, R.L. Contextual sensitivity in beginning readers. *Elementary School Journal,* 1978, *78,* 325-331.

Miller, S.P. *Writing: Process and product.* Cambridge: Winthrop, 1976.

Minsky, M. A framework for representing knowledge. In P.H. Winston (Ed.), *The psychology of computer vision.* New York: McGraw-Hill, 1975.

Miron, M.S., & Brown, E. The comprehension of rate incremented aural coding. In E. Foulke (Ed.), *Proceedings of the second Louisville conference on rate and/or frequency-controlled speech.* Louisville, Kentucky: University of Louisville, 1971.

Mitchell, D.C., & Green, D.W. The effects of context and content on immediate processing in reading. *Quarterly Journal of Experimental Psychology*, 1978, *30*, 609-
636.

Monteith, M. Taped books and reading materials. *The Reading Teacher*, 1978.

Morgan, J. Toward a rational model of discourse comprehension. *Theoretical issues in
natural language processing 2*. Champaign-Urbana: University of Illinois, 1978.

Morton, J. (Ed.), *What could possibly be innate: Biological and social factors in psycholinguistics*. London: Logos, 1971.

Morriss, E.C., & Halverson, D. *Idea analysis technique*. Teachers College, Columbia
University, 1938. In J.S. Chall, *Readability: An appraisal of research and
application*. Columbus, Ohio: Ohio State University Press, 1958.

Mowbray, G.H. Simultaneous vision and audition: The comprehension of prose passages
with varying levels of difficulty. *Journal of Experimental Psychology*, 1953, *46*,
365-372.

Myers, M., & Paris, S.G. Children's metacognitive knowledge about reading. *Journal of
Educational Psychology*, 1978, *70*, 680-690.

Myerson, R. *A study of children's knowledge of certain word formation rules and the rela-
tionship of this knowledge to various forms of reading achievement*.
Unpublished doctoral dissertation, Harvard University, Graduate School of
Education, 1976.

National Assessment of Educational Progress. *Reading Rate and Comprehension, 1970-
1971 Assesement*. Report 02-R-09. Denver, Colorado: State Education
Commission, 1972.

Nelson, K. The syntagmatic-paradigmatic shift revisited: A review of research and theory.
Psychological Bulletin, 1977, *84*, 93-116.

Neville, M.H., & Pugh, A.K. Context in reading and listening: Variations in approach to
cloze tasks. *Reading Research Quarterly*, 1976-1977, *12*, 13-31.

Ngandu, K. What do remedial high school students do when they read? *Journal of Reading*, 1977, *21*, 231-234.

Norman, D. Perception, memory, and mental processes. In L.G. Nilsson (Ed.), *Perspectives on memory research*. Hillsdale, New Jersey: Erlbaum, 1979.

Norman, D., & Rumelhart, D. *Explorations in cognition*. San Francisco: Freeman, 1975.

O'Connell, D. One of many units: The sentence. In S. Rosenberg (Ed.), *Sentence production*. Hillsdale, New Jersey: Erlbaum, 1977.

Olshavsky, J. Reading as problem-solving: An investigation of strategies. *Reading Research Quarterly*, 1976-1977, *12*, 654-674.

Olshavsky, J. Comprehension profiles of good and poor readers across materials of
increasing difficulty. In P.D. Pearson & J. Hansen (Eds.), *Reading: Disciplined
inquiry in process and practice*, 27th Yearbook of the National Reading
Conference. Clemson, South Carolina: NRC, 1978.

Olson, D.R. The languages of instruction: On the literate bias of schooling. In R.C.
Anderson, R.J. Spiro, & W.E. Montague (Eds.), *Schooling and the acquisition
of knowledge*. Hillsdale, N.J.: Erlbaum, 1977.

Olson, G.M., Duffy, S., & Mack, R. *The reader's knowledge of the conventions of story
writing*. Paper presented at the Psychonomic Society meetings, San Antonio,
November 1978.

Oppenheim, P. *Selected relationships between linguistic processing skills and reading*.
Unpublished doctoral dissertation, Boston University, 1981.

Ortony, A., & Anderson, R. On putting apples into bottles: A problem of polysemy. *Cognitive Psychology*, 1975, *7*, 167-180.

Osherson, D., & Markman, E. Language and the ability to evaluate contradictions and
tautologies. *Cognition*, 1975, *3*, 213-226.

Owings, R.A., Peterson, G.A., Bransford, J.D., Morris, C.D., & Stein, B.S. Spontaneous
monitoring and regulations of learning: A comparison of successful and less
successful fifth graders. *Journal of Educational Psychology*, 1980, *72*, 250-256.

Pace, A.J. *Further explorations of young children's sensitivity to world knowledge story information discrepancies.* Paper presented at the meeting of the Southeastern Conference on Human Development, Alexandria, April 1980.

Pace, A.J. *The ability of young children to correct comprehension errors: An aspect of comprehension monitoring.* Paper presented at the annual meeting of the American Educational Research Association, Boston, April 1980.

Paige, J.M., & Simon, H.A. Cognitive processes in solving algebra word problems. In B. Kleinmutz (Ed.), *Problem solving: Research, method, and theory.* New York: Wiley, 1966.

Paris, S.G., & Myers, M. *Comprehension monitoring of good and poor readers.* Unpublished manuscript, University of Michigan, 1980.

Patterson, C.J., & Cosgrove, J.M., & O'Brien, R.G. Nonverbal indicants of comprehension and noncomprehension in children. *Developmental Psychology*, 1980, *16*, 38-48.

Pearson, P.D. (Ed.), *Handbook of reading research.* New York: Longman, in press.

Piaget, J. *The language and thought of the child.* London: Routledge & Kegan Paul, 1926.

Pichert, J.W. *Sensitivity to what is important in prose.* Technical Report #149. University of Illinois, Center for the Study of Reading, November 1979.

Pike, Kenneth. *Language in relation to a unified theory of the structure of human behavior.* The Hague: Mouton, 1967.

Polanyi, M. Life's irreducible structure. *Science*, 1968, *160*, 1308-1312.

Pollack, I., & Pickett, J. Intelligibility of excerpts from fluent speech: Auditory vs. structural content. *Journal of Verbal Learning and Verbal Behavior*, 1964, *3*, 79-84.

Popham, W.J. Two decades of educational technology: Personal observations. *Educational Technology*, 1980, *20*, 19-21.

Pribram, K.H. Localization and distribution of function in the brain. In J. Orbach (Ed.), *Neuropsychology since Lashley*, in preparation.

Rayner, K. Eye movements in reading and information processing. *Psychological Bulletin*, 1978, *85*, 618-660.

Reder, L.M. The role of elaboration in the comprehension and retention of prose: A critical review. *Review of Educational Research*, 1980, *1*, 5-53.

Rieger, C.J. Conceptual memory and inference. In R. Schank, N. Goldman, C. Rieger, & C. Riesbeck. *Conceptual information processing.* Amsterdam: North Holland, 1975.

Ritchie, D.M., & Thompson, K. The UNIX time-sharing system. *Communications of the* ACM, 1974, *17*, 365-375.

Roberts, C.S. Partial-Match retrieval via the method of superimposed codes. *Proceedings of the* IEEE, 1979, *67*, 1624-1642.

Robinson, H.A. *Teaching reading and study strategies: The content areas.* Boston: Allyn and Bacon, 1975.

Robinson, H.M. Developing critical readers. In R.G. Stauffer (Ed.), *Dimensions of critical reading.* Newark, Delaware: University of Delaware, 1964.

Rogers, P.C. A discourse-centered rhetoric of the paragraph. *College Composition and Communication*, 1966, *17*, 2-11.

Rothkopf, E.Z., & Billington, M.J. Goal-guided learning from text: Inferring a descriptive processing model from inspection times and eye movements. *Journal of Educational Psychology*, 1979, *17*, 310-327.

Rubenstein, H.H., Lewis, S.S., & Rubenstein, M.A. Evidence for phonemic recoding in visual word recognition. JVLVB, 1971, *10*, 645-657.

Rumelhart, D. *Introduction to human information processing.* New York: Wiley, 1977.

Rumelhart, D. Notes on a schema for stories. In D. Bobrow & A. Collins (Eds.), *Representation and understanding: Studies in cognitive science.* New York: Academic Press, 1975.

Rumelhart, D. Schemata: The building blocks of cognition. In R. Spiro, B. Bruce, & W. Brewer (Eds.), *Theoretical issues in reading comprehension*. Hillsdale, New Jersey: Erlbaum, 1980.

Rumelhart, D.E. Understanding and summarizing brief stories. In D. LaBerge & S.J. Samuels (Eds.), *Basic processes in reading: Perception and comprehension*. Hillsdale, New Jersey: Erlbaum, 1977.

Rumelhart, D.E., & Ortony, A. The representation of knowledge in memory. In R.C. Anderson, R.J. Spiro, & W.E. Montague (Eds.), *Schooling and the acquisition of knowledge*. Hillsdale, New Jersey: Erlbaum, 1977.

Ryan, E.B. Identifying and remediating failures in reading comprehension: Toward an instructional approach for poor comprehenders. In T.G. Waller & G.E. MacKinnon (Eds.), *Advances in reading research*, vol. 2. New York: Academic Press, in press.

Salus, M.W. *The hierarchy of strategies in word association responses*. Unpublished paper, Boston University, 1980.

Salus, M.W., & Salus, P.H. Cognition, opposition, and the lexicon. *Toronto semiotic circle monographs, working papers*, and *prepublications #3*, 1978.

Salus, P.H. A realistic view of the mental lexicon. *Semiotica*, in preparation.

Santa, C.M., & Hayes, B.L. (Eds.), *Children's prose comprehension*. Newark, Delaware: International Reading Association, 1981.

Schallert, D.L., & Kleiman, G.M. *Why the teacher is easier to understand than the textbook*. Reading Education Report #9, University of Illinois, Center for the Study of Reading, June 1979.

Schank, R.C. *Interestingness: Controlling inferences*. Department of Computer Science, Yale University, Research Report #145, 1978.

Schank, R.C. *Inference in the conceptual dependency paradigm: A personal history*. Department of Computer Science, Yale University, Research Report #141, 1978.

Schank, R.C. *Reminding and memory organization: An introduction to MOPs*. Department of Computer Science, Yale University, Research Report #170, 1979.

Schank, Roger C. *Dynamic memory: A theory of learning in computers and people*, in press, a.

Schank, Roger C. *Reading and understanding: Teaching from the perspective of artificial intelligence*, in press, b.

Schank, R.C., & Abelson, P. *Scripts, plans, goals, and understanding*. Hillsdale, New Jersey: Erlbaum, 1977.

Schank, R., Goldman, N., Rieger, C., & Riesbeck, C. *Conceptual information processing*. Amsterdam: North Holland, 1975.

Schank, R., & Wilensky, R. Response to Dresher and Hornstein. *Cognition*, 1977, *5*, 133-145.

Schustack, M.W., & Anderson, J.R. Effects of analogy to prior knowledge on memory for new information. *Journal of Verbal Learning and Verbal Behavior*, 1979, *18*, 565-584.

Selfridge, O.G., & Neisser, U. Pattern recognition by machine. *Scientific American*, 1960, *203*, 60-68.

Selinker, L., Trimble, R.M.T., & Trimble, L. Presuppositional rhetorical information in EST discourse. *TESOL Quarterly*, 1976, *3*, 281-290.

Selinker, L., Trimble, L., & Vroman, R. Presupposition and technical rhetoric. *English Language Teaching*, 1974, *29*, 59-65.

Shannon, C., & Weaver, W. *The mathematical theory of communication*. Urbana: University of Illinois Press, 1949.

Shuy, R. Some language and cultural differences in a theory of reading. In K. Goodman & J. Fleming (Eds.), *Psycholinguistics and the teaching of reading*. Newark, Delaware: International Reading Association, 1969.

Shuy, R.W., & Larkin, D.L. Linguistic considerations in the simplification/clarification of insurance policy language. *Discourse Processes*, 1978, *1*, 305-321.

Simons, H.D. Reading comprehension: The need for a new perspective. *Reading Research Quarterly*, 1971, *6*, 340-363.

Sinclair, J. Beginning the study of lexis. In Bazell, et al. (Eds.), *In memory of J.R. Firth*. London: Longman, 1966.

Singer, H. Active comprehension from answering to asking questions. *Reading Teacher*, 1978, *31*, 901-908.

Singer, H. The SEER Technique: A noncomputational procedure for quickly estimating readability levels. *Journal of Reading Behavior*, 1975, *7*, 255-257.

Slobody, Laurie. The effects of questioning on prose comprehension and retention. Qualifying paper, Harvard Graduate School of Education, June 1981.

Smiley, S.S., Oakley, D.D., Worthen, D., Campione, J.C., & Brown, A.L. Recall of thematically relevant material by adolescent good and poor readers as a function of written versus oral presentation. *Journal of Educational Psychology*, 1977, *69*, 381-387.

Smith, E.E., Shoben, E.J., & Rips, L.J. Structure and process in semantic memory: A featural model for semantic decisions. *Psychological Review*, 1974, *81*, 214-241.

Smith, F. *Understanding Reading*. New York: Holt, Rinehart, & Winston, 1972.

Smith, H.K. The responses of good and poor readers when asked to read for different purposes. *Reading Research Quarterly*, 1967, *3*, 53-84.

Smith, N.B. Patterns of writing in different subject areas, Part I. *Journal of Reading*, 1964, 31-37.

Smith, N.B. Patterns of writing in different subject areas, Part II. *Journal of Reading*, 1964, 97-102.

Smith, R.J., & Barrett, T.C. *Teaching reading in the middle grades*. Reading, Massachusetts: Addison-Wesley, 1974.

Snow, D. *Classroom practices in reading comprehension*. Technical Note 2-80/12, Southwest Regional Laboratory, Los Alamitos, California, 1980.

Sokolov, A.N. *Inner speech and thought*. New York: Plenum Press, 1972.

Spache, G.D. The Spache readability formula. In G.D. Spache (Ed.), *Good reading for poor readers*. Champaign, Illinois: Garrard, 1974.

Spiro, R.J. Etiology of reading comprehension styles. In M.L. Kamil & A.J. Moe (Eds.), *Reading research: Studies and applications*. Clemson, South Carolina: National Reading Conference, 1979.

Spiro, R.J., Bruce, B., & Brewer, W.F. (Eds.), *Theoretical issues in reading comprehension*. Hillsdale, New Jersey: Erlbaum, 1980.

Spiro, R.J. Remembering information from text: The state of schema approach. In R.C. Anderson, R.J. Spiro, & W.E. Montague (Eds.), *Schooling and the acquisition of knowledge*. Hillsdale, New Jersey: Erlbaum, 1977.

Spiro, R.J. Constructive processes in prose comprehension and recall. In R.J. Spiro, B.C. Bruce, & W.F. Brewer (Eds.), *Theoretical issues in reading comprehension*. Hillsdale, New Jersey: Erlbaum, 1980.

Spiro, R.J. *The uses of subjectivity: The role of felt experience in cognition*, in preparation.

Spiro, R.J., & Esposito, J. Superficial processing of explicit inferences in text. *Discourse Processes*, in press.

Spiro, R.J., & Taylor, B.M. *On investigating children's transition from narrative to expository discourse: The multidimensional nature of psychological text classifications*. Technical Report No. 195, Center for the Study of Reading, University of Illinois, December 1980.

Springston, F.J. *Some cognitive aspects of presupposed coreferential anaphora*. Dissertation, Stanford Psychology Department, 1975.

Stein, N.L., & Glenn, C.G. An analysis of story comprehension in elementary school children. In R.O. Freedle (Ed.), *Discourse processing: Multidisciplinary perspectives*. Norwood, New Jersey: Ablex, 1979.

Stevens, A., & Rumelhart, D. Errors in reading: Analysis using an augmented transition network model of grammar. In D. Norman & D. Rumelhart, *Explorations in cognition*. San Francisco: Freeman, 1975, 136-155.

Sticht, T.G. Learning by listening. In R.O. Freedle & J.B. Carrol (Eds.), *Comprehension and the acquisition of knowledge*. Washington, D.C.: V.H. Winston and Sons, 1972.

Sticht, T.G. Some relationships of mental aptitude, reading ability, and listening ability using normal and time-compressed speech. *Journal of Communication*, 1968, *18*, 243-258.

Sticht, T.G. *The acquisition of literacy by children and adults*. Paper presented at the Second Delaware Symposium on Curriculum, Instruction, and Learning, University of Delaware, June 1975.

Sticht, T.G. with Gaylor, J., Fox, L. and Ford, J. *Methodologies for determining reading requirements of military occupational specialities*. Washington, D.C.: Human Resources Research Organization, 1973.

Sticht, T., Beck, L., Hauke, R., Kleiman, G., & James, J. *Auding and reading: A developmental model*. Alexandria, Virginia: HumRRO Press, 1974.

Strang, R., & Rogers, C. How do students read a short story? *English Journal*, 1965, *54*, 819-823, 829.

Stolz, W.S., & Tiffany, J. The production of child-like word associations by adults to unfamiliar adjectives. JVLVB, 1972, *11*, 38-46.

Sullivan, J. Comparing strategies of good and poor comprehenders. *Journal of Reading*, 1978, *21*, 710-715.

Swanson, D.E. Common elements in silent and oral reading. *Psychological Monographs*, 1937, *48*, 36-50.

Taft, M. *Detecting homphony of misspelled word*. Unpublished paper, Monash University, 1973.

Taylor, S.E. An evaluation of forty-one trainees who have recently completed the reading dynamics program. *Problems, programs, and projects in college adult reading*, 11th Yearbook of the National Reading Conference, 1962, 41-56.

Taylor, W. Cloze procedure: A new tool for measuring readability. *Journalism Quarterly*, 1953, *30*, 415.

Terman, L.M., & Merrill, M.A. *Measuring intelligence: A guide to the advancement of the new revised Stanford-Binet tests of intelligence*. Boston: Houghton Mifflin, 1937.

Thorndike, E.L. Reading as reasoning: A study of mistakes in paragraph reading. *Journal of Educational Psychology*, 1917, *8*, 323-332.

Thorndike, Robert L. Reading as reasoning. *Reading Research Quarterly*, 1973-1974, *9*, 135-147.

Thorndyke, P.W. Cognitive structures in comprehension and memory of narrative discourse. *Cognitive Psychology*, 1977, *9*, 77-110.

Thorndyke, P., & Yekovich, F. A critique of schemata as a theory of human story memory. *Poetics*, 1980, *9*, 23-49.

Trager, G. Review of K.L. Pike, *Phonemics, Language*, 1950, *26*, 152-158.

Vacca, R. *An investigation of a functional reading strategy in seventh grade social studies*. Unpublished doctoral dissertation, Syracuse University, 1973.

van Dijk, T.A. Context and cognition: Knowledge frames and speech act comprehension. *Journal of Pragmatics*, 1977, *1*.

Vygotsky, L.S. Mind in society and the development of higher psychological processes. M. Cole, V. John-Steiner, S. Scribner, & E. Souberman (Eds.). Cambridge: Harvard University Press, 1978.

Waller, T.G., & MacKinnon, G.E. (Eds.), *Advances in reading research*, Vol. 2. New York: Academic Press, in press.

Warren, Beth M. *Readability reconsidered*. Unpublished paper for reading, schools and social policy, Harvard Graduate School of Education, 1980.

Warren, W., Nicholas, D., & Trabasso, T. Event chains and inferences in understanding narratives. In R. Freedle (Ed.), *New directions in discourse processing.* Norwood, New Jersey: Ablex, 1979, 23-52.

Weber, R.M. A linguistic analysis of first grade reading errors. *Reading Research Quarterly,* 1970, *5,* 427-451.

Wechsler, David. *Wechsler intelligence scale for children revised.* New York: Psychological Corporation, 1974.

Wellman, H.M., Rysberg, J., & Suttler, H.E. *The development of accurate assessment of comprehension readiness: A study of cognitive monitoring in young readers.* Unpublished manuscript, University of Michigan, 1980.

Whimbey, A. *Intelligence can be taught.* New York: Dutton, 1975.

Wilensky, R. *Understanding goal based stories.* Doctoral dissertation, Department of Computer Science, Yale University, Research Report #140, 1978.

Wilensky, R. PAM. In Schank, R., & Riesbeck, C. (Eds.), *Inside computer understanding.* Hillsdale, New Jersey: Erlbaum, 1981.

Wilson, K. *Inference and language processing in hearing and deaf children.* Unpublished doctoral dissertation, Boston University, 1979.

Winograd, P., & Johnston, P. *Comprehension monitoring and the error detection paradigm.* Technical Report #153, University of Illinois, Center for the Study of Reading, January 1980.

Wolf, M. The word retrieval process and reading children and aphasics. In K. Nelson (Ed.), Children's language, Vol. III. New York: Gardner, in press.

Woods, W. Transition network grammars for natural language analysis. *Communications of the Association for Computing Machinery,* 1970, *13,* 591-606.

Woods, W. Generalizations of ATN grammars. In W. Woods & R. Brachman, *Research in natural language understanding,* Technical Report #3963. Cambridge: Bolt, Beranek & Newman, 1978.

Wozniak, R. Verbal regulations of motor behavior. *Human Development,* 1972, *15,* 13-57.

Young, R.Q. A comparison of reading and listening comprehension with rate of presentation controlled. *AV Communication Review,* 1973, *21,* 327-336.

Yussen, S.R., Mathews, S.R. Buss, R.R., & Kane, P.T. Developmental changes in judging important and critical elements of stories. *Developmental Psychology,* 1980, *16,* 213-217.